Freedom
As
A Value

Freedom
As
A Value

A Critique
of the
Ethical Theory
of
Jean-Paul
SARTRE

David
Detmer

Open  Court
La Salle, Illinois 61301

✹

OPEN COURT and the above logo are registered in the U.S. Patent and Trademark Office.

© 1986 by David Detmer

First printing 1988

Printed and bound in the United States of America.

Library of Congress Cataloging-in-Publication Data
Detmer, David, 1958-
      Freedom as a value: a critique of the ethical theory of Jean-Paul Sartre/David Detmer.
      p. cm.
      Bibliography: p.
      Includes index.
      ISBN 0-8126-9082-6: $29.95. ISBN 0-8126-9083-4 (pbk.): $15.95
      1. Sartre, Jean Paul, 1905-   —Ethics. 2. Sartre, Jean Paul, 1905-   —
Contributions in concept of freedom. 3. Free will and determinism—
History—20th century. I. Title.
B2430.S34D45 1988
171'.2—dc19   88-17757
                                                                          CIP

Acknowledgements

Many people have aided me in the preparation of this book. I would like to acknowledge their assistance here.

First of all, it is a pleasure to thank David Michael Levin, James M. Edie, John Deigh, and Robert C. Solomon for reading earlier drafts of this work, and for offering many helpful criticisms and suggestions which have improved it.

I would also like to thank the teachers from whom I have learned most: Erazim Kohák, Alasdair MacIntyre, the late John N. Findlay, and the aforementioned Professors Levin, Edie, and Deigh.

Sometimes one can learn as much from peers as from teachers. In this regard, I would like to thank Kerri Mommer, John Pfleiderer, Lisa Heldke, and Allan Wall.

The extremely competent Marcia Wroblewski expertly performed several tasks related to transforming the raw manuscript into publishable form. In addition, she caught and brought to my attention several errors in my manuscript.

Randa Duvick kindly agreed to check some of my translations from the French and rescued me from at least one major blunder.

It is also my pleasure to thank Rol Mommer for his art and design work on the cover and interior of the book.

Also deserving of thanks are the scholars who have generously taken the time to read and comment on the final version of the book: Thomas C. Anderson, Hazel E. Barnes, Thomas R. Flynn, Lisa Heldke, David Michael Levin, William Leon McBride, Anthony R. Manser, and Robert C. Solomon.

On a more personal level, I would like to thank Kerri, Eva, and Rol Mommer, and Kris and Letha Detmer for their multifaceted support and encouragement throughout the period during which I was working on this book.

I am very grateful to my former colleagues, John Leigh Smith of Valparaiso University and Theodore Scharle of Bradley University, and even more so to my present colleague, Kenneth Klein of Valparaiso University, for their many kindnesses and acts of friendship.

Finally, I offer my sincerest thanks to all people who read.

Contents

Introduction

The purpose of this book is twofold. On the one hand, it attempts to provide a critical exposition of the ethical theory of Jean-Paul Sartre. On the other hand, it strives to explain, and in a limited way to defend, the central thesis of that theory, namely, that freedom is the "highest," or most important, value.

But why, to begin with the first of my two purposes, is there a need for yet another exposition of Sartre? And why, more specifically, should we be concerned with his ethical views?

In the first place, I would argue that Sartre's philosophy is still, despite the great amount of critical attention that has been devoted to it, not well understood. In my view, Sartre's thought has historically been, and today still is, obscured by a consensus interpretation of it which is in many essential détails erroneous. I am, incidentally, not alone in reaching this conclusion. Thus, according to Thomas W. Busch, "granted that misunderstanding and misrepresentation are occupational hazards of the study of a philosopher, the abuse done to Sartre in this regard, even by critics of obvious good will, is exceptional."[1] And Thomas C. Anderson adds, "I sometimes think that few philosophers of our century have had their views so regularly distorted and misrepresented as has he."[2] In any case, whether or not the reader shares this conviction that Sartre is widely misunderstood, one justification for the present work is that it does *not* simply restate the mainstream, already widely accessible, reading of Sartre's thought, but rather provides an alternative interpretation. Of course, it is up to the reader to determine which interpretation is more accurate.

A second justification for reexamining Sartre is that it is little realized, even by those who respect Sartre and read him carefully, just how much he has to say about ethics. The impression that Sartre does not have an ethical theory derives largely from the fact that he failed to publish any systematic work on ethics during his lifetime, though at one point, at the conclusion of *Being and Nothingness,* he promised to do so.[3] This unfortunate fact certainly makes my task more difficult, as it becomes necessary to reconstruct Sartre's theory from partial discussions which are scattered throughout his writings. Still, I would hold that a Sartrean ethical theory can be found. And, once again, the reader is the one who must judge whether the search for it has been worthwhile.

A third justification for focusing on Sartre stems from a combination of the first two justifications, for, as it happens, those elements of Sartre's philosophy which are most widely misunderstood are precisely those which are most central to the proper understanding of his ethics. Thus, even those who are interested in Sartre's ethics fail to understand it if they, for example, think that Sartre recognizes no limitations to freedom, or that he does not distinguish between different senses of freedom, or that his later philosophy is inconsistent with his earlier thought, or that his doctrine of "radical conversion" refers to the abandonment of existentialism in favor of Marxism. The present work attempts to correct all of these misunderstandings.

A final justification for my concern with Sartre is that he offers the provocative thesis that freedom is the highest value. This brings us to my second purpose, that of clarifying and evaluating that thesis. I regard this project as an important and worthwhile undertaking for at least two reasons. First, I trust that Sartre's thesis bears a certain initial plausibility. After all, is it not a commonplace that morality is possible only insofar as human beings are free? And is it not the case, moreover, that many ethical theories have included freedom as *one* of the important values to be upheld? Thus, it seems to me that the thesis that freedom is the *highest* value will, at the very least, not be immediately dismissed as wildly implausible.

Secondly, I believe that a careful examination of the value of freedom can throw a great deal of light on some of the most vexing problems of ethical theory. In this work I take up one such problem, that of the subjective or objective nature of value-judgments, at some length, and discuss many others in a less extensive manner as they arise naturally in the course of the argument. In every case I try to show that a proper understanding of the value of freedom can increase our understanding of the problem at hand.

Finally, something should be said about the organization of this book. The first chapter is concerned with freedom. It begins by taking up Sartre's arguments for freedom, and then, in its consideration of his theory of the *nature* of freedom, defends Sartre against a number of widespread objections. The second chapter, which is much more critical of Sartre, is devoted to values. It considers Sartre's arguments for the subjectivity of values and distinguishes that doctrine from ethical subjectivism, which Sartre also endorses. All of Sartre's arguments are subjected to criticism, as is his general position on values and value-judgments. Finally, the work concludes, on the basis of what has been established in the first two chapters, with an explanation and defense of the thesis that freedom is the highest value. This final chapter discusses objectivist elements in Sartre's ethics, develops in regard to ethics Sartre's general theory of knowledge, and shows how the notion of freedom as a value not only underlies both the subjectivist and the objectivist phases of Sartre's ethical thought, but also suggests that these two phases can be reconciled in a conception of ethics as a dialectic of invention and discovery. This conception is then defended by way of a brief discussion of its advantages over rival ethical theories, which neglect one or the other of the stages of this dialectic.

CHAPTER 1
Freedom

1.1 Introduction

Perhaps it is fitting to begin a discussion of the nature of freedom by considering the contribution of Jean-Paul Sartre, a philosopher for whom "freedom is both starting point and ultimate goal."[1] Obviously, the sheer bulk of Sartre's output precludes the possibility of an encyclopedic or comprehensive treatment of his views, so I have had to be somewhat selective in my coverage. I have chosen to concentrate on what I take to be Sartre's most important contributions to the present topic: his arguments for the freedom of consciousness, his analyses of the meaning and scope of this freedom, and his descriptions of its varieties and limitations. A number of other subjects, such as Sartre's rejection of both the phenomenological reduction and the transcendental ego, and his descriptions of imagination, perception, and the experience of absence are also touched upon in the course of the exposition of these major topics. Finally, it should be noted that the present chapter begins with a discussion of Sartre's "early" philosophy, with the greatest emphasis being accorded to *Being and Nothingness* (hereafter cited as *BN*).[2] The justification for this initial concentration on the early works is twofold. First, since later sections of the present chapter are also partially devoted to Sartre, the most convenient manner of presentation seems to be to begin with his early thought and to introduce later developments and modifications in his thinking, as well as material from sources other than Sartre, as they are pertinent to the subsequent critical discussion. Such an approach best facilitates the transition from an exposition of Sartre's views to a critical evaluation of them, and of the issues raised by them. A further justification for this procedure lies in my conviction, to be defended in some detail in this chapter, that Sartre's later philosophy can only be understood by reference to his early views, since it is, for the most part, a *development* of these views, a continuation of the early philosophy which takes that philosophy as its foundation; it is not, as some commentators have thought,[3] a repudiation of, or a "radical conversion" from, his previous outlook. Let us turn, then, to an examination of some of the salient features of Sartre's early philosophy.

1.2   Sartre's Arguments for Freedom

Sartre's arguments for the freedom of consciousness are all founded on an alleged connection between consciousness and negativity—a connection which Sartre never tires of attempting to demonstrate, and which is so basic for him that he does not hesitate to define consciousness as the reality that "is not what it is and is what it is not."[4] But what on earth can Sartre possibly mean by this paradoxical and perplexing definition? An answer to this question should take us a long way toward understanding why Sartre conceives of consciousness as free, since all of his arguments for freedom, superficially diverse though they may be, can for the most part be profitably understood as variations on two basic arguments, corresponding to the two components of the above-stated definition. Let us begin, then, by examining the first of Sartre's arguments, which stems from his attempt to show that consciousness "is not what it is."

1.2.1   The First Argument: Consciousness is Not What it Is

Consciousness is not what it is, because it is not any *thing* at all. It is not any kind of substance; it is not an ego; it cannot be identified with its objects, nor with its states, its moods, or its emotions. Moreover, it is not in any sense a *container* of things. Rather, all of its objects, whether physical or mental, perceived or imagined, "real" or "unreal," are *external* to it. Indeed, *literally everything* is external to it. In itself, it is nothing at all. Consequently, consciousness is completely independent from the world of things and from the causal order; consciousness is completely, or as Sartre would say, "absolutely," free.

This conception of consciousness results from Sartre's radical interpretation of Edmund Husserl's doctrine of intentionality: the doctrine that consciousness is always consciousness *of* something.[5] The point of this principle is that consciousness is always *directional*; that consciousness, in every one of its acts and in every one of its modes, always points toward some object. Thus, if I see, I see *something*; if I imagine, I imagine *something*; if I question, I question *something*; and if I am not conscious of anything, I am simply *un*conscious.

What makes Sartre's interpretation of this doctrine radical is his insistence, as against Husserl, that it has "realistic" ontological implications. Thus Sartre, in an article devoted entirely to the concept of intentionality, refers to the "necessity for consciousness to exist as consciousness *of something other than itself.*"[6] So interpreted, the principle of intentionality becomes Sartre's main instrument for "ejecting" all contents from consciousness.

A good example of Sartre's procedure is his critique of the "alimentary" psychologists, who had attempted to describe knowledge as a process in which consciousness assimilates objects and makes them contents of itself. As Sartre puts it in his splendid metaphorical description of this theory, "we have all believed that the spidery mind trapped things in its web, covered them with a white spit and slowly swallowed them, reducing them to its own substance."[7]

The chief difficulty with this theory is that it clashes violently with our experience, both of things and of our own consciousnesses. As for things, it is clear that they do not present themselves in experience as existing in consciousness. Rather, the tree that I see is plainly given as existing "at the side of the road, in the midst of the dust, alone and writhing in the heat, eight miles from the Mediterranean coast."[8] This alone is for Sartre a clear indication that the tree "could not enter into . . . consciousness, for it is not of the same nature as consciousness."[9]

The same conclusion is reached when we turn to examine our own consciousnesses, only to find an obscure, shadowy realm which, again, simply cannot be compared to the realm of objects. For in the latter realm we have found that certain objects, like the tree, present themselves with a degree of clarity, solidity, and sheer massive obtrusiveness that has no analogue in our experience of our own consciousnesses.

It would seem, then, that the alimentary theory cannot serve as an adequate theory of knowledge. But where, specifically, does it go wrong?

The main source of the alimentary theory's difficulties is, for Sartre, its acceptance of the Cartesian assumption that consciousness must be some kind of substance, or "thing," albeit a thing whose nature differs radically from that of physical objects. The acceptance of this assumption accounts for: (1) the very need for the alimentary theory to be invented in the first place, since the assumption makes it difficult to understand, and thus necessary to explain, how such unlike things as consciousnesses and physical objects can ever enter into the kinds of relationships which seem required in order for knowledge to be possible; (2) the final form which the theory takes, since the assumption renders interaction between the two substances impossible unless one substance is reduced to another, as when consciousness is conceived of as a kind of thing which *contains* other kinds of things; and (3) the principal weakness of the theory, since it is precisely this reduction of one substance to another, necessitated by the Cartesian assumption, which is so starkly contradicted by experience. What is needed, then, is a theory which can account for knowledge without vainly trying to put things *into* consciousness, but which instead recognizes the reality of things *outside of* consciousness. The chief virtue of Husserl's notion of intentionality, as Sartre understands it, is that it alone is capable of founding such a theory.

The principle of intentionality shows that consciousness need not be viewed as a thing which confronts other things, or which tries to assimilate them. Instead, it reveals the possibility, which is more in keeping with our experience, of conceiving of consciousness as a *process* of "shooting out" toward, and thereby revealing, objects. It is not that consciousness is a *thing*, one of whose *features* is intentionality; rather, as Sartre sees it, consciousness itself *is* intentionality. To know is to know *something*; but this means, not that consciousness *does* the knowing, but that consciousness in this instance *is* the act of knowing. Consciousness can be understood, not as a thing, but only as an irreducible fact which no physical image, "except perhaps the quick, obscure image of a burst," can capture. Thus, "to know is to 'burst toward.'"[10]

This conception of consciousness obviously excites Sartre:

> All at once consciousness is purified, it is clear as a strong wind. There is nothing in it but a movement of fleeing itself, a sliding beyond itself. If, impossible though it be, you could enter "into" a consciousness you would be seized by a whirlwind and thrown back outside, in the thick of the dust, near the tree, for consciousness has no "inside". It is just this being beyond itself, this absolute flight, this refusal to be a substance which makes it a consciousness.[11]

We are now in a position to see precisely why Sartre finds Husserl's notion of intentionality so liberating. Here at last is a doctrine which can free consciousness from the constraints of its own subjectivity, injecting it back into the real world. The fact that consciousness is essentially intentional guarantees, for Sartre, that it can be brought into a direct confrontation with real things in the world, rather than merely with its own contents.

1.2.1.1   The rejection of the phenomenological reduction

At this point, Sartre would seem to be open to an obvious objection from within the phenomenological tradition, namely, that his realistic interpretation of intentionality, which is so crucial to his argument for the freedom of consciousness, is in fact a violent and completely illegitimate distortion of that Husserlian doctrine. As Herbert Spiegelberg explains, Sartre, in his article on intentionality,

> credited Husserl's intentionality with having destroyed the idea of immanence, since consciousness-of referred essentially to something beyond, thus "expelling" the things from consciousness and "liberating" it. Sartre did not mention the fact that according to Husserl the intended object is constituted by consciousness and certainly not independent of it.[12]

By the time of *BN,* however, Sartre had come to realize that the principle of intentionality

> can be taken in two very distinct senses: either we understand by this that consciousness is constitutive of the being of its object, or it means that consciousness in its inmost nature is a relation to a transcendent being.[13]

The principal task of the introduction to *BN,* then, is precisely to affirm the latter interpretation of intentionality as against the former, which is attributed to Husserl. Before examining his arguments, it might prove useful to take a brief look at Husserl's position.

While the passage by Spiegelberg quoted above represents a somewhat idealistic interpretation of Husserl's views,[14] it is clear that Husserl has always, even in his least idealistic moods, insisted that the question of the actual existence of the intentional object must be "bracketed," or "placed in suspension." This is the famous procedure which is known as "the phenomenological reduction." Husserl argues, on strictly phenomenological grounds, that "any experience, however extensive, leaves open the possibility that what is given does *not* exist."[15] I can only know with certainty that I *experience* an object; I cannot be certain that the object actually exists. Thus, while I *know* that I *see* a desk, for this is an absolute datum, I can only *conjecture* that *there is* a desk, for this is a matter of contingent fact which is affirmed only by going beyond what is strictly given in experience. So if philosophy is to be conceived, with Husserl, as a radically experiential discipline to be founded on descriptive fidelity, the obvious conclusion is that the question of the actual existence of intentional objects must, at least initially, be bracketed.

The rejection of this Husserlian reduction, and the reaffirmation of the world's existence, are major themes, not only in the introduction to *BN,* but also in Sartre's early, "phenomenological," writings, written at a time when Sartre apparently was less clear about the degree of his divergence from Husserl. Perhaps Sartre's most fundamental argument stems from his attempt to demonstrate, contra Husserl, that the existence of the world is indeed a datum of our experience, rather than an inference from it, that the objects of our perceptual experience clearly do present themselves as overwhelmingly and irreducibly real. (This, to a large extent, is the point of Roquentin's encounter with the chestnut tree in Sartre's great philosophical novel, *Nausea*.[16]) Maurice Merleau-Ponty, who agrees with Sartre on this issue, goes so far as to claim that "the most important lesson which the reduction teaches us is the impossibility of a complete reduction. This is why Husserl is constantly re-examining the possibility of the reduction."[17]

Now Sartre does not merely *assert* that the existence of the world is an irreducible datum of experience; he also argues against the reduction on the grounds that the distinction on which it depends, that between object-as-experienced and object-as-existing, or if you prefer, between appearance and reality, is untenable. Thus, he claims that

> the being of an existent is exactly what it *appears* . . . [The phenomenon] does not point over its shoulder to a true being which would be, for it, absolute. What it is, it is absolutely, for it reveals itself as it is. The phenomenon can be studied and described as such, for it is *absolutely indicative* of itself.[18]

To be sure, the distinction which Sartre is here denying does seem to have an obvious basis in experience. We are often fooled in our perceptions of things, and it is tempting to think of this in terms of being fooled by *mere appearances*. "You can't judge a book by its cover" is an old homily which captures the insight that the essences of things are often missed when we look at them hurriedly or superficially. And yet, as Husserl points out,[19] the corrective to faulty seeing is simply more (and better) seeing. Frequently we need to "look again," from several different angles, and often we need to consult others who, through their arguments, examples, and elaborations, *point out* to us what they see so that we might see it as well.[20] Through this process of coming to see things more and more clearly, and comprehensively, we may begin to think that we are finally seeing things "as they are." But it is clear that we have not moved beyond the plane of phenomena. Thus, the distinction which we find *in experience* between appearance and reality is not that between, say, the desk as it appears and the desk itself; rather, there is only a distinction between this or that appearance of the desk and the *infinite series of all possible appearances of the desk*.

And if the reality of the desk is thus to be understood solely in terms of its possible appearances, there can be no question of some underlying, unperceived desk, the existence of which would need to be bracketed.[21] Here again, Merleau-Ponty perhaps exceeds Sartre in expressing the move that has just been made: "we must not . . . wonder whether we really perceive a world, we must instead say: the world is what we perceive."[22]

At this point the reader is likely to be troubled by an apparent contradiction in Sartre's reasoning, as I have been presenting it. On the one hand, Sartre claims that the real existence of the world is an irreducible and un-bracketable datum of our experience. On the other hand, he rejects the existence/appearance distinction altogether, partly on the grounds that we cannot move beyond the realm of phenomena! Surely the former claim cannot be rescued from utter triviality if existence is held to be identical to appearance; yet this is precisely what the latter claim seems to hold. And this latter claim appears to trivialize the entire dispute over the reduction by giving it a definitional solution; for if "the being of an existent" is simply defined as being "exactly what it appears," there obviously can be no question of bracketing the existence of a thing so as to focus on its appearance. But Sartre does not intend his arguments to be taken as trivial elaborations of the consequences of the definitions of words. How, then, are we to understand them?

Perhaps the first issue standing in need of clarification is Sartre's attempt to equate being with phenomena. The central point here is that "the being of that which *appears* does not exist *only* in so far as it appears."[23] Clearly, there is more to my desk than what I see when I look at it right now, as there is more to it than is given in any single act of consciousness. But to say that the desk cannot be equated with any one of its appearances is not to say that its existence transcends the phenomenal realm altogether. Rather, the way is cleared for an identification of the table with the series of its appearances, and such an identification seems necessary if we are to account for our experience without appealing beyond it.

Consider, once again, my desk. I now perceive it as brown in color, standing upright to my left, on its four feet, etc. But the following is also a datum of my experience: this desk that I now see is the same desk that I *would* see if I were to look at it through rose-colored glasses, or move it to my right, or turn it upside-down, or cut off one of its legs. Indeed, if I were conscious of the desk only through one of its attributes, say, its uprightness, in abstraction from all of its other perceivable aspects, I would not be conscious of a *desk* at all, but only of the property "uprightness." Thus, since I most certainly am conscious of a *desk*, I must be identifying the desk with a series of its appearances; and since this series cannot be limited to a finite number—there are always additional perspectives from which to perceive an object—the desk must be identified with the infinite series of its possible appearances.

It is now apparent, then, that Sartre equates reality with an infinite series of appearances, rather than with a single appearance, and so his position is readily distinguishable from Berkeley's "to be is to be perceived." The object always surpasses not only our individual experiences of it but also our knowledge of it (since there are always more perspectives from which to observe it). The path is thus laid clear for an investigation of the *transphenomenal being* of the phenomenon.

It would seem, then, that the previously mentioned objections to Sartre's reasoning can be answered after all. First of all, the rejection of the existence/appearance dualism does not contradict the claim that existence is a datum of experience. While it is true that we cannot move beyond the realm of appearances, we can see that the object transcends any finite series of its appearances; and this transphenomenality, which is itself grounded in our experience, is identical to the being of the object. Moreover, the claim that being is experienceable can no longer be regarded as trivial, for there might, after all, have been no experiential grounding of transphenomenality.

The remaining objection is that Sartre has simply eliminated the possible need for the reduction through sheer linguistic fiat. Indeed, it is by no means obvious that his definitional identification of being with transphenomenality eliminates all possibility of the existence of a hidden noumenal realm, or of realities entirely distinct from appearances. It is, of course, this possibility which Husserl "brackets," and such bracketing at least implies an acknowledgement of a possibility which Sartre denies.

In one sense, Sartre's disagreement with Husserl on this point is less radical than it seems. Both philosophers endeavor to be experientialists; neither has room for unexperienceable entities in his thinking. Husserl gets rid of such entities by bracketing them; Sartre disposes of them by denying them. Moreover, insofar as Husserl's insistence upon the reduction does not appear in any way to have been motivated by real doubts about the existence of the world,[24] his rejection of Sartre's subsequent route might be attributed more to methodological differences, and to differences in interest, than to significant ontological disagreements between the two thinkers.

Let us also remember that Sartre's main reason for rejecting the phenomenological reduction is that it leaves open as a possibility what Sartre regards as manifestly impossible, namely the "idealistic" thesis that "consciousness is constitutive of the being of its object." Now, whatever other kind of being any given object might be said to have, its transphenomenality alone is enough, according to Sartre, to show that it has some kind of existence apart from any constituting consciousness. Thus, even this arguably minimal conception of being is sufficient to establish a phenomenological realism, and thereby to eliminate the need for (and the possibility of) a reduction.

What we have not yet seen, however, is the reason why this phenomenon of transphenomenality is sufficient to guarantee the real existence of objects apart from any consciousness. One of Sartre's arguments, as summarized by Frederick A. Olafson, is that

> since objects, whatever their status, are never exhaustively given to an instantaneous intuition, a "constitutive consciousness," as conceived by Husserl, could reproduce this central feature of our consciousness of objects only by intending the infinite series of appearances that compose the object and at the same time not intending all those that are not presently given. This it manifestly cannot do, and thus . . . the transcendence of objects is established.[25]

Leaving aside questions pertaining to the soundness of this piece of reasoning, one of its noteworthy features is that it illustrates Sartre's familiar technique of grafting a "regressive" argument onto a phenomenological description.[26] Sartre typically begins by describing certain phenomena, and then asks what else, besides what is given directly in experience, *must* be the case given these particular phenomena. In this instance, Sartre begins by describing the phenomenon of transphenomenality, and then argues that the phenomenon described cannot be *explained* except through reference to real beings existing outside of consciousness.

Sartre uses similar reasoning in his chapter on Husserl in *Imagination*.[27] There he moves from a detailed description of the experienced difference between perception and imagination to the conclusion that this difference cannot be explained except on the assumption that the perceived object really exists. Unlike the imagined object, which can be called to mind and altered at will, the perceived object presents itself with a certain stubborn obtrusiveness. It *resists* my conscious attempts to alter it, to deny it, or even to "bracket" it; and this "coefficient of resistance," Sartre argues, surely cannot be held to originate from my conscious act, since, as we have seen, it is given in experience as arising *against* my conscious acts. Thus, the existence of the perceived object must be granted, rather than bracketed.[28]

As a final illustration of Sartre's regressive method in arguing against the reduction, consider the following passage from *The Psychology of Imagination*:

> phenomenological descriptions can discover . . . that the very structure of the transcendental consciousness implies that this consciousness is constitutive *of a world*. But it is evident that they will not teach us that consciousness must be constitutive *of* such a world, that is exactly the one where we are, with its earth, its animals, its men and the story of these men. We are here in the presence of a primary and irreducible fact which presents itself as a contingent and irrational specification of the noematic essence of the *world*.[29]

Sartre's point is that an idealistic interpretation of intentionality becomes implausible as soon as we turn our attention away from eidetic structures of experience and toward matters of fact. That is, while certain general patterns of experience might well be seen as stemming from essential structures of consciousness, this cannot reasonably be said of the "factical" dimension of our experience. Thus, while it might be of the very nature of consciousness that it have perceptual experiences of a world, this is no explanation of the specific perceptual patterns, or of the "world," that we do in fact perceive. Rather, this dimension of our perceptual experience can only be explained by the actual existence of the perceived world apart from our consciousness of it.

It is through arguments such as these that Sartre attempts to safeguard his conception of consciousness, and by extension his argument for freedom, from objections arising from the phenomenological reduction. There is nothing inside of consciousness, since its objects exist *independently* of it, outside in the world.

1.2.1.2   The transcendence of the ego

But intentional objects are not the only candidates for inhabitancy in consciousness. To the contrary, Sartre himself acknowledges that "for most philosophers the *ego* is an 'inhabitant' of consciousness."[30] Once again Sartre finds himself in opposition to Husserl, for whom there is a "transcendental ego" that stands behind all conscious acts, accounting for their origin and their directedness.[31] The purpose of Sartre's essay, *The Transcendence of the Ego* (hereafter cited as *TE*), is precisely to refute this view and to show, contra Husserl, "that the ego is neither formally nor materially *in* consciousness: it is outside, *in the world*. It is a being of the world, like the ego of another."[32] The relevance of this issue to our discussion consists in the fact that any identification of consciousness with an ego would tend to threaten Sartre's conception of consciousness as that which is not what it is; and this conception of consciousness, as we have seen, forms the basis of Sartre's first argument for freedom. So it should prove useful to examine briefly Sartre's reasoning in this essay, as it will allow us, not only to see how he answers the Husserlian threat, but also to witness the completion of Sartre's project of evacuating all entities from consciousness.

According to Sartre, "it is ordinarily thought that the existence of a transcendental *I* may be justified by the need that consciousness has for unity and individuality. It is because all my perceptions and all my thoughts refer themselves back to this permanent seat that my consciousness is unified."[33] But surely the fact that consciousness is unified and individuated is not by itself a proof that the transcendental ego is *responsible* for this unification and individuation. Rather, there is still a need to ask the following question: "is the *I* that we encounter in our consciousness made possible by the synthetic unity of our representations, or is it the *I* which in fact unites the representations to each other?"[34]

Sartre comes down strongly in favor of the former alternative, attributing to consciousness the unity and individuality of the ego, rather than the other way around.[35] Sartre's view here echoes that of the early Husserl, who, in the first edition of the *Logical Investigations,* had written that the contents of conscious acts

> have, as contents generally have, their own law-bound ways of coming together, of losing themselves in more comprehensive unities, and, in so far as they thus become and are one, the phenomenological ego or unity of consciousness is already constituted, without need of an additional, peculiar ego-principle which supports all contents and unites them all once again. Here as elsewhere it is not clear what such a principle would effect.[36]

Thus, Sartre upholds the early Husserl against his later self when he concludes that

> the phenomenological conception of consciousness renders the unifying and individualizing role of the *I* totally useless. It is consciousness, on the contrary, which makes possible the unity and the personality of my *I*. The transcendental *I*, therefore, has no *raison d'être.*[37]

Spiegelberg objects that "Sartre's main reason for denying the 'I' transcendental status is that he found it to be unnecessary and hence useless, a reason which sounds more like the logic of Occam's razor than like phenomenology."[38] But this objection loses its force when we realize that Sartre is here responding to what might be called a "regressive" argument for the existence of the transcendental ego. At this stage Sartre is not addressing himself to the claim that the transcendental ego is a datum of experience—this would call for a response strictly on the plane of descriptive phenomenology. Rather, Sartre is addressing himself to the claim that *there must be* a transcendental ego to explain the unity and individuality of consciousness. He is responding to the Husserl who admits that

> we shall not encounter the pure Ego anywhere in the flux of manifold mental process. . . . In contradistinction, the pure Ego would, however, seem to be something essentially *necessary*; and, as something absolutely identical throughout every actual or possible change in mental processes, *it cannot in any sense be a really inherent part or moment* of the mental processes themselves.[39]

Husserl's claim, then, is not that *we find* a transcendental ego, but that there *must be* a transcendental ego, given some other things that we find. Thus, it is only appropriate for Sartre at this stage to take up, not the factual issue, but the question of whether there is a theoretical *need* for the transcendental ego. His conclusion, that this ego is superfluous, unnecessary, and useless, is not an appeal to Occam's razor; it is an attempt to answer Husserl on his own terms.

Well then, what *about* the question of fact? Even if there is no theoretical need for the transcendental ego, might not its existence nonetheless be affirmed simply as a datum of experience?

At first glance an affirmative answer would seem inescapable, for whenever we reflect upon any of our experiences we always find them to be connected to an experiencing "I." Thus, I might describe some of my experiences by saying "*I* have been running after a streetcar," "*I* am looking at the time," "*I* have been contemplating a question," etc. Indeed, the presence of an I in each of my experiences is given with such clarity and distinctness that Descartes did not hesitate to affirm it as the foundation for all other knowledge.[40] Thus, while I might well doubt the correctness of any thought that I might be thinking, what cannot in any case be doubted is that *I* am the one doing the doubting—*I* am thinking.

Sartre's objection to this claim is that it depends upon giving an illegitimate priority to reflection, which is in fact a secondary mode of consciousness. While I am unreflectively engaged in thinking, my consciousness is entirely directed toward and bound up with the object of my thought. It is only subsequently, when I take a step back and directly focus upon my previous act of thinking, that I first discover an "I"; and this is, of course, an entirely new act of consciousness. "Thus the consciousness which says *I think* is precisely not the consciousness which thinks."[41]

Sartre's conclusion, based on the fact that there is no I in unreflected consciousness, and on the further fact, acknowledged by Husserl,[42] that reflection modifies the spontaneous consciousness, is that the I is *brought into existence* by reflection:

> There is no *I* on the unreflected level. When I run after a streetcar, when I look at the time, when I am absorbed in contemplating a portrait, there is no *I*. There is consciousness *of the streetcar-having-to-be-overtaken*, etc. . . . In fact, I am then plunged into the world of objects; it is they which constitute

the unity of my consciousnesses; it is they which present themselves with values, with attractive and repellent qualities—but *me,* I have disappeared. . . . There is no place for *me* on this level. And this is not a matter of chance, due to a momentary lapse of attention, but happens because of the very structure of consciousness.[43]

What Sartre proposes, then, is a non-egological conception of consciousness.[44] Thus, we must not say " '*I have* consciousness of this chair,' but 'There is consciousness of this chair.' This content is sufficient to constitute an infinite and absolute field of investigation for phenomenology."[45]

Now Sartre adds that, in addition to there being neither theoretical nor experiential justification for the transcendental ego, its existence would also be a positive hindrance.

If it existed it would tear consciousness from itself; it would divide consciousness; it would slide into every consciousness like an opaque blade. The transcendental *I* is the death of consciousness. Indeed, the existence of consciousness is an absolute because consciousness is consciousness of itself. And consciousness is aware of itself *in so far as it is consciousness of a transcendent object.* All is therefore clear and lucid in consciousness: the object with its characteristic opacity is before consciousness, but consciousness is purely and simply consciousness of being consciousness of that object. This is the law of its existence.[46]

At least three elements of the above passage stand in need of clarification: (1) Why is the transcendental ego "the death of consciousness"? (2) In what sense is consciousness always conscious of itself? and (3) what is the justification for (2)?

(1) The problem here is that Sartre insists upon a highly metaphorical presentation of his argument. Thus, we are told that the ego would be a "center of opacity" which would "congeal" and "darken" consciousness, spoiling the "lightness" and "translucence" of the latter. The I would "load consciousness down," making it "heavy and ponderable."[47]

Perhaps the key to Sartre's argument, obscured by this procession of metaphors, is that the introduction of the transcendental ego destroys "the fruitful definition" of consciousness as intentionality.[48] We must remember that under Sartre's realistic interpretation of intentionality, consciousness is brought into a direct encounter with real objects existing in the world. But consciousness cannot encounter things *as they are* unless it is itself totally transparent. Consciousness must bring nothing to the encounter if the thing encountered is to be the pure, unadulterated object. If, on the other hand, consciousness were to bring some excess metaphysical baggage, like the transcendental ego, into the encounter, this baggage would inevitably interfere with consciousness's access to the object, partially obscuring or even distorting it. Thus, Sartre's rejection of the transcendental ego may be seen as completing his attempt to purify consciousness; just as his realistic interpretation of intentionality had purified consciousness by ridding it of the object known, now his rejection of the transcendental ego purifies consciousness by ridding it of the knowing subject.[49]

(2) The difficulty here is that, on the one hand, Sartre rejects the transcendental ego on the grounds that consciousness is originally pre-reflective, with no ego appearing; and yet, on the other hand, we are now told that consciousness is always consciousness of itself, and this sounds perilously close to saying that consciousness is always reflective.

Sartre's answer to this dilemma is that pre-reflective consciousness is "non-positionally," or "non-thetically," aware of itself, which is to say that consciousness is implicitly aware of itself *without taking itself for an object.*[50]

(3) Sartre's first argument for this conception of consciousness is that implicit self-consciousness is both a necessary and a sufficient condition for a knowing consciousness to be knowledge of its object.

> This is a necessary condition, for if my consciousness were not consciousness of being consciousness of the table, it would then be consciousness of that table without consciousness of being so. In other words, it would be a consciousness ignorant of itself, an unconscious consciousness—which is absurd. This is a sufficient condition, for my being conscious of being conscious of that table suffices in fact for me to be conscious of it.[51]

At best, this argument shows that consciousness must be aware of itself. But it does not show that this self-consciousness is merely implicit. What is to prevent us from claiming that consciousness is always explicitly an object for itself, as is clearly the case in reflection?

Sartre's answer, of course, is that a careful inventory of the objects of a pre-reflective consciousness does not include consciousness itself. Thus, if I am engrossed in some activity, say, counting cigarettes, my attention is entirely directed toward, and occupied with, the cigarettes. There is no "I" here; my consciousness simply is not explicitly focused on itself.

Now, however, a problem seems to arise. On the one hand, Sartre provides an argument showing that consciousness must be aware of itself; but this argument cannot establish the implicitness of this awareness. On the other hand, Sartre's descriptions of pre-reflective experience—the cigarettes, the streetcar, etc.—show that there is no explicit self-awareness; but these descriptions do not by themselves entail *any* kind of self-awareness. What is needed, then, is an argument which can establish both that prereflective consciousness is aware of itself, and that this awareness is "non-positional."

Perhaps one could maintain that just such an argument can be fashioned simply by conjoining Sartre's two arguments. Thus, Sartre's first argument shows that consciousness is always aware of itself, while the second argument shows that consciousness does not always take itself explicitly as an object. The obvious conclusion is that consciousness sometimes is aware of itself without taking itself explicitly as an object. That is, while consciousness is *always* self-*aware,* it is only *sometimes* self-*reflective.*[52]

Sartre attempts to prove this in yet another way by drawing out the implications of what is involved in passing from pre-reflective to reflective consciousness. Let us return to the example of counting cigarettes. As we have seen, my consciousness is initially concerned exclusively with the cigarettes, and there is no explicit self-awareness. And yet, if suddenly someone were to burst into the room and ask me what I have been doing, I could reply at once, "I am counting cigarettes."[53] Where does this knowledge come from? Clearly, my consciousness must have had some awareness of itself all along, even though this awareness of itself was not explicit. Moreover, this same phenomenon can be witnessed in all shifts from the pre-reflective to the reflective mode of consciousness. "The 'I' that is so seldom present is always available, on call."[54]

> If, for example, I want to remember a certain landscape perceived yesterday from the train, it is possible for me to bring back the memory of that landscape as such. But I can also recollect that *I* was seeing that landscape. . . . In other words, I can always perform any recollection whatsoever in the personal mode, and at once the *I* appears.[55]

Thus, the "I" can always be brought into being by an act of reflective consciousness, but, prior to reflection, there is no "I." Consciousness, therefore, cannot be identified with an ego;[56] nor, as we have seen, can it be equated with its objects. Are we justified in concluding, then, that consciousness cannot be identified with *anything*, that it is *nothing* at all, that it "is not what it is"?

1.2.1.3   Acts, Roles, Psychic States, and Emotions

At this point such a conclusion would be premature. "We could still identify consciousness with its acts, its roles, its psychic states, with its emotions perhaps."[57] But Sartre will not allow such identification. He claims, rather, that the above-named items, like the ego itself, are merely objects which consciousness, that great "clear wind," freely passes over and leaves behind.

This is perhaps easiest to see in the case of emotions and other "psychic" states. I cannot identify myself with, say, my sadness, for the simple reason that my state of being sad is, with any luck at all, a transitory phenomenon. Moreover, the separability of my consciousness from my emotional state can be demonstrated by the simple move from the pre-reflective to the reflective level of consciousness. Thus, as James M. Edie explains,

> Sartre shows that whenever and as soon as I can reflexively say to myself "I am sad," or "I hate," or "I love," for instance, I . . . *am* no longer sad or hateful or in love, because I have become the consciousness of a state of being sad, of a state of being in love, and so on. My consciousness cannot *be* sad, since sadness is a state that affects the being (in this case myself) of which I am conscious.[58]

Similar reasoning is used to establish that consciousness cannot be identified with its acts, its roles, its decisions, etc. Suppose that I am a gambler who has resolved to give up gambling, but now find myself in the presence of the gaming table. The overwhelming presence of my temptation establishes clearly that I *am not* my past resolution. My resolution

> is there doubtless but fixed, ineffectual, surpassed by the very fact that I am conscious *of* it. The resolution is still *me* to the extent that I realize constantly my identity with myself across the temporal flux, but it is no longer *me*—due to the fact that it has become an object *for* my consciousness. I am not subject to it, it fails in the mission which I have given it . . . I should have liked so much not to gamble anymore; yesterday I even had a synthetic apprehension of the situation (threatening ruin, disappointment of my relatives) as *forbidding me* to play. It seemed to me that I had established a *real barrier* between gambling and myself, and now I suddenly perceive that my former understanding of the situation is no more than a memory of an idea, a memory of a feeling. In order for it to come to my aid once more, I must remake it *ex nihilo* and freely. The not-gambling is only one of my possibilities, as the fact of gambling is another of them, neither more nor less. I *must rediscover* the fear of financial ruin or of disappointing my family, etc., I must re-create it as experienced fear. . . . After having patiently built up barriers and walls, after enclosing myself in the magic circle of a resolution, I perceive with anguish that *nothing* prevents me from gambling.[59]

Several noteworthy points are raised in this unusually rich passage. First of all, the reason for the non-identification of consciousness with its acts is shown to be the same as that which separates consciousness from its emotions: both of these can be turned into objects *for* consciousness. Thus, my resolution ceases to *be* me at the precise moment when it becomes an object *for* me.

Secondly, the passage underscores quite clearly the essential connection between freedom and negativity. I am free from my past resolution only because I *am not* that resolution.

Moreover, in this instance my freedom is experienced negatively in yet a different sense: I find it a painful burden. I wish that my past resolution had causal efficacy; I wish I were not free to gamble. But, as my futile attempt to escape from my freedom indicates, I am not free not to be free—I am, in Sartre's famous phrase, "condemned to be free."[60]

This painful experience of the inalienability of freedom is at the root of two other famous Sartrean themes: bad faith and anguish. Bad faith, at least in the form with which we are now concerned, consists in the attempt to deny one's freedom, and to take oneself for some kind of "thing": solid, immutable, unfree. Anguish, on the other hand, is that from which one flees in bad faith, since "it is in anguish that man gets the consciousness of his freedom."[61]

While one might well wonder why Sartre considers anguish to be *the* consciousness of freedom,[62] there can be no doubt that it is *a* consciousness of freedom. We have already seen this in the case of the gambler, but it can perhaps be brought out even more plainly by reflecting on the experienced difference between anguish and fear. As Sartre explains, "a situation provokes fear if there is a possibility of my life being changed from without; my being provokes anguish to the extent that I distrust myself and my own reactions in that situation."[63] For example, suppose that I am on a narrow path, without a guard rail, which goes along a precipice. If I am worried that I might fall because of a sliding stone, a gust of wind, or a patch of ice—this is fear. If I am worried that I might hurl myself over the precipice—this is anguish. Or, should this example appear extreme, consider that nearly any threatening situation is experienced through an oscillation of fear and anguish, "according to whether we envisage the situation as acting on the man or the man as acting on the situation."[64] Thus,

> The man who has just received a hard blow—for example, losing a great part of his wealth in a crash—can have the fear of threatening poverty. He will experience anguish a moment later when nervously wringing his hands . . . , he exclaims to himself: "What am I going to do? But what am I going to do?"[65]

The phenomenon of anguish, then, would seem to count as an independent argument for freedom. True, Sartre admits that "anguish has not appeared to us as a *proof* of human freedom,"[66] but in another work he quotes with approval Descartes' declaration that freedom is "known without proof and merely by our experience of it;"[67] and, as we have seen, Sartre finds this experience of freedom in the phenomenon of anguish. Moreover, this intuitive argument for freedom is perhaps strengthened by the realization that there is no counterbalancing intuition of determinism.

In any case, the phenomenon of anguish supports the general argument for freedom that we have been considering—namely, that I am free because I am a consciousness which is not what it is. We have already seen that I am not my objects, my ego, or my emotions. And now my anguish reveals that I cannot be identified with any one of my acts or roles. Unlike a stone, which simply "is what it is," I "overflow" all of my individual roles. I can step back from them, taking them for objects; I can ignore them, focusing instead on other matters; I can renounce them, and create other roles for myself. Thus, I am free.

1.2.2   The Second Argument: Consciousness Is What it is Not

To this point we have been examining in some detail, with a few detours, what it means to say that consciousness is not what it is, and why this characterization amounts to an argument for the freedom of consciousness. Let us now attempt to unravel the second half of Sartre's definition: "consciousness is what it is not." In the process, we will come to see that this confusing formulation implies the second of Sartre's two major arguments for freedom.

Consciousness is what it is not, because consciousness is characterized by its negative activities. It is only through such "nihilating" behaviors as imagining, doubting, abstracting, questioning, denying, etc., that non-being emerges in the world. And since consciousness is "the being by which Nothingness comes to the world," Sartre argues that "it must be its own Nothingness,"[68] and that "it must arise in the world as a No."[69] Thus, consciousness not only is (negatively) not what it is (e.g., its objects, the ego, its acts, roles, states, decisions, emotions, etc.), but it also is (positively) what it is not (e.g., the source of all "negativities," which it brings about through its multifarious nihilating activities).

We have already seen that, for Sartre, freedom is to be understood in terms of the connection between consciousness and negativity. Are we to assume, then, that these nihilating behaviors of consciousness are examples of what he regards as freedom? His answer is unequivocal: "nihilation is precisely the being of freedom."[70]

Sartre's procedure in arguing for this claim is "regressive" in the sense which I have already discussed. He begins by describing the

various nihilating behaviors of consciousness through which negativities are brought into being, and then asks, "what must man *be*
. . . in order that through him, nothingness may come to being?"[71]
Sartre's answer, at least in part, is that man must be free. In order
better to understand this, let us examine briefly Sartre's analyses of
some of these nihilating behaviors.

1.2.2.1 Imagination

Unlike the object of perception, which is experienced as really
existing, the imagined object is "posited as non-existent or as
absent or as existing elsewhere or not posited as existing."[72] Thus,
the essential characteristic of the image which distinguishes it from
the object of perception is that "the image involves a certain
nothingness."[73]

Let us consider an example. When I open my guitar case and
look inside, my guitar immediately presents itself with that certain
obtrusiveness, that "resistance," which characterizes objects of
perception. I *encounter* the guitar; I experience it *as being present,*
really existing out there in the world. Now suppose that, having lent
my guitar to a neighbor, I go back and reopen its case. I now
experience the *absence* of the guitar. This cannot be explained
simply by the fact that I do not perceptually encounter my guitar in
its case, for, speaking abstractly, there are also an infinite number
of other things—pink elephants, books, nails, etc.—that I do not
perceptually encounter there. Rather, I have an image of the guitar
only because my imaginative consciousness actively *places beside*
what I do perceive in the case (e.g., sheet music, some guitar picks,
and an extra set of strings) an image which presents the guitar *as
being absent.*[74] The guitar is therefore encountered as a *negativity,*
as an objective correlate of my *negative act.* Thus, the image of the
guitar, like all images, is given with "a certain nothingness."

Sartre next asks the question, "what must a consciousness be in
order for it to possess the power to imagine?"[75] He answers: "For a
consciousness to be able to imagine it must be able to escape from
the world by its very nature, it must be able by its own efforts to
withdraw from the world. In a word it must be free."[76]

We have already seen some of the reasons for this conclusion.
We have seen, for instance, that what distinguishes perception from
imagination in our experience is that the image is presented as to

some degree under the free control of consciousness, unlike the perceived object, which resists such control. Sartre adds to this argument that if images were in fact produced by a strict causality, there would be no distinguishing them from objects of perception. If something were at any time to *guarantee* that an image would be brought before my consciousness, I would be utterly incapable of distinguishing this image from a perceptual object. Moreover, we have seen that being *in-itself* is fully positive, containing no gaps, skips, or absences. My guitar case is transphenomenal; it gives itself as a source of an infinite number of perspectivally distinct perceptions. Negativities appear in it only following a free act of my consciousness. To be sure, it is somewhat misleading to say that my act *produces* or *creates* the absence of my guitar, for this absence cannot appear in my experience if my guitar is in fact present in my case. I can *experience* my guitar's absence only if it *really is* absent. My free act of consciousness is therefore a necessary, but not a sufficient, condition for the appearance of a negativity; but at least it *is* necessary, and therefore it is only because I am "transcendentally free that [I] can imagine."[77]

1.2.2.2 Doubt

Sartre agrees with Descartes that methodical doubt is "the very model of the free act."[78] On the basis of what we have already seen, the meaning of this statement should be clear. I can doubt only because I am able to tear myself apart from the world. As Sartre puts it, "doubt is a breaking of contact with being."[79] Were I completely engulfed in the world, bound by the chains of a thorough-going causal determinism, it would be quite impossible for me to effect that degree of separation from the world which is necessary if I am to call that world into question. It is only because I am *not* the world, and because I am *free from* the world, that I am able to effect that nihilating withdrawal from being that is involved in doubt. For this discovery Sartre credits Descartes: "no one before Descartes had stressed the connection between free will and negativity. No one had shown that freedom does not come from man as he is . . . , but rather from man as he *is not*."[80]

1.2.2.3 Destruction

Sartre attempts to extend this Cartesian insight by analyzing, characteristically, a much more extreme form of negativity, namely destruction. He begins with the seemingly outrageous claim that "man is the only being by whom a destruction can be accomplished. . . . *It is man* who destroys his cities through the agency of earthquakes . . . (and) who destroys his ships through the agency of cyclones."[81] As with many of Sartre's hyperbolic statements, most of the apparent preposterousness of the above claim evaporates once one realizes the precise, limited meaning which he intends his dramatic words to convey. In this case, the key point to understand is that Sartre is making a conceptual, rather than a causal, claim.[82] He is not submitting the absurd assertion that nature contains only benign and preservative forces, which human beings alone are capable of negating; nor does he argue that storms, earthquakes, volcanoes, and cyclones are illusory or "mere ideas." Rather, Sartre's claim is that the results which are brought about by these very real forces cannot properly be called "destruction," except through reference to a witness who can "nihilate" these results by recalling what is *not* (the state of affairs prior to, say, the tornado) and by comparing it to the present as that which is *no longer*. In-itself the storm is only capable of rearranging and redistributing matter, but such rearrangement and redistribution, in the absence of a nihilating consciousness, is not destruction. Thus, destruction cannot come into being without nihilating acts of consciousness; and nihilating acts of consciousness, as we have seen, are possible only for a *free* consciousness. The conclusion, strange though it may sound, is that destruction is possible only on the condition of the freedom of consciousness, and that the phenomenon of destruction is therefore a kind of evidence, or even proof, of freedom.[83]

1.2.2.4   Interrogation

The phenomenon of interrogation encompasses at least three distinct negativities, each of which reveals the nihilating capacity, and therefore the freedom, of consciousness. First of all, the asking of a question presupposes an ignorance on the part of the questioner. When I ask a question, *I do not know* whether the reply will be affirmative or negative.[84] Sartre calls this negativity "the non-being of knowledge in man."[85] Secondly, there always exists "for the questioner the permanent objective possibility of a negative reply."[86] This Sartre calls "the possibility of non-being in transcendent being."[87] Finally, negativities are introduced even in an affirmative reply, since we can always say of that reply that "it is thus *and not otherwise.*"[88] This is "the non-being of limitation."[89]

Sartre concludes, on the basis of his by now familiar "regressive" argument, that the appearance of these negativities can only be explained on the assumption of freedom:

> It is essential . . . that the questioner have the permanent possibility of dissociating himself from the causal series which constitutes being and which can produce only being. If we admitted that the question is determined in the questioner by universal determinism, the question would thereby become unintelligible and even inconceivable. . . . Thus in so far as the questioner must be able to effect in relation to the questioned a kind of nihilating withdrawal, he is not subject to the causal order of the world; he detaches himself from Being.[90]

The obvious objection to this sort of reasoning is that such nihilating behaviors as imagining, doubting, questioning, etc., *might,* contrary to appearances, prove to be determined after all. For example, at some stage in the future we might discover that our behavior is determined down to the last detail by external and "internal" causal forces. And yet, as Ian Craib argues,

> this very argument . . . is an example of freedom in the sense that Sartre uses the word: it nihilates the present state of what we call 'knowledge', where the freedom/determinism argument is unsettled and posits a state in which it is settled; it then nihilates the future state as not yet existing. . . . To say that Sartre's argument might, at some time, be open to a scientific proof of its rightness or wrongness is in fact itself a proof that his argument is correct.[91]

1.2.2.5   Perception

It may seem odd to regard perception as an *act* of consciousness, let alone as a *nihilating* act. To many, nothing could be more obvious than that perception is an essentially passive process in which physical objects, or "data" given off by them, are directly recorded in all their positivity by consciousness. Clearly, such a view differs radically from Sartre's, since it recognizes neither the activity nor the negativity of consciousness in perception. Why does Sartre dissent from such a view, and why does his disagreement with it amount to an argument for freedom?

Sartre assigns an active role to consciousness in perception because no alternative account can be reconciled with the data of experience. To say that my consciousness is passive when I perceive something is to say that what I perceive is *completely* determined by such factors as the physical features of the objects in front of me and the light rays which reach my eyes. But this is manifestly not the case, as can be easily shown.

Let us consider, for example, what is involved in "singling out" a sheet of paper.[92] Suppose that on my desk right now there are several books, sheets of paper, pens and pencils, a stapler, a clipboard, and a cup of tea, all arranged in a very close proximity to one another. Clearly, when I single out from this background and look at an individual sheet of paper, this is something that *I* do— something that the world, or the objects on the desk, cannot do for me. As proof of this, consider that, without the objects themselves physically changing in any way, and without their position changing or my physical position changing with respect to them, I can single out in perception first one, then another, then yet another, etc., at will. Thus, objects in the world cannot completely determine, either individually or collectively, what I perceive. Rather, another factor must come into play, and this factor is the activity of consciousness.

For Sartre, the fact that consciousness is active in perception can also be understood as an aspect of the intentionality of consciousness. As we have seen, Sartre's first argument for the freedom of consciousness stems from his conception of consciousness as consciousness of something, with emphasis on the fact that consciousness is distinct from, and therefore liberated from, the "of something" which is its object. This new facet of the intentionality of consciousness also amounts to an argument for freedom, though the emphasis now is on the free activity implicit in the "consciousness of" part of the equation. This needs to be explained more clearly. Why does the activity of consciousness in perception imply its freedom, and, moreover, why is this activity to be characterized as a *nihilating* behavior?

Let us return, once again, to the singling out of a sheet of paper on my desk. To see the paper, to make it "stand out" against the background of the other objects on the desk, it is necessary to relegate these other objects to the background, to *nihilate* them, and to envelop the sheet of paper in nothingness. In other words, in order to see the sheet of paper, in order for it to emerge against the background of the other objects, it is necessary to see it as *not* the books, *not* the stapler, *not* the cup of tea, etc., and as *not* my consciousness. Being in-itself, without regard to consciousness, is simply an undifferentiated mass. Individual objects emerge only when a consciousness, through its nihilating acts, establishes limits and boundaries such that *just these* objects are elevated to the foreground, while others sink into the background. Thus, the activity of consciousness in perception implies the freedom of consciousness, not only for the straightforward reason that my focusing on first one object and then another is directly experienced as being under my free control, but also because such singling out is always accomplished through the introduction of negativities; and these negativities in turn, for reasons which we have already discussed, can only be regarded as having their origin in free acts of consciousness.[93]

1.2.2.6   The experience of absence

Many of the themes which we have been examining concerning the relationship between freedom and nihilating acts of consciousness can perhaps most clearly be seen in the phenomenon of absence. Suppose, for example, that I have an appointment to meet my always-punctual friend Pierre at the café at four o'clock.[94] I arrive at the café fifteen minutes late and begin to look for Pierre. Will he have waited for me? As I continue my search, I have the experience of encountering a negativity, namely Pierre's absence. Finally, having surveyed the entire café, I arrive at a negative judgment: "Pierre is not here."

It should be noted, first of all, that negativity appears in the café only after my conscious act of looking for Pierre. In-itself the café contains no negativities.

> It is certain that the café by itself with its patrons, its tables, its booths, its mirrors, its light, its smoky atmosphere, and the sounds of voices, rattling saucers, and footsteps which fill it—the café is a fullness of being. And all the intuitions of detail which I can have are filled by these odors, these sounds, these colors, all phenomena which have a transphenomenal being. . . . We seem to have found fullness everywhere.[95]

Secondly, my search for Pierre illustrates quite clearly the fact that the world cannot completely determine what I see, that what I see is largely a function of the directedness or intentionality of my consciousness, through which I freely nihilate some portions of the plenitude of being which stands before me, while elevating others to the foreground. Sartre's discussion of these matters is worth quoting at some length:

> We must observe that in perception there is always the construction of a figure on a ground. No one object, no group of objects is especially designed to be organized as specifically either ground or figure; all depends on the direction of my attention. When I enter this café to search for Pierre, there is formed a synthetic organization of all the objects in the café, on the ground of which Pierre is given as about to appear. This organization of the café as the ground is an original nihilation. Each element of the setting, a person, a table, a chair, attempts to isolate itself, to lift itself upon the ground constituted by the totality of the other objects, only to fall back once more into the undifferentiation of this ground; it melts into the ground. For the ground is that which is seen only in addition, that which is the object of a purely marginal attention. Thus the original nihilation of all the figures which appear and are swallowed up in the total neutrality of a *ground* is the necessary condition for the appearance of the principle figure, which is here the presence of Pierre. This nihilation is given to my intuition; I am witness to the successive disappearance of all the objects which I look at—in particular of the faces, which detain me for an instant (Could this be Pierre?) and which as quickly decompose precisely because they "are not" the face of Pierre. Nevertheless if I should finally discover Pierre, my intuition would be filled by a solid element, I should be suddenly arrested by his face and the whole café would organize itself around him as a discrete presence.[96]

Thirdly, while Pierre's absence cannot occur without a consciousness expecting or hoping to find his presence, this does not render his absence "purely subjective." My expectation does not *cause* Pierre to be absent from the café—he might have waited for me; he might have been there. Rather, "it is an objective fact at present that I have *discovered* this absence, and it presents itself as a synthetic relation between Pierre and the setting in which I am looking for him."[97]

Finally, my encounter with Pierre's absence establishes that it is my positive intuition of negativity that founds my ability to make negative judgments, rather than the other way around. This point is crucial since so many critics, especially English-speaking analytical philosophers, have rejected Sartre's conception of negativity on the grounds that he has mistakenly granted ontological status to the purely linguistic category of negation. This objection is forcefully stated by the logical positivist A. J. Ayer, in one of the first critiques of Sartre's philosophy to appear in English:

> Sartre's reasoning on the subject of *le néant* seems to me exactly on a par with that of the King in 'Alice through the Looking-glass'. 'I see nobody on the road,' said Alice. 'I only wish I had such eyes,' remarked the King. 'To be able to see Nobody! And at that distance, too!' And again, if I remember rightly: 'Nobody passed me on the road'. 'He cannot have done that, or he would have been here first.' In these cases the fallacy is easy enough to detect, but although Sartre's reasoning is less engagingly naïve, I do not think that it is any better. The point is that words like 'nothing' and 'nobody' are not used as the names of something insubstantial and mysterious; they are not used to *name* anything at all. To say that two objects are separated by nothing is to say that they are *not* separated; and that is all that it amounts to. What Sartre does, however, is to say that, being separated by Nothing, the objects are both united and divided. There is a thread between them; only it is a very peculiar thread, both invisible and intangible.[98]

I do not think that this criticism is sound since Sartre, I believe, cannot plausibly be read as committing the same error as is committed by the King, that of misconstruing a quantifier as a name. Perhaps Ayer is led to this mistake by his failure to notice Sartre's distinction between an abstract negative judgment on the one hand, and a specific experience of a negativity on the other. Sartre's reasoning on the subject of nothingness is *not* "exactly on a par with that of the King," since Sartre is well aware, as the King is not, of the difference between the absence of a presence ("Nobody passed me on the road") and the presence of an absence ("He cannot have done that, or he would have been there first"). Thus, Sartre explicitly contrasts my concrete experience of Pierre's absence with

> judgments which I can make subsequently to amuse myself, such as "Wellington is not in this café, Paul Valéry is no longer here, etc."—these have a purely abstract meaning; they are pure applications of the principle of negation without real or efficacious foundation, and they never succeed in establishing a *real* relation between the cafe and Wellington or Valéry. Here

> the relation "is not" is merely *thought*. This example is sufficient to show that non-being does not come to things by a negative judgment; it is the negative judgment, on the contrary, which is conditioned and supported by non-being.[99]

Moreover, Ayer's criticism seems to me to depend upon an ill-conceived linguistic prescriptivism, as when he insists that "words like 'nothing' and 'nobody' are not used to *name* anything at all." Even if one were to grant that Ayer is correct in his analysis of the ordinary usage of these words and their French cognates, it by no means follows that Sartre is making a *mistake* by using these words differently. Ayer simply assumes this, ignoring the possibility, which seems in fact to be the case, that Sartre uses *"le néant"* as a technical term, with a consistent, clearly explained meaning of its own within his philosophy. That this meaning may not be identical to that of *"le néant"* in ordinary French usage is simply irrelevant.[100]

In any case, it should be plain from what has already been said that "nothingness" designates for Sartre what is introduced by consciousness through its acts of imagining, doubting, questioning, and perceiving, and through its experiences of destruction and absence. This list could be expanded indefinitely, as "nothingness" also denotes that which is introduced through conscious acts of denying, abstracting, isolating, etc., and through conscious experiences of the lacking, the possible, the ideal, and so on. These acts and experiences establish the freedom of consciousness since, as we have seen, nothing in the world external to consciousness is capable of determining or producing them. Thus, consciousness is free since it is what it is not (e.g., the source of all negativities, which it brings about through its free nihilating activities).

To this point we have examined some of Sartre's reasons for regarding consciousness as free, and we have seen that these stem from his conception of consciousness as that which is not what it is and is what it is not. In order to facilitate further discussion, it should now be pointed out that Sartre sometimes refers to consciousness as "being-for-itself,"[101] a fundamental ontological category which he often contrasts with "being-in-itself." Since we have already examined in some detail the (mainly negative) features of consciousness, perhaps all that remains to be said about being-for-itself at this stage is that it is so named principally because (aside from the fact that the term was handily available, having been used by Hegel) part of its nature is to be aware of itself and to be unable to exist without such self-awareness.[102]

By contrast, being-in-itself refers to that which does not exist for-itself, having no self-awareness or consciousness of its own, but which exists for some alien consciousness.[103] Other than this, little can be said about being-in-itself, and it should be clear from our discussion of the nihilating behaviors of consciousness why this is so. We can say that being-in-itself coincides with itself in a way that the for-itself (which is what it is not, etc.) does not. We can say that being-in-itself is all positivity, since consciousness is the source of all negativity. Beyond this, however, almost any statement that we might attempt to make about "brute being" as it exists apart from our consciousness of it is bound to involve some surreptitious introduction of that which is introduced through nihilating acts of consciousness. For example, we cannot say that being-in-itself contains sticks and stones, since sticks and stones can emerge *as* sticks and stones only subsequently to the introduction of a consciousness which can nihilate everything else given with them in a perceptual field while elevating the sticks and stones themselves to the foreground. Similarly, we cannot say that being-in-itself contains objects of various shapes and sizes and spatial locations, etc., since these facts also depend for their emergence upon the introduction of a consciousness capable of such nihilating behaviors as abstracting and isolating. Thus, being-in-itself must be conceived of as an opaque, massive, undifferentiated existence. It is sheer "being," in the strong sense of the word; it becomes a *world* only when a consciousness involves itself with it. Strictly speaking, all that can be said about "being" in this sense is this: "Being is. Being is in-itself. Being is what it is."[104]

1.3   The Nature of Freedom

Bearing all of this in mind, let us now return to see if we can achieve a clearer and more complete understanding of Sartre's theory of freedom. In doing so, however, it will be necessary to depart from the presentation which has been adopted thus far, in which we have restricted ourselves to exposition, with only an occasional foray into criticism. Rather, since, as I will attempt to show, Sartre's theory of freedom has become hopelessly obscured by the widespread acceptance of certain erroneous criticisms of it, it is no longer possible to explain Sartre's theory accurately without at the same time demonstrating that these criticisms are unsound. Thus, given the currently prevailing understanding of Sartre's theory of freedom, to explain that theory accurately *is* to provide a limited defense of it. The following discussion is intended to reflect that fact.

The biggest obstacle facing our attempt to clarify Sartre's theory of freedom is, however, probably *not* the widespread critical misunderstanding of it, but rather Sartre's own rather hyperbolic summations of his doctrine, which have undoubtedly precipitated this misunderstanding. Thus, we are repeatedly told in Sartre's writings that human beings are "absolutely free,"[105] "totally free,"[106] "condemned to be free,"[107] free "in any circumstances, in any period, and at any place,"[108] "even in the most crushing situations, the most difficult circumstances,"[109] that we are "wholly and forever free,"[110] and that "the slave in chains," therefore, "is as free as his master."[111] These statements represent Sartre's famous doctrine of "absolute freedom," for which he is so often censured.[112] Indeed, these statements, if taken at face value, do seem sufficiently preposterous as to leave little wonder why many philosophers, especially English-speaking members of the "analytical" school, have tended not to take Sartre seriously, or even to ridicule him.[113] Let us see if we can determine whether or not they are right to do so.

1.3.1   The Omnipotence Objection

According to Sartre, "the decisive argument which is employed by common sense against freedom consists in reminding us of our impotence."[114] This is also the "decisive argument" which is used by Sartre's critics against his doctrine of "absolute freedom," as any quick perusal of the secondary literature on Sartre will readily establish.[115] The argument usually runs something like this: First, we are told that Sartre's theory of freedom regards human beings as "totally" (or "completely," "absolutely," "entirely," etc.) free. This statement is then interpreted as meaning that human freedom is unlimited, facing no restrictions or constraints of any kind, and that you and I are therefore utterly free to do whatever we want, whenever we want, wherever we want. (This interpretation is so widespread that I feel no shame in henceforth referring to it, for purposes of ready identification, as "the official interpretation" of Sartre's theory of freedom.) Finally, Sartre's critics bring their argument to its conclusion: the complete and decisive refutation of Sartre's theory of freedom. This is accomplished by simply referring the reader to the apparently limitless supply of counterexamples to that theory that can be culled from everyday experience and from ordinary knowledge. Thus, Sartre's theory is refuted by such simple observations as that prisoners are not free to come and go as they please, that the blind are not free to see, that the poor are not free to lead lives of luxury, and that no one is free to fly like a bird, to swim like a fish, or to bring back the dead, or to exist in two places or times at once; the wrongheadedness of Sartre's doctrine is similarly manifested, say his critics, in the recognition that, as a result of the stubborn independence of the world around us, of other people, and of social institutions and arrangements, many of our actions are certain to fail completely, while even our successes will undoubtedly be incomplete at best; or again, the critics point out that I am not free to act except within a context of factual givens, that I am not free to eliminate or change any more than a few of these givens, and finally, that I am doomed eventually to die, irrespective of my wishes.

I call this argument "the omnipotence objection" because it relies so heavily on the claim that Sartre's defense of "absolute freedom" is scarcely distinguishable from a defense of human omnipotence. And, as we have seen, if Sartre's theory of freedom is to be interpreted as tantamount to a defense of human omnipotence, one has only to "remind us of our impotence" to show that Sartre's theory is not only false, but truly stupid or crazy, or at least wildly implausible and entirely unenlightening. This is indeed the conclusion that many of Sartre's critics seem to have reached, as the following four brief passages clearly indicate:

Sartre claims that man is totally, unconditionally free. Nothing whatsoever restricts his freedom. This claim clashes with everything we know about human behavior. And it clashes with everything we do. It clashes with our practice of education. It clashes with our attempts at rehabilitation. It clashes with our hope for the progress of civilization. Sartre's task is therefore quite Quixotic. He must try to convince us, in spite of all we know and do, that nothing whatsoever can influence our actions.[116]

[According to Sartre] man is free because he can make himself be whatever he wants to be, merely by looking at himself in a different way. I think of this as the ostrich view of the human condition.[117]

Sartre's extravagant emphasis on man's complete freedom was a bracing challenge to his early readers, but it was at odds . . . with the facts of life.[118]

[Sartre] offers no proof whatsoever of man's freedom. One finds in his works only flat assertions that man is free, absolutely free, condemned to be free, and so on. Such statements sound all right in his plays, but they do not hold up so well in a philosophical treatise, where one is obliged to support statements with relevant facts and valid reasons. . . . As far as I know, Sartre's extreme doctrine of absolute freedom is unique in the annals of philosophy. All other doctrines in favor of freedom at least acknowledge some limitation or other.[119]

No one can deny that there are many passages in Sartre's writings which at least *seem* to justify such harsh criticisms as these. Still, in the face of the almost universal acceptance of the soundness of such criticisms, it must be pointed out that Sartre's "absolute freedom" doctrine *does not* represent his complete teaching on the subject of freedom. In fact, Sartre has been known to say things about freedom which seem flatly to contradict the grandiose statements quoted in the paragraph immediately preceding the beginning of section 1. 3. 1. In one passage, for example, he assigns to freedom a truly modest role, defining it as "the small movement which makes of a totally conditioned social being someone who does not render back completely what his conditioning has given him."[120] Similarly, he asserts that "you become what you are in the context of what others have made of you,"[121] and submits, as an illustration, that "Flaubert is free to become Flaubert, but he didn't have all that many possibilities of becoming something else."[122] Elsewhere, Sartre seems even less impressed with the efficacy of freedom, as when he declares that "freedom

. . . does not mean the possibility of choice, but the necessity of living the constraint."[123] Finally, in the *Critique of Dialectical Reason* (hereafter cited as *CDR*) Sartre seems at times to deny that *anyone* is free: "It would be quite wrong to interpret me as saying that man is free in all situations, as the Stoics claimed. I mean the exact opposite: all men are slaves in so far as their life unfolds in the practico-inert field and in so far as this field is always conditioned by scarcity."[124] Lest we think that this statement is simply a case of Sartre getting carried away with his rhetoric, it should be noted that he addresses this issue head-on in a subsequent interview, and states bluntly: "I believe we are not free."[125]

How are we to make sense of these two seemingly incompatible lines of thought on freedom? One possibility, of course, would be simply to deny that they are reconcilable. On such a view Sartre's theory of freedom would obviously be open to the simple and decisive refutation that it is self-contradictory, and thus incoherent. After all, it makes little sense to say *both* that we are free *and* not free, or that our freedom is both unlimited *and* limited.

Other critics, however, have arrived at a different conclusion. These critics, noticing that the "absolute freedom" theory is usually found in Sartre's earlier writings, while the "restricted freedom" theory is more prominent in the later works, have tended to conclude that there is a sharp break in Sartre's thought, that there are *two* Sartres, each with his own theory of freedom. Thus, the "absolute freedom" theory is ascribed to the early, "existential-ist," Sartre, while the "restricted freedom" theory is attributed to the later, "Marxist," Sartre. In fact, one critic, Mary Warnock, sees in Sartre's later thinking a complete repudiation of the earlier doctrine, arising from Sartre's "radical conversion" to Marxism.[126]

I will address these interpretations in due time. First, however, in an effort to expose the one-sidedness of "the official interpreta-tion," and in so doing to refute "the omnipotence objection," let us now turn our attention to Sartre's discussions of freedom's limitations.

1.3.1.1 Limitations to freedom

It must be emphasized, first of all, that Sartre has *always* recognized the existence of constraints upon, and limitations to freedom. This is doubly significant. The fact that he *acknowledges* limitations undermines the official interpretation and the omnipotence objection; the fact that he has *always* done so undermines the view that there is a sharp break between the early "absolute freedom" theory and the later "restricted freedom" theory. I propose to document both of these facts by examining briefly four concepts which are introduced in Sartre's early works: "facticity," "coefficient of adversity," "situation," and "human condition." Familiarity with Sartre's analyses of these concepts, all of which concern freedom's bounds, should completely dispel the notion that Sartre's early theory of freedom is an "absolute" one, in the sense of claiming that freedom is utterly without limitations. Following the examination of these concepts, I will briefly discuss two related notions from his later works, namely, "practico-inert" and "counter-finality," in order to give some initial idea as to the degree to which Sartre's later thought is continuous with his earlier thinking on the subject of freedom's limitations.

1.3.1.1.1   Facticity

"The facticity of freedom is the given which [human-reality] *has to be* and which it illumines by its project."[127] Thus, my facticity refers to the set of "facts" which my consciousness encounters, in every one of its acts, as already present. Of course, different facts are brought to the forefront by different acts of consciousness; and these foreground facts can never completely encompass the inexhaustible realm of the given which underlies each and every one of my acts. This realm of the given may be said to comprise the context out of which my freedom operates. It is this realm which Sartre designates with the term "facticity."

My facticity includes, then, such facts as the time and place of my birth, the socio-economic status of the family into which I was born, my sex, the color of my skin, my current height and weight, all of my past acts, the attitudes that others have towards me, the locations of my current and previous residences, my ability to see better with one eye than with another, etc., etc.

It is important for those who ascribe to Sartre a crude theory of "absolute freedom" to notice that he does acknowledge the existence of facticities which I did not originate and which I cannot change (e.g., the date of my birth). Moreover, Sartre also recognizes states of affairs which do owe their origin to my free activity but which contain a certain irreducible, factual element that resists my subsequent freedom (e.g., I insulted my friend yesterday—although I am remorseful and will apologize, I cannot change the fact that I *did* insult him). Finally, while I can change some of my facticities (e.g., I can move to another city, I can get glasses, I can even, perhaps, get a sex-change operation), it is nonetheless true that these acts are all possible for me only insofar as I now, in fact, live in Chicago, have certain abilities and disabilities of eyesight, and am male. Freedom, then, always presupposes facticity, and a free act cannot occur, nor can the idea of a free act even be rendered intelligible, except against a background of facticity.

Freedom's dependence upon facticity is not one-sided, however. Rather, the relationship between freedom and facticity is one of interdependence. An example should help to make this clear: If a river is an obstacle for me, this is partly because I choose to go to the other side (freedom), and partly because the water is deep, the current is strong, there is no bridge, and I am a weak swimmer (facticity). Clearly, these facticities emerge as obstacles only in the light of my freely-chosen project. Equally clearly, my free choice can occur only on the condition that I am a finite being who cannot have everything at once, that I have certain desires or needs rather than others, that these desires or needs can only be satisfied through, let us say, possession of certain objects, that these objects can be found only on the other side of the river, etc. This example illustrates "the inextricable connection of freedom and facticity . . . Without facticity freedom would not exist—as a power of nihilation and of choice—and without freedom facticity would not be discovered and would have no meaning."[128]

Perhaps, then, what misleads some of those critics who are unimpressed by Sartre's concessions to facticity is his insistence that I am always free to *interpret* my facticities in a wide variety of ways. Suppose, for example, that I have been born blind. At first glance this might appear to count as a severe limit to freedom (and we will later see that Sartre himself thinks so, at least with respect to one legitimate sense of "freedom"). Nonetheless, Sartre is quick to point out that (at least in one sense) my disability serves, not as a limitation to my freedom, but as the occasion for its exercise. His point is that "I *choose* the way in which I constitute my disability (as 'unbearable,' 'humiliating,' 'to be hidden,' 'to be revealed to all,' 'an object of pride,' 'the justification for my failures,' etc.)."[129] Thus, "there is an unchangeable element in the past" (e.g., I was born blind) "and an element which is eminently variable (the meaning of the brute fact in relation to the totality of my being)."[130] Moreover, Sartre finds the relationship between these changeable and unchangeable elements of facticity to be so complex that he does not hesitate to draw the provocative conclusion that "it is impossible to grasp facticity in its brute nudity, since all that we will find of it is already recovered and freely constructed."[131] Or again, "it is . . . impossible for me to distinguish the unchangeable brute existence from the variable meaning which it includes."[132]

Thus, the relationship between freedom and facticity is one of ambiguity, as well as one of interdependence. This ambiguity becomes readily apparent when we ask whether or to what extent facticity limits freedom, for the answer seems to be that facticity both limits freedom and makes it possible in the first place: "freedom can exist only as *restricted* since freedom is choice. Every choice . . . supposes elimination and selection; every choice is a choice of finitude. Thus freedom can be truly free only by constituting facticity as its own restriction."[133] Or again,

> the very project of a freedom in general is a choice which implies the anticipation and acceptance of some kind of resistance somewhere. Not only does freedom constitute the compass within which in-itselfs otherwise indifferent will be revealed as resistances, but freedom's very project in general is to *do* in a resisting world by means of a victory over the world's resistances.[134]

For our purposes it is of paramount importance that we not let this discussion of the ambiguous nature of the relationship between freedom and facticity (e.g., facticity limits and restrains freedom, but facticity emerges *as* a limit and a restriction only in the context of freely chosen projects) obscure the fundamental fact that *facticity does limit freedom*. We have seen that I cannot choose the date of my birth, that I cannot eradicate my past actions, that while

I can change my residence, I cannot move *from* anywhere but from where I currently live. Moreover, and perhaps more importantly, facticity can prevent me from *succeeding* in various of my freely chosen projects, as we saw in the example of being unable to cross a river. As Sartre himself emphasizes,

> far from being able to modify our situation at our whim, we seem to be unable to change ourselves. I am not "free" either to escape the lot of my class, of my nation, of my family, or even to build up my own power or my fortune or to conquer my most insignificant appetites or habits. I am born a worker, a Frenchman, an hereditary syphilitic, or a tubercular. *The history of a life, whatever it may be, is the history of a failure.*[135]

Finally, it should be noted that facticity limits our freedom even when it appears to enable our success! As Howard R. Burkle so clearly explains,

> facticity contains just as many pleasant, ennobling, and supporting traits as it does negative ones, and they are no less dangerous to freedom. The world negates our freedom not because it is absurd or crushes our hopes but because it inolves us in two ontological conditions which Sartre regards as the antithesis of freedom, namely, "actuality" and "givenness." Actuality *is* unfreedom; actuality *as such* is "failure." It is not so because it is unsuccessful, painful, repulsive, or whatever, but because it is past, finished, objective, static (all pejorative epithets). Even success is failure! because as actuality it is *not* potential, dynamic, fluid and projective (all auspicious epithets and roughly synonymous with freedom).[136]

Thus, in a radical departure from traditional Sartrean scholarship, Burkle urges that we must curb "Sartre's over-stated attitudes towards facticity" if we are to see that "man is capable of widening his foothold and extending his range of autonomy."[137]

1.3.1.1.2 *Coefficient of adversity*

"The coefficient of adversity in things is such that years of patience are necessary to obtain the feeblest result."[138] Thus, the concept of "coefficient of adversity" (also called "coefficient of resistance"), which Sartre borrows from Gaston Bachelard, refers not simply to the requirement of my freedom always to find itself operating within a realm of external facts (facticity), but rather to the fact that these external objects and states of affairs may put up *actual resistance* to my freely undertaken projects.

One way of seeing the difference between facticity and the coefficient of adversity is that the latter, unlike the former, admits of degrees. That is, while there are always an infinite number of facts which apply to me and to my situation, no matter what my project may happen to be, the degree to which my project is restricted by factors external to my consciousness clearly depends upon the project I choose and upon the nature of these external factors. The coefficient of adversity, then, is a doubly relative concept. It is relative to my freedom, since one and the same set of external factors will be either adverse or helpful depending upon my project. On the other hand, it is relative to external factors, since one and the same project will be either difficult or easy depending upon which external factors happen to be present.

Let us take up one of Sartre's examples, in order to see this more clearly.

> A particular crag, which manifests a profound resistance if I wish to displace it, will be on the contrary a valuable aid if I want to climb upon it in order to look over the countryside. In itself—if one can even imagine what the crag can be in itself—it is neutral; that is, it waits to be illuminated by an end in order to manifest itself as adverse or helpful.[139]

Thus, the coefficient of adversity manifested by a single object, a particular crag, varies in accordance with the project that is adopted with respect to it. On the other hand, the coefficient of adversity confronting a single project, that of displacing rocks from a field, will vary in accordance with the number and nature of the different rocks currently lying in that field.

Of course, this is an overly simplified analysis, and Sartre is the first to recognize that in cases of any appreciable complexity it is difficult or even impossible to determine to what extent the adversity arises from consciousness and to what extent it arises from "the brute existent."[140] Thus, if we return to the example of the crag, and now factor in the *degree* to which I desire to climb it, we find that

> the rock will not be an obstacle if I wish *at any cost* to arrive at the top of the mountain. On the other hand, it will discourage me if I have freely *fixed limits* to my desire of making the projected climb. Thus the world by

coefficient of adversity reveals to me the way in which I stand in relation to the ends which I assign myself, so that *I can never know if it is giving me information about myself or about it.*[141]

As if this were not enough, a more complex analysis of the situation would have to include such considerations as the strength and endurance of my body and my skill as a climber; and these considerations concerning the condition of my body would in turn raise questions regarding the extent to which I had freely trained or neglected my body; these in turn would raise questions about my native constitution, etc., etc. Thus, according to Sartre, the complexity of the situation clearly is such that it is impossible to determine *precisely* the role of consciousness and of factors external to consciousness in any particular case of adversity.

Let us conclude this discussion of the coefficient of adversity by taking up what is for our purposes the most important point, namely, that this concept illustrates, once again, Sartre's acknowledgement of limitations to our freedom.[142] Thus, while it is true that the crag cannot dictate to me what project I am to undertake with regard to it—whether I will attempt to displace it, to scale it, or merely to regard it aesthetically as a beautiful or ugly object— what the crag can determine is whether it "will or will not lend itself to scaling. This is part of the brute being of the rock."[143]

Now one might conclude from this that I am completely free to choose the manner in which I am to regard the crag, and to choose any project concerning the crag, so that the coefficient of adversity of the crag limits my freedom only in the sense that it *might* prevent me from achieving *success* in realizing my chosen ends. This would not be correct, however, since the coefficient of adversity also places limits upon both my manner of regarding the crag and my range of choices concerning it. This can be easily grasped by considering that, while I can freely regard the crag as an obstacle to be cleared away, as an aid to be climbed, or as a beautiful or ugly configuration, I cannot regard it as, for instance, a poached egg which is singing an aria. If I were able so to regard it, I would be "plunged in a world like that of a dream in which the possible is no longer in any way distinguished from the real."[144] Thus, while I am free to confer significance upon the crag in a wide variety of ways, its coefficient of adversity prevents me from conferring *any kind of significance whatever* upon it.

As a consequence of this, it is plain that the coefficient of adversity of the crag also limits the range of projects that I might choose to undertake with respect to it. Because I cannot regard the crag as a poached egg which is singing a song, I can undertake neither the project of putting it on toast and eating it for breakfast, nor that of joining its singing while accompanying it on guitar. Thus, the coefficient of adversity of a thing limits me (a) in my manner of regarding it, (b) in the range of choices of action that I might undertake with respect to it, and (c) in my possibility of achieving success with respect to the action that I have chosen to undertake.

1.3.1.1.3   Situation

"The situation is the organized totality of the being-there, interpreted and lived in and through being-beyond."[145] "Situation," then, refers not merely to the set of all facts external to my consciousness which confront me (facticity), but rather to the *product* of this facticity and my way of consciously interpreting and acting upon it. Thus, to return to our example, my "situation" refers neither to the sum total of "objective facts" about myself and the crag, nor to my project of attempting to reach a point from which to get a good look at the countryside, at least if this is conceived without reference to those facts about my body and the crag which give to my project its coefficient of adversity. Rather, "my situation" refers precisely to the *result of the confrontation* between my consciousness and facts external to it at this particular time and place. Consequently, "the situation is neither objective nor subjective," and

> can be considered neither as the free result of a freedom nor as the ensemble of the constraints to which I am subject; it stems from the illumination of the constraint by freedom which gives to it its meaning as constraint.[146]

These observations, along with other considerations discussed in connection with the ambiguous nature of facticity and of the coefficient of adversity, show us that "the *situation,* the common product of the contingency of the in-itself and of freedom, is an ambiguous phenomenon in which it is impossible for the for-itself to distinguish the contribution of freedom from that of the brute existent."[147]

Let us now take up the question of whether or to what extent my situation can be considered a limitation on my freedom. The first point that needs to be made is that, for Sartre, *all freedom is situated*; he holds no doctrine of "absolute freedom" if that phrase is taken, as it is by some commentators, to refer to a freedom which can be contrasted with situated freedom.[148] That so many critics have thought otherwise is truly quite astonishing (and scandalous), given Sartre's repeated declarations that "I am never free except *in situation*,"[149] that "for the for-itself, to exist and to be situated are one and the same,"[150] that "'being-in-situation' . . . characterizes the For-itself,"[151] and that "*being situated* is an essential and necessary characteristic of freedom."[152] Indeed, it is precisely the inescapably situated character of freedom that Sartre calls

> the paradox of freedom; there is freedom only in a *situation,* and there is a situation only through freedom. Human-reality everywhere encounters resistance and obstacles which it has not created, but these resistances and obstacles have meaning only in and through the free choice which human-reality *is*.[153]

We are now in a position to see precisely how it is that my situation can be said to limit my freedom. Quite simply, because I am situated, I can never do just *anything* that I might want to do; rather, my situation limits me in the sense that only a certain range of choices are possible within any situation, and this range will vary as my situation varies. An example from Robert C. Solomon should make this clear:

> I may today decide whether or not to volunteer for military service and, provided that I fulfill the physical and antispiritual requirements for acceptance, I have absolute freedom to volunteer or not. If I decide to volunteer today and two months hence I begin to reconsider my decision, my situation does not provide me with the freedom to choose simply, as I did before, whether to volunteer or not. My new situation demands that my decision, not to be in the military any longer, entails the most grave of alternatives. I may face prison or death as alternatives to continued service. *I do not have the freedom to choose, as I once did, simply to be an uncommitted civilian*. My . . . choice is now restricted by the fact that I am in the military.[154]

It must be pointed out that my situation, while clearly *limiting* my range of choices, does not *determine* my choice. Though I am not free to be an uncommitted civilian, my situation does not *force* me to remain in the military. After all, I can always choose imprisonment or even death as alternatives to fulfilling my military commitments. Thus, as Solomon points out, "the situation is the *basis* for my choice (my already being in the military is the basis for my decision to desert or to remain there), but it is never a sufficient condition for my choice (it cannot compel me to desert or stay)."[155]

Another important point in the analysis of my situated freedom is that my choice of action within any situation depends, to a large extent, on how I interpret my situation. However, this point introduces yet another layer of ambiguity into our understanding of "situation." We have already seen that the relationship between my consciousness and facticity is one of such complexity and thoroughgoing interdependence as to render any analysis of the individual contribution to the situation made by each impossible. Now we are in a position to see that the relationship between my interpretation of my situation and my choice within that situation is ambiguous in precisely the same sense and for the same reasons. Thus, to return to our crag example, I choose to attempt to climb the crag in part because I notice certain of its features rather than others (e.g., its height and the angle of its incline, rather than its width and color); and I notice certain features of the crag rather than others in part because I choose one particular project rather than others (e.g., to attempt to climb the crag, rather than to displace it or to contemplate it aesthetically). Which takes precedence, the interpretation of the situation, or the choice of action? Perhaps there are situations in which a positive answer can be clearly determined. For the most part, however, especially in the case of more complex projects, there would appear to be no way to distinguish the influence of the choice upon the interpretation of the situation from the influence of the interpretation of the situation upon the choice.

Finally, we should notice that just as my situation limits my freedom by restricting my range of choices (recall Solomon's example of the military volunteer), so does the coefficient of adversity of things limit my range of possible interpretations of my situation (recall that I cannot interpret the crag as a poached egg which is singing an aria). This is precisely what we should expect, of course, given the intimate nature of the relationship between interpretation and choice.

1.3.1.1.4 *Human condition*

While Sartre is famous for denying the existence of "human nature," understood as a universal human essence, he does affirm the existence of a universal "human condition," which refers to the sum total of all elements which are found in *every* human situation:

> What men have in common is not a "nature" but a condition, that is, *an ensemble of limits and restrictions*: the inevitability of death, the necessity of working for a living, of living in a world already inhabited by other men. Fundamentally this condition is nothing more than the basic human situation, or, if you prefer, the ensemble of abstract characteristics common to all situations.[156]

Elsewhere Sartre defines "human condition" as "all the *limitations* which *à priori* define man's fundamental situation in the universe," and cites as examples "the necessities of being in the world, of having to labor and to die there."[157] Still elsewhere he defines it as "all the *constraints* which limit [men] *a priori*," and adds "the necessity of being born and . . . of being *finite*" to his list of examples.[158]

Now it is clear that Sartre conceives of the human condition as one of freedom's bounds, as can readily be seen from the fact that he defines it in terms of "limitations," "restrictions," and "constraints." But *why* should we think of the presence of certain characteristics in all human situations as constituting a restriction of our freedom? And how does this concept of a human condition enlarge our understanding of the limitations to human freedom beyond what we have already achieved through our analysis of other concepts?

To answer the first question we need only reflect on the fact that our freedom can be curtailed in a variety of ways in *any* situation. In any situation I might, for example, find limitations in my range of possible interpretations of my situation, in my range of possible choices of action with respect to that situation, and in the possibility of success with regard to the particular action chosen. As these limitations can be brought about by *any* characteristics of my situation, so might they be brought about by those specific characteristics which happen to be present in *all* situations. The concept of a universal human condition enlarges our knowledge of the limitations to human freedom, then, simply in that it shows both that certain limitations are present for me in *all* situations, and that I *share* these limitations with all other human beings, who are also subject to them in all circumstances. Thus, like all other human beings, my situation always constrains me from interpreting my arms as wings; it constrains me from selecting as my choice of action the project of flapping my wings and flying to the moon; and if despite these constraints I, through some sort of madness, do interpret my arms as wings and do choose to undertake the project of flapping my wings and flying to the moon, my situation will most assuredly prevent my success in seeing this project through to its desired conclusion.

1.3.1.1.5 *Practico-inert*

In *CDR* Sartre claims to "discover an equivalence between alienated *praxis* and worked inertia," and proposes to "call the domain of this equivalence the *practico-inert*."[159] Let us see if we can render this mysterious sentence intelligible. First of all, "praxis" refers to purposeful human activity, that is, "the activity of an individual or group in organising conditions in the light of some end."[160] Praxis becomes "alienated" when the matter or conditions that we have "worked over" in order to bring about some end begin to absorb our past actions toward them and to reflect back to us the meanings that we have inscribed in them. This process results in a kind of inertia, since the material and social structures that we have worked over begin to *resist* our freedom to assign new meanings to them. "Practico-inert," then, refers to all of those worked-over structures which alienate (reappropriate) our freedom from us, and which restrict our present freedom by thrusting upon us only those meanings which we have already introduced into them. Thus, the relationship between praxis and practico-inert might most clearly be stated this way: we shape the world (praxis); and the world, on the basis of the manner in which we have shaped it, comes back to shape us (practico-inert).

All of this can be simply, if somewhat trivially, illustrated by a return to our crag example. We have already seen that if I come across a crag, under normal circumstances, I have a wide variety of choices as to how to "interpret" the crag. I might, for example, see it as something to climb, as something to displace, as something to contemplate, etc. But what if I were to come across a crag which had already been "worked on" to facilitate climbing—a crag, let us say, into which steps had been carved, and on which hand-rails and a platform for standing had been erected? While it is true that I might still be able to think of the crag as something-to-be-displaced-so-that-the-field-might-be-farmed, is it not obvious that what I would *immediately* observe would be something *to climb,* something *from which to look*? Is it not clear that my interpretation of the crag as something to be displaced would be brought about and sustained only through some *effort* on my part—that the obvious interpretation of the crag would have to be, in some sense, resisted? Thus, there is an inertia about the crag, such that my attempt to constitute it as something other than a staircase and observation tower is resisted by it. And this *inertia,* in turn, is clearly the result of purposeful human activity, that is to say, of *praxis*—hence the aptness of the term "practico-inert."

We are now in a position to see how this concept of practico-inert enlarges our understanding of freedom's bounds. We have already seen that the coefficient of adversity of the crag limits my possible interpretations of the crag (e.g., I cannot interpret it as a poached egg which is singing an aria). The concept of practico-inert, however, enables us to understand that *our freedom to interpret the crag can be limited even further by our own alienated freedom.* We *are not free* (or, more precisely, we are less free than we were before) to assign new meanings to things, because we find their meanings to be already present in them, having been put there through previous acts of freedom.[161]

This point reinforces one of Sartre's most persistent claims (recall the discussion of anguish), namely that freedom, though precious, is a *dangerous* thing. Our freedom, once it has escaped from us and become encrusted in things or in social arrangements, can come back to haunt us. This insight is perhaps obscured by our choice of this trivial crag example. The justice of Sartre's claim can be more readily seen by shifting our attention away from physical objects and toward more complex human institutions and social arrangements. One has only to think of such things as advertising, organized religions, laws, news media, public opinion, manners, customs, formal education, etc., to see the extent to which we are "molded" by the very structures that we freely invent. Nonetheless, for those who are still not convinced of our freedom's potential to strike back at us, let us move on to a consideration of Sartre's concept of "counter-finality."

1.3.1.1.6 Counter-finality

The fact that my freedom can escape from me, become encrusted in things, and come back to limit my freedom, is perhaps most clearly illustrated through Sartre's concept of "counter-finality," which is defined as the "contradiction . . . which develops within an ensemble, in so far as it opposes the process which produces it."[162] As an example of this, Sartre cites the case of Chinese peasants who, in an effort to increase the number of cultivable acres, have comprehensively deforested the Chinese mountains and hillsides. Far from bringing about the desired result, this action has, of course, resulted only in massive flooding and the further erosion of the peasants' land. Indeed, "if some enemy of mankind had wanted to persecute the peasants of China as a whole, he would have ordered mercenary troops to deforest the mountains systematically. The positive system of agriculture was transformed into an infernal machine."[163] And yet, as Sartre notes, the enemy who brought about this counter-finality was "the peasant himself."[164]

The conclusion to be drawn from all of this is that my freedom, when brought to bear upon that which is external to it, frequently yields results which are diametrically opposed to those which I had intended to effect. Moreover, and more importantly, these unanticipated and undesired results often have lasting consequences, as when they limit my freedom to undertake a new action which would bring about the effects that I had originally intended (e.g., it will be much harder *now* for the Chinese peasants to create a larger number of cultivable acres than it would have been had they never deforested the mountains). Thus, I must be extremely careful in the exercise of my freedom, lest I should unwittingly *diminish* that freedom!

It is clear, then, that counter-finalities restrict my freedom in a much more radical sense than does the practico-inert. For while the practico-inert limits my freedom to interpret "worked-over" objects (e.g., the fact that steps have been carved into the crag makes it harder for me to conceive of it as an obstacle to be displaced), it does not *necessarily* diminish my possibility of *succeeding* in bringing about my freely chosen ends (e.g., the fact that steps have been carved into the crag does not make it harder for me to displace it, should I choose to do so; moreover, I might have chosen in any event to attempt to climb the crag, in which case the steps would actually be an *aid* to me).

Thus, the relationship of "practico-inert" to "counter-finality" may profitably be viewed as comparable to that of "facticity" to "coefficient of adversity." In both pairs, the first term refers to certain facts which help to define my situation, and which, therefore, place limits upon my freedom to interpret my situation, and upon my range of choices of action within that situation, while the latter term suggests a much more positive *interference* with me in my attempt to succeed in carrying out certain acts—it suggests, indeed, a type of obstruction which might very well *prevent* my success altogether.

However, it must not be thought that these two pairs of terms refer to the *same* distinction, and that Sartre, therefore, has not in any way evolved in his understanding of the limitations to freedom. Rather, as Hazel E. Barnes points out, Sartre has much more to say in his later works than in his earlier ones

> about the way in which material things by their presence or absence circumscribe my action or "steal it from me." This change is illustrated by the shift from stress on the "coefficient of resistance" in things to the "counterfinalities" which acts may evoke. "Coefficient of resistance" suggests simply that which must be overcome by a freedom in process of realizing itself. A "counterfinality" is a result opposite to that which I expected.[165]

1.3.1.1.7 My relations with others

Let us conclude our discussion of freedom's bounds by
mentioning a limitation of a somewhat different kind. It should be
recalled that all six of the concepts that we have just been
considering are concerned with the limitations to my freedom
which arise when my consciousness interacts with that which is
external to it. Moreover, they are primarily concerned with such
limitations as arise when my consciousness interacts with what is
not itself a consciousness. It is significant that Sartre takes such
pains in analyzing these limitations, since it is clear that, on his
view, my relationship with things is in many respects *enhancive* of
my freedom. After all, it is precisely my ability to nihilate things—
to interpret them in a variety of ways and to form and carry out
projects with respect to them—that comprises my freedom. My
relations with *other people,* on the other hand, are quite another
matter, at least according to the early Sartre.[166] Far from *enhancing*
my freedom, such relations act as a unique kind of *limitation* to my
freedom. For one thing, as we have seen, my freedom to assign
meanings to objects in the world is severely curtailed by the fact
that, through my interactions with others, I am constantly confronted with the meanings which they have inscribed, and are
inscribing onto things. But what is even more important in the
context of our present discussion is the fact that the other, in
addition to being able to confer meanings onto the *things* of my
experience, can also directly interfere with my freedom by
conferring meanings *onto me.* For this reason, as Solomon points
out, "my relations with *other people* . . . do constitute a threat to
my freedom, for the other has the ability *to make me into an
object.*"[167]

Thus, in my relations with others I stand always in danger of
having the tables turned on me; rather than having the ability
myself to interpret and to assign meanings to that which is external
to me, I am vulnerable to the ability of those external entities called
people to interpret and to assign meanings *to me.* "It is because of
the other that we have an alienated outwardness: I am ruler, slave,
teacher, or student, beautiful or ugly, because of the other. Tribes
are not aware of themselves as black, tall, or short until they are
aware of others recognizing them as such."[168] As Sartre puts it,

the Other's existence brings a factual limit to my freedom. This is because of the fact that by means of the upsurge of the Other there appear certain determinations which I *am* without having chosen them. Here I am—Jew, or Aryan, handsome or ugly, one-armed, etc. . . . We must recognize that we have just encountered a *real* limit to our freedom—that is, a way of being which is imposed on us without our freedom being its foundation.[169]

1.3.1.2   The omnipotence objection answered

In the preceding discussion of Sartre's seven analyses of freedom's limitations we have gathered ample evidence to show that "the official interpretation" of Sartre's theory of freedom is inaccurate and that "the omnipotence objection" to that theory is unjust. We have seen that Sartre, though his critics deny it,[170] *does* acknowledge, repeatedly and insistently, restrictions and limitations to human freedom. Where, then, do the critics go wrong?

In fairness to Sartre's detractors, it must be noted (as indeed I *have* already noted)[171] that Sartre *does* sometimes claim that we are "absolutely free," "totally free," "completely free," etc. But the crucial mistake made by the omnipotence objection critics is that they behave *as if this were the whole story*! The fundamental methodological error underlying the official interpretation and the omnipotence objection consists, then, in *the failure to consider any evidence which runs counter to one's thesis.* It is not the case that the omnipotence objection critics offer *reasons* and *arguments* for regarding *one strand* of Sartre's theory of freedom as representing the *entirety* of that theory, to the exclusion of other, apparently incompatible, strands. Rather, they tend simply to *ignore* these contrary strands. Thus, when Reinhold Grossmann attributes to Sartre the view that "nothing whatsoever restricts (human) freedom,"[172] he does not even *mention,* much less discuss or analyze, Sartre's repeated insistences in *BN* that "freedom can exist *only* as restricted";[173] when Risieri Frondizi claims that Sartre acknowledges no limitations to freedom,[174] he himself fails to acknowledge, much less defend his interpretation against, Sartre's claim in *BN* that "the Other's existence brings a factual limit to my freedom . . . (this is) a *real* limit to our freedom—that is, a way of being which is imposed on us without our freedom being its foundation,"[175] or his references elsewhere to "all the *limitations* which *à priori* define man's fundamental situation in the universe";[176] when Grossmann attributes to Sartre the claim that "man is free because he can make himself be whatever he wants to be, merely by looking at himself in a different way,"[177] he fails to address Sartre's explicit rejection of such a conception of freedom as one which would plunge us into "a world like that of a dream in which the possible is no longer in any way distinguished from the real";[178] and Frondizi neatly solves all of the difficulties of interpretation which one encounters in Sartre's arguments in defense of freedom by denying that Sartre has ever offered any such arguments![179]

The omnipotence objection completely overlooks the *real* problem with Sartre's theory of freedom: the problem of figuring out how to reconcile (if indeed they *are* reconcilable) the two seemingly antithetical strands of that theory—the "absolute freedom" strand and the "restricted freedom" strand. The omnipotence objection "solves" this crucial problem by ignoring the latter strand. Perhaps it is time for us to ignore the omnipotence objection, and to get on with the business of facing this issue squarely.

1.3.2   The Inconsistency Objection

The rejection of the omnipotence objection brings into sharp focus the perplexing problem of interpretation that Sartre's writings on freedom pose. On the one hand, we have just seen that, contra the omnipotence objection critics, Sartre repeatedly insists upon the fact that my freedom is limited by my facticity, by the coefficient of adversity in things, by the practico-inert, etc. On the other hand, and on this point I am in agreement with the omnipotence objection critics, we have seen that Sartre also insists upon the "absolute" nature of my freedom—that I am "totally free," "condemned to be free," free "in any circumstances, in any period, and at any place," etc. If we are to hold that the omnipotence objection critics' solution to this dilemma is inadequate—that it will not do simply to ignore one or another of the major strands of Sartre's theory of freedom—we are left with the following problem: How are we to reconcile the two major strands of that theory—how are we to reconcile Sartre's theory of absolute freedom with his theory of restricted freedom?

The response to this question which seems initially the most plausible is that the two strands *cannot* be reconciled, and that Sartre's theory of freedom is therefore simply an incoherent muddle. On such a view Sartre's theory would clearly be vulnerable to the objection that it is self-contradictory and, indeed, ultimately unintelligible. After all, Sartre says both that we are free and unfree; he says that our freedom is both unlimited and limited; and, perhaps worst of all, he says both that we are *always* absolutely free and that we are *always* constrained. Surely all of this constitutes the sort of deep nonsense which all sober minds feel compelled to reject.

Thus, the criticism which readily suggests itself, once we have seen what is wrong with the omnipotence objection, is that Sartre's theory is simply inconsistent. I propose therefore to call this criticism "the inconsistency objection," for purposes of ready identification. Let us see if this objection is sound.

1.3.2.1 Different senses of freedom

According to Maurice Cranston, we should

> consider how much—or rather how little—you say if you say you are free. Imagine a meeting with a stranger. You know nothing about him or his predicament. He approaches you and says: 'I am free.' You are baffled. Has he just escaped from prison, from his debts, from his wife, from his sins? He has told you he is free, but he has not told you what he is free *from*. He has confided remarkably little.
>
> Yet if the stranger had said: 'I am hungry', you would have known only too well what he meant. . . . For whereas 'I am hungry' has one meaning, 'I am free' *might have any one of a vast range of possible meanings.*[180]

This passage suggests a *possible* strategy to be employed in reading Sartre's many and varied writings on freedom—a strategy which *might* allow us to understand his theory of freedom in such a way as to absolve it of self-contradiction. That is, given that "freedom" could "have any one of a vast range of possible meanings," might not Sartre's apparently inconsistent claims about freedom—e.g., his claims that we both are and are not free, and that our freedom is both unlimited and limited, etc.—be more plausibly and accurately read as mutually consistent claims about *different kinds* of freedom? In other words, might it not be the case that Sartre's statements about "freedom" are not mutually *inconsistent* statements about *one* thing (freedom), but rather mutually *consistent* statements about *different* things (all of which are called "freedom")?

To be sure, such a reading would immediately raise the question as to why Sartre (or anyone, for that matter) would want to use the same word to represent different meanings. But this question admits of an obvious reply—that, as both the dictionary and the history of philosophy amply demonstrate, ordinary people and philosophers alike often find it useful to refer to different *but related* ideas with the same term. Why should Sartre be any different?[181]

Thus, let us consider the following thesis as a reply to "the inconsistency objection": when Sartre declares that freedom is absolute, he is referring to a different (though related) sense of "freedom" than that to which he refers when he declares freedom to be limited.

The first point which needs to be made about this thesis, however, is simply that a possibility is not necessarily a reality; given that we have discovered a *possible* strategy for interpreting Sartre's theory of freedom and for acquitting it of charges of inconsistency, we have yet to see whether or not this way of reading Sartre is accurate (or even plausible), and, if accurate, whether or not it really gives us sufficient ammunition to enable us satisfactorily to refute the inconsistency objection. Let us investigate these matters.

1.3.2.1.1 *Does Sartre recognize a need to distinguish between different senses of freedom?*

We have seen that Cranston recognizes a need to distinguish between different senses of "freedom," and I have suggested that Sartre can be read not only as acting upon this suggestion, but also, in so doing, as acquitting himself of charges of inconsistency. But surely this suggestion is premature. We have yet to establish that Sartre even *shares* Cranston's recognition, let alone that he acts upon it. Well then, *does* Sartre acknowledge a need to distinguish between different senses of freedom? Consider the following passage from *What is Literature?*:

> In 1947 the proprietor of a public swimming pool refused to admit a Jewish captain, a war hero. The captain wrote letters of complaint to the newspapers. The papers published his protest and concluded: 'What a wonderful country America is! The proprietor of the pool was *free* to refuse admittance to a Jew. But the Jew, a citizen of the United States, was *free* to protest in the press. And the press, which, as everybody knows, is free, mentions the incident without taking sides. Finally, everybody is free.' The only trouble is that the word *freedom* which covers these very different meanings—and a hundred others—is used without anyone's thinking that he ought to indicate the meaning he gives it in each case.[182]

In answer to our question, then, we have found a passage in which Sartre does call for the careful distinguishing of different meanings of "freedom" from one another. But then, this is only one passage. Perhaps it is an aberration. Are there other passages in which Sartre calls for such distinctions? Better yet, does he himself follow through on his suggestion—is he himself careful to indicate what he means by "freedom" in each case?

1.3.2.1.2 *Does Sartre in fact distinguish between different senses of freedom?*

The question, does Sartre in fact distinguish between different senses of freedom, can be clearly, accurately, and decisively answered with a simple "yes." While Sartre seldom calls a great deal of attention to it, and while many of his critics evidently have not noticed it, Sartre does *repeatedly* and *explicitly* draw distinctions between different senses of "freedom." Thus, we find that he distinguishes between "freedom" and "power";[183] between "freedom of choice" and "freedom of obtaining";[184] between the freedom we are and the freedom we can become;[185] between "metaphysical," "artistic," and "political and social" freedom;[186] between "metaphysical freedom" and "practical freedom";[187] between "abstract freedom" and "concrete freedom";[188] between "political and intellectual freedom" and "economic and social freedom";[189] and between "ontological freedom" and "conditioned and limited freedom,"[190] to name only a few.

It might be objected, and with justice, that not all of these distinctions are really between different *senses* of freedom, as opposed to, say, different areas of a human life in which freedom can be exercised.[191] Still, it is clear that Sartre recognizes, throughout his philosophy, at least two distinct senses of "freedom," which I shall refer to as "ontological freedom" and "practical freedom," but which Sartre calls in *BN* "freedom of choice" and "freedom of obtaining." Sartre's distinction between these two fundamental senses is in my view the generic distinction which underlies most of the specific distinctions cited in the preceding paragraph. It is also the distinction which appears to offer the most promise of supplying us with the ammunition needed to refute "the inconsistency objection." Thus, we will have to explore this distinction carefully. But first, let us ask whether there are any initial reasons for supposing that Sartre's distinctions between different senses of freedom are indeed relevant to our assessment of the soundness, or lack thereof, of the inconsistency objection.

1.3.2.1.3   Are Sartre's distinctions between different senses of freedom relevant?

Many readers, while granting from the textual documentation presented above that Sartre does indeed distinguish different senses of freedom, might well wonder, nonetheless, whether these distinctions can save Sartre from inconsistency in his various statements about absolute and restricted freedom. That is, even if we grant that Sartre recognizes the need to distinguish between different senses of freedom, that he does in fact draw such distinctions, and that it might be theoretically possible to acquit him of charges of self-contradiction by systematically assuming, in each and every instance wherein he appears to be issuing contradictory statements about freedom, that he is really referring to different senses of freedom, we might still wonder if this assumption is *warranted*—whether such an interpretive strategy really captures Sartre's thought accurately, or whether it is simply a handy interpretive device which may be readily superimposed on his thought from without in order to (falsely) save him from (genuine) inconsistency. In short, even if we grant (what has not yet been demonstrated) that it is theoretically *possible* to read Sartre as *not* inconsistent and *not* confused, might it not be the case that he nonetheless *is* inconsistent and confused?

Aside from the general interpretive principle that, all else equal, an interpretation which yields coherence is to be preferred to one that does not, two other points can immediately be made in defense of my interpretive strategy. First, there are simply too many passages in which, if we deny the presence of implicit distinctions between different senses of freedom—"implicit" in the sense that they are not explicitly drawn or referred to in the passage in question, not in the sense that they are *never* explicitly drawn or referred to—Sartre must be thought to contradict himself so flatly, so bluntly, and so directly that we would have to assume him an idiot not to have noticed. For example, in a passage detailing "our concrete goal," Sartre prescribes "making [man] aware of his *total freedom* and his duty to struggle against everything which tends to limit his freedom"; and, two sentences later, he proposes for us the task of "liberating the oppressed and other men."[192] Surely it is too much to believe that a thinker of Sartre's ability, immediately after saying that "man" is totally free, could continue to say in the same breath that, *in the same sense of "freedom,"* our freedom is limited and at least some of us have yet to be liberated!

Secondly, and far more importantly, Sartre himself sometimes *explicitly* draws distinctions between different senses of freedom *precisely in order to refute charges of inconsistency.* For example, in taking up what he regards as "the decisive argument which is employed by common sense against freedom," which "consists in reminding us of our impotence,"[193] Sartre does not hesitate to admit that we *are* impotent, and, in that sense, unfree.[194] And yet, at the same time, he is here concerned to defend his doctrine of absolute freedom. How does he claim to be able to do this without falling into contradiction?

It is at this stage that Sartre introduces a distinction between, on the one hand, "the technical and philosophical concept of freedom" called "freedom of choice," in which "success is not important to freedom," with, on the other hand, "the empirical and popular concept of 'freedom'" called "freedom of obtaining," in which success *is* important to freedom.[195] Thus, Sartre *claims* to avoid contradiction by saying that while we are totally free in the sense of "freedom of choice," we are free only in varying degrees, and are often quite unfree, in the sense of "freedom of obtaining." Of course, we are not yet in a position to assess the adequacy of Sartre's claim, since we have not yet examined his distinction between two fundamental senses of freedom. Let us now take up this task.

1.3.2.1.4   *Ontological freedom and practical freedom*

In order to illustrate the distinction between ontological freedom and practical freedom concretely, let us consider one of Sartre's most famous statements about freedom, namely, his scandalous declaration that "the slave in chains is as free as his master."[196] Now, those who reject the notion that Sartre acknowledges different senses of freedom, and who therefore deny that there might be *other* senses of freedom in which Sartre would regard the slave as *not* as free as his master, are likely to reject his assertion as both obviously false and ethically pernicious: obviously false, because the contrast between a slave and his master is precisely the sort of thing that we would point to as clearly exhibiting the distinction between unfreedom and freedom—so that the falsity of Sartre's statement would be apparent from the fact that it obliterates the distinction embodied in a paradigm case; ethically pernicious, because, if the slave in chains really is as free as his master, it would seem just as pointless to exhort the slave to seek greater freedom as it would be to insist that the master grant more freedom to him. Thus, it is easy to sympathize with Herbert Marcuse's complaint that

> if philosophy, by virtue of its existential-ontological concepts of man or freedom, is capable of demonstrating that the persecuted Jew and the victim of the executioner are and remain absolutely free and masters of a self-responsible choice, then these philosophical concepts have declined to the level of a mere ideology, an ideology which offers itself as a handy justification for the persecutors and executioners.[197]

Sartre has responded to criticisms of this sort many times. Before proceeding in our discussion, let us pause to examine a representative sampling of his briefer replies:

> You call us social traitors, saying that our conception of freedom keeps man from loosening his chains. What stupidity! When we say a man who's out of

work is free, we don't mean that he can do whatever he wants and change himself into a rich and tranquil bourgeois on the spot. *He is free because he can always choose to accept his lot with resignation or to rebel against it.* And undoubtedly he will not be able to avoid great poverty; but in the very midst of his destitution, which is dragging him under, he is able to choose to struggle . . . against all forms of destitution.[198]

But, say the Marxists, if you teach man that he *is* free, you betray him; for he no longer needs to *become* free; can you conceive of a man free from birth who demands to be liberated? To this I reply that *if man is not originally free, but determined once and for all, we cannot even conceive what his liberation might be.*[199]

It is not true that a free man cannot hope to be liberated. *For he is not free and bound in respect to the same things.*[200]

The prisoner is always free to try to run away, if it is clearly understood that he risks death in crawling under the barbed wire. *Is his jailor any less guilty on that account*?[201]

But what would it mean to liberate a man whose actions were determined? *If man were not free, it would not be worth moving a finger for him.*[202]

Thus, the slave, the unemployed worker, and the prisoner are free in one sense of the word, that designated by such expressions as "freedom of choice" and "ontological freedom," but relatively unfree in another sense, that designated by "freedom of obtaining" and "practical freedom." Moreover, according to Sartre, it is precisely *because* the slave, the unemployed worker, and the prisoner are free in the first sense, that it is possible to (1) describe them as being unfree in the second sense, (2) condemn those who render them unfree in this sense, (3) encourage them to become free in this sense, and (4) help them to do so.

In order to see why this is so, however, it will be necessary to understand (1) what it means to be ontologically free, (2) what it means to be practically unfree, and (3) what is the connection between ontological freedom and practical unfreedom.

(1) First of all, we need to understand how, *exactly,* the slave, the unemployed worker, and the prisoner can be ontologically free, and how they, or we, or anybody can be *absolutely* free. Sartre's answer is that any consciousness, no matter what its situation, is absolutely

free in the sense that it is *not* its situation—that, through its nihilating behaviors, it can separate itself from all that is external to it, and from whatever might attempt to ensnare or enslave it, and, in so doing, disentangle itself from the chain of causal determinism. Thus, no matter what situation I am in, nothing can *determine* which features of that situation I will focus on, which I will relegate to the background, which I will accept, which I will attempt to eliminate, which I will employ as aids to assist me in the undertaking of some project, which, in virtue of the project that I have chosen, will be revealed as obstacles to me, which I will regard only in terms of their positive aspects, which I will "color with insufficiency" by regarding them as *not* some alternative state which I constitute through an act of imagination, etc. I am absolutely free because no situation can *completely determine* how I will interpret that situation, what project I will form with respect to that interpretation, or how I will act in attempting to carry out that project. To be sure, there are any number of external forces which "push" me in various directions; but these forces cannot *by themselves,* without my complicity, determine my action. The connection between freedom and negativity is nowhere more clearly illustrated than in the simple fact that, with respect to any external force, insofar as I am conscious of it, I can always say "no" to it, and choose to undertake the project of acting in opposition to it.

(2) But if we are *absolutely* free in *any* situation, how can it ever be accurately said that we are unfree, even in some "practical" sense? To answer this question we must remember, as we have exhaustively seen in our discussion of the limitations to freedom, that Sartre's "absolute freedom" must not be confused with omnipotence. The unemployed worker "is free because he can always choose to accept his lot with resignation or to rebel against it," but he is *not* free, for example, "to change himself into a rich and tranquil bourgeois on the spot." Similarly, the prisoner is always free to attempt an escape or to adopt an attitude of resignation, but not simply to make the prison bars disappear without effort or risk. Or again, a poor working woman is free to regard her salary strictly in positive, factual terms, as "X dollars a week," or to regard it as "not enough," and attempt to change her situation; but she is not

free to double her salary merely by wishing or imagining it to be so. Finally, a man who has just been blinded in an automobile accident is free to interpret his permanent blindness as a reason for committing suicide, or as the occasion for taking advantage of those years of piano lessons and beginning a career as a musician, but not as a sign that the time has finally arrived to pursue his dream of becoming a baseball umpire.

Thus, in addition to his famous concept of "absolute freedom," Sartre also recognizes another fundamental sense of freedom which is not absolute but limited, and which is present in varying degrees in varying circumstances—a freedom in which failure is possible, and in which the slave is less free than the slaveholder. As we recall, while I am (absolutely) free to constitute a rock as "scalable," and to attempt to scale it, "what my freedom can not determine is whether the rock 'to be scaled' will or will not lend itself to scaling. This is part of the brute being of the rock."[203] Clearly, if my *freedom* to scale rocks is to be equated with my *success* in scaling them (and Sartre admits that this is a legitimate sense of the term), then it is only *possible* in any given case that I will be free. I certainly cannot always be free in this sense, and it would therefore be folly to suggest that I am "absolutely" free to reach the top of any rock that I might attempt to scale.

We are now in a position to see that "the inconsistency objection," at least when it is presented as a *general* criticism of Sartre's theory of freedom rather than as an objection to certain specific individual passages, is unsound. In previous sections we have seen that Sartre recognizes a *need* to distinguish between different senses of freedom, that he does *in fact* draw such distinctions, and that he draws them *in order to* refute charges of inconsistency. Moreover, in the immediately preceding discussion we have seen that Sartre's concepts of "ontological freedom" and "practical freedom," whatever their defects, are at the very least of such a nature as to make it possible for him to say, without inconsistency, that one and the same individual in one and the same situation is both free and unfree. Thus, while it may be true that there are inconsistencies, and even outright contradictions, to be found in Sartre's writings on freedom—indeed, given the astonishing amount of attention that he has given to the subject of freedom, and given the inherent difficulty of that subject, it would be amazing were he not to issue some nonsense with regard to it from time to time—there seems to be no basis for the claim that his theory of freedom is *in general* inconsistent merely because it both affirms and denies that we are free, holds that our freedom is both unlimited and limited, claims that we are both absolutely free and yet impotent, etc. Of course, readers will have to decide for themselves whether the foregoing considerations are sufficient, in any particular case of suspected inconsistency, to point out a way of accurately reading Sartre which would absolve him of the inconsistency. I would claim only to have shown that Sartre is innocent of charges of general inconsistency, and to have done so by showing that the specific passages discussed in connection with Sartre's distinctions between different senses of freedom—passages which, by the way, are among the most frequently cited by critics alleging to document inconsistency—are not inconsistent.

(3) But why is Sartre not content merely to claim that absolute ontological freedom is *compatible* with practical unfreedom, and that he is therefore not guilty of inconsistency? Why does he also insist that there is a *connection* between the two freedoms? Why, to be more specific, does he assert that ontological freedom is *foundational* to practical unfreedom, that practical unfreedom is only possible against a background of ontological freedom, with the implication that only an ontologically free being can *be* practically unfree, or, for that matter, practically free? Why, finally, does he say that "if man is not originally free, but determined once and for all, we cannot even conceive what his liberation might be"?[204]

Sartre's reasoning on these matters is perceptively explained by Thomas C. Anderson:

> If man is *by nature* determined, chained to being and its causal influence, then to speak of increasing his freedom in the concrete is absurd. Only what is by nature free can become more free in the concrete situations of the world.[205] . . . True, [man's] situation could be improved so that he can more readily attain the goals of his choices and desires. His freedom to attain could be increased. Still, if his nature is such that his very choices and desires remain the product of causal forces, he remains ontologically no more than a robot.[206]

Anderson's last point needs to be underscored. To be sure, one *could* adhere to a sense of "practical freedom" according to which

one's practical freedom or unfreedom would be entirely unconnected with one's ontological freedom or unfreedom. For example,
one could say that I am free to read secret government documents if
I have the *ability* to read them and am *not constrained* from doing
so. It is to be noticed that such a conception of practical freedom is
perfectly compatible with ontological unfreedom, since it is
entirely conceivable that the fact that I am not constrained from
reading secret government documents, together with both my ability and my desire to do so, might be the effect of a thoroughgoing
causal determinism. But this is not Sartre's sense of "practical
freedom." For him, "practical freedom" means freedom to obtain
our freely (in the ontological sense) chosen ends. Thus, for Sartre,
if I *have to* read secret government documents, if I am *determined*
to do so, then I am not *free* to read secret government documents, in
either the ontological or the practical sense. It follows that only an
ontologically free being can be enslaved, or liberated from enslave-
ment. True, even if I am determined to have a strong desire to read
secret government documents, it is just as possible to *thwart* me in
my attempt to realize this desire as it would have been had my
desire been free. But this can be no objection to Sartre, since there
is nothing in his theory of freedom which would preclude him from
considering such thwarting to be both possible and, under certain
conditions, undesirable. It is only that he would not regard such
thwarting as a limitation of "freedom," or its elimination "liberation," properly speaking.

But given that it is possible, as we have seen, to develop a
coherent sense of practical freedom which is entirely unconnected
with ontological freedom, why does Sartre insist upon connecting
the two? Furthermore, why should we prefer Sartre's concept of
practical freedom to the hypothetical alternative which I have
mentioned? Granted, it is probably not a question of deciding
whether Sartre's way of distinguishing between ontological freedom and practical freedom is "right" or "wrong." Surely conceptual classificatory schemes are to *some* degree arbitrary, so that
more than one scheme is capable of doing everything that we want
a scheme to do (e.g., enable us to see important differences and
similarities between the phenomena in question, reveal connec-
tions between these phenomena and others, make clear what had
been obscure, be easy, rather than cumbersome, to use, etc.).

Still, I believe there is something to be said for Sartre's way of drawing the distinction between ontological freedom and practical freedom. In order to bring Sartre's rationale into sharper focus, and to expose some of what I consider to be its intuitive appeal, let us compare Sartre's views on this point with those of Herbert J. Muller, whose theory of freedom is in many respects remarkably similar to Sartre's.[207] According to Muller, freedom is to be understood as "the condition of being able to choose and to carry out purposes."[208] Muller goes on to explain that "this definition has three immediate implications: (1) . . . the absence of external constraints; (2) practicable purposes, or an actual ability with available means; and (3) a power of conscious choice, between significant, known alternatives."[209] The importance of "a power of conscious choice" to freedom can be seen by considering whether birds are free to fly and sing. Clearly, birds have two of Muller's three necessary conditions of freedom: absence of external constraints—nobody *prevents* birds from flying and singing, and actual ability with available means—birds *can,* are *able to,* fly (after all, no one *constrains* me from flying, but I am nonetheless *not* free to fly). But Muller is quick to point out that "actually, of course, birds are not simply free to fly and sing—they *have* to fly and sing."[210] Thus, birds lack the third necessary condition of freedom, the power of conscious choice, and thus are not, after all, free to fly and sing.

We are now in a position to see that Sartre's reasons for insisting that ontological freedom is a prerequisite to practical freedom are basically the same as Muller's reasons for holding the power of conscious choice to be a necessary condition of freedom. Thus, while Muller maintains that one cannot be free without the power of conscious choice, Sartre underscores essentially the same point by drawing out its logical corollaries—namely, that a being who lacks the power of conscious choice cannot be enslaved, nor can the freedom of such a being be enhanced or diminished. Clearly, such a being cannot be enslaved, since the concept of slavery makes no sense if there is not some *capacity* for freedom which is being thwarted; and the freedom of such a being cannot be enhanced or diminished, because one cannot alter the *quantity* of a *quality* which is not present in the first place.

Such is Sartre's justification (a plausible one in my view) for holding ontological freedom to be foundational to practical freedom. But now that we are aware of the nature of, and the rationale for, Sartre's distinction between these two senses of freedom, let us continue our inquiry into the soundness (or lack thereof) of that distinction. Toward that end, it will be necessary to examine difficulties in Sartre's reasoning. Let us now take up that task.

1.3.2.1.5   *An objection to Sartre's ontological freedom*

By far the most common objection to Sartre's doctrine of absolute ontological freedom is "the omnipotence objection," which I have already discussed. We have seen that Sartre does *not* believe that human beings are "absolutely" free to realize their ends instantly or without effort; indeed, he acknowledges that we are often not free to realize our ends *at all*. Thus, the "absolute" freedom of prisoners and slaves is a freedom which by no means insures that they will be able to escape from their lot. Theirs (and ours) is a freedom which is perfectly compatible with the condition of remaining permanently imprisoned or enslaved.

But this reply to the omnipotence objection merely serves to raise a new objection to the concept of "ontological freedom." If such a freedom is indeed perfectly compatible with imprisonment, slavery, failure, and impotence, surely it can only be a rather inconsequential freedom, an inner freedom, that is, a freedom of attitude, of thinking, of judging, desiring, and wishing—in short, a completely *ineffective* freedom having nothing to do with *acting* in the world.

The trouble with this objection, which has been raised by Warnock,[211] and repeatedly by Merleau-Ponty,[212] is that it rests on a misrepresentation of Sartre's concept of ontological freedom. Nowhere does Sartre endorse such an empty, inconsequential freedom; nor, as I hope a careful reading of the preceding section makes clear, does an analysis of what he explicitly says about ontological freedom *entail* that it must be understood in this diluted sense; nor is it the case that the only kind of freedom which would be compatible with imprisonment, slavery, and impotence would be such a freedom.

Moreover, and more importantly, Sartre explicitly disowns such a conception of freedom, calling it an "inner freedom" which is "a pure idealist hoax," because "care is taken never to present it as the necessary condition of the *act*."[213] As against this view of freedom, and against the claim that the only kind of freedom which would be compatible with imprisonment would be the idle freedom to wish for release, Sartre distinguishes ontological freedom from both "the license to do everything we want" and "a kind of inner refuge which we could enjoy even while enchained."[214] Rather, Sartre insists that any freedom worthy of the name

> supposes a commencement of realization in order that the choice may be distinguished from the dream and the wish. Thus *we shall not say that a prisoner is always free to go out of prison, which would be absurd,*[215] *nor that he is always free to long for release, which would be an irrelevant truism,* but that he is always free to try to escape (or get himself liberated); that is, that whatever his condition may be, he can project his escape and learn the value of his project by undertaking some action.[216]

Thus, by distinguishing the formation of a project, together with the undertaking of an action, from both *successful* action, on the one hand, and idle wishing, on the other, Sartre seems to render himself invulnerable to the present objection. To press the objection, then, a critic would have to show that Sartre's answer is inadequate, perhaps that the passages quoted above are not representative of his views, or that the conception of freedom advocated in them really is, Sartre's protests to the contrary notwithstanding, indistinguishable from an idle "inner" freedom of longing. But Warnock and Merleau-Ponty do not address these passages, or any others like them, and proceed as if they are unaware that such passages exist.

1.3.2.1.6 *Some difficulties with Sartre's practical freedom*

Let us ask *why* it is that the slave in chains is "practically" unfree, or at least *less* "practically" free than (most) people who are not slaves in chains. At first glance it would appear that this question can be easily answered. After all, Sartre's "practical freedom" is the sense of freedom in which "success is important to freedom," and the slave cannot possibly succeed, or at least, can succeed only with great effort and at great risk, in carrying out his project—that of escaping from the master's control.

The problem with this answer is that, on Sartre's view, ontological freedom would seem to preclude *this* kind of practical unfreedom. For, as we recall, part of what is meant by ontological freedom is the freedom to interpret one's situation variously, and to select from a range of possible projects with respect to one's situation as one has interpreted it. Thus, the slave's chains cannot *by themselves* bring about his practical unfreedom (understood as inability to succeed in one's chosen project), for he can always choose a project in which he *can* succeed. For instance, as Anderson points out, if the slave

> chooses masochism . . . , his chains will be of great assistance. Thus, it would seem that all that is necessary in the concrete in order for a man to change the character of his situation (its "coefficient of adversity") is for him to change his projects. As the stoics believed freedom is achieved not by changing the situation of men, but by changing their goals.[217]

An obvious response to this argument would be to claim that the master's situation is *inherently* freer than that of the slave, and that the project of resigning oneself to a life in chains is therefore, despite the fact that it admits of a high possibility of success, an inferior project stemming from a debased practical freedom.[218]

And yet, Sartre explicitly rejects this response:

> The situation of the slave *can not be compared* with that of the master. Each of them in fact takes on its meaning only for the for-itself in situation and in terms of the free choice of its ends. A comparison could be made only by a third person . . . only in the light of a project freely chosen by this third person. There is no absolute point of view which one can adopt so as to compare different situations, each person realizes only one situation—*his own*.[219]

Another possible answer to our question is that the slave's practical freedom or unfreedom lies not in his ability to succeed in the particular project that he has *in fact* chosen to undertake, but rather in the *range* of possible choices of realizable projects which are presented to him by his situation. Thus, we may say even of a slave who succeeds completely in carrying out the project of resigning himself to a life of slavery that he is unfree, since he is presented only with the pitifully limited choice of either resigning himself to slavery or risking almost certain death in an attempt to escape.

But this answer is unsatisfactory for at least two reasons. First, it is very difficult to see by what criteria we would decide what counts as a wide range of choices and what counts as a narrow range. For, as Isaiah Berlin points out, the method of counting how many possibilities are open to me "can never be more than impressionistic" since "possibilities of action are not discrete entities like apples, which can be exhaustively enumerated."[220]

Part of the problem here, as we have seen in our discussion of the human condition, is that there are, at least from an abstract point of view, an infinite number of restrictions which pertain to all human beings in all situations. We cannot flap our wings and fly to the moon, or change the color of our skin at will, or run one hundred yards in one second flat. Moreover, in addition to the restrictions which we all share, each of us faces innumerable personal restrictions which pertain to us in all situations. The dwarf is *always* unable to become a center in the National Basketball Association. The tone-deaf woman is *always* unable to become a professional singer. The blind man is *always* unable to become a baseball umpire, etc., etc.

Again, at least from an abstract point of view, I am presented with an infinite number of possible choices in any situation—an infinite number of possible projects which I can reasonably expect to be able to carry out successfully. Thus, even if I am a slave, I can choose the project of writing songs and singing them a capella—a project that I can easily undertake while in chains; or I can deliberately undereat, so as to perfect "that gaunt look"; or I can simply choose the project of becoming the most obedient servant the world has ever seen, etc., etc. So, in addition to facing an infinite number of *restrictions* in every situation, I am also faced with an infinite number of *possibilities* in every situation. But if I face both an infinite number of restrictions *and* of possibilities in *each and every situation,* it is difficult to see how a purely quantitative evaluation of the range of choices available to me can reveal that I am freer in any one situation than in any other.[221]

To be sure, it sounds strained and forced, even if abstractly true, to say in this manner that I have an infinite range of choices in any situation. But I suspect that the reasons *why* this claim strikes us as implausible only underscore the basic point that there is a problem about the criteria by which we distinguish a wide range from a narrow range of choices. For one thing, projects are hierarchically related to one another—some are more fundamental than others. If I choose, for example, to become a doctor, this more basic project is foundational to my project of going to medical school; and my desire to become a doctor, in turn, might itself be founded in my more fundamental desire for wealth and prestige, etc. Perhaps, then, the implausibility of the claim that we always have an infinite range of choices lies in the fact that it ignores this hierarchical structure. Thus, it would seem that the most natural way to describe the choices facing the slave would not be to say that he faces an infinity of possible choices—to attempt to escape, to write and sing songs, to perfect the gaunt look, to be perfectly obedient, etc., etc., but that he faces an extremely limited range of *fundamental* choices—to attempt to escape or to accept his lot—and an infinite range of *secondary* choices—to write and sing songs, etc.

The difficulty arises, however, when we ask *why* it is that this description seems more natural to us. Is it not because we move beyond *quantitative* criteria, and introduce *qualitative* criteria into our analysis? Is it not, indeed, because we *value* the escape from slavery so highly that we see the choice between acquiescence and escape as *more important* than the choice between, say, escape and singing? Indeed, if singing were what I valued most, would I not view my range of possibilities in terms of "singing or not" as the fundamental choice, with "in chains or not" as a secondary choice? And if, for some reason, the life of a slave were more conducive to the project of singing than most others, would I not then regard such a life as one which promised a relatively *large* amount of practical freedom?

This brings us to the second difficulty with the view that practical freedom is a function of the (quantitative) range of possible choices of realizable projects which are present in a situation. The problem is that even if one is not convinced that qualitative criteria *must* be invoked in order to render such a quantitative analysis possible, it can also be argued, *on independent grounds,* that evaluative criteria are essential to a determination of the degree of freedom which I have in any situation. In other words, my freedom depends not only on the *quantity* of choices available to me, but also their *quality*—how *good* they are, or at least, how much I *value* them. P. H. Partridge explains this well:

> Does it follow . . . that the extent of freedom is related to the number of available alternatives, in that the more alternatives there are for choice, the freer a man is? Clearly there can be no simple or direct relationship between the range of available alternatives and the extent of freedom. However numerous the alternatives between which a man may choose, he will not admit himself to be free if the one alternative that he would most prefer is the one which is excluded. In a society that forbids the preaching of Catholic doctrine and the practice of Catholic forms of worship, Catholics will not concede that they are free just because they are still free to be either Anglicans, Methodists, or Buddhists.[222]

One possible objection to Partridge's statement is that it places exclusive emphasis on the *subjective* value of choices (how much do I *value* X) while ignoring their *objective* value (how *good* is X, irrespective of the degree to which I value it). I have in mind the fact that we would probably be less inclined to call "unfree" a person who is well-fed, rich, well-educated, and healthy, but whose strongest desire, to own a Mercedes Benz, has been utterly unfulfilled, then we would a person who is hungry, poor, ignorant, and diseased, and whose strongest desire is for food. Moreover, I think that this would be our judgment even if, for whatever reason, the wealthy person's unfulfilled desire for a Mercedes Benz were every bit as strong, or even stronger, than the poor person's desire for food, or even, to vary our example, if the poor person, as a result of disease, had no remaining appetite mechanism, and thus no desire for food at all, or even, finally, if the poor person's desire for food were *partially* (but inadequately) satisfied, while the wealthy person's desire for a Mercedes Benz went *totally* unfulfilled.[223] This suggests that, while we do regard the quality of choices available as relevant to practical freedom, the determination of the quality of a given choice cannot be settled *solely* by reference to whether or to what extent that choice is *valued* by the person in question. Rather, I think we must regard the presence of some choices as *intrinsically* more important to freedom than the presence of others—which partially explains why we talk of "freedom of speech" and "freedom from hunger," but not of "freedom of fingernail polish" or "freedom from lint"—so that there is at least a rough objective hierarchical order of choices as far as their relevance to freedom is concerned, perhaps with the greatest importance being assigned to choices which allow for the fulfillment of fundamental human needs.

But can Sartre, whose ethical subjectivism is well-known, be expected to go along with anything like this? Consider the following three texts:

> Freedom—not metaphysical but practical freedom—is conditioned by proteins. Life will be human on the day that everyone can eat his fill and every man can work at a job under suitable working conditions.[224]

> [Freedom] is a word that lends itself to numerous interpretations. In the West it is taken to mean abstract freedom. But to me it means a more concrete freedom—the right to have more than one pair of shoes and to eat when one is hungry.[225]

> Alienation, exploitation of man by man, under-nourishment, [relegate] to the background metaphysical evil which is a luxury. *Hunger is an evil: period.*[226]

One *suspects* from reading these passages, especially Sartre's claim about the evil of hunger, that he is prepared to admit the objectivity of at least *some* value-judgments, such as, perhaps, those contained in Howard Zinn's declaration that "the experiences of millions of lives over centuries of time, relived by each of us in those aspects common to all men, *prove* to us that love is preferable to hate, peace to war, brotherhood to enmity, joy to sorrow, health to sickness, nourishment to hunger, life to death.[227] If so, the judgment that the slave has comparatively little practical freedom arises from our judgment that what the slave lacks is something of great (objective) value, and that the *choice* of slavery would, therefore, be strictly speaking an "error."

However, to return to an issue raised previously, no matter how we arrive at the judgment that the slave is unfree, and that the slaveholder is responsible for this unfreedom, it still does not seem to follow straightforwardly that we must (as Sartre does) *condemn* the slaveholder. Rather, it would seem that we could approve the slaveholder's actions, or, even if we disapproved, we could hold our disapproval to be merely a matter of personal taste, having no objective validity.[228] But Sartre does disapprove of the slaveholder, and in a manner which leaves little doubt as to his view that *any other attitude would be* (objectively?) *morally reprehensible.* Indeed, the severity of Sartre's moral judgments illustrates (arguably) a tension, if not an actual inconsistency, in his thought. Thus, as Peter Caws points out, Sartre is "passionately committed, ready to judge in the most scathing terms bad faith, failures of authenticity, the behaviour of bosses and anti-semites, still Sartre can find no objective ground for these judgments."[229]

The problem, then, is clear. Both in declaring the slave to be "practically" unfree, and in condemning the slaveholder for enslaving him, Sartre seems (arguably) to be committed to the objectivity of certain moral or evaluative judgments. And yet, as is widely known, he appears to be deeply committed, on the theoretical level, to the view that no such objectively valid moral judgments can possibly be found. This problem, however—if, indeed, it truly *is* a problem—is much too complex and controversial to be fully pursued here. Rather, since its complexity is matched by its importance and interest, we shall devote to it a fuller treatment in subsequent sections.[230]

1.3.2.2   The inconsistency objection answered

We have seen that "the omnipotence objection" is unsound, and that it rests upon a fundamental methodological error, consisting in the failure to consider any evidence which runs counter to one's thesis. I am now ready to argue that "the inconsistency objection" is also unsound, and that it too rests upon a basic methodological error: *the failure to inquire into the nature of the question to which a given philosophical assertion is proposed as an answer.*

To clarify this, consider the following assertion: "Everyone in this room is free." Clearly, this assertion means one thing when uttered during a political conversation, in response to a questioner who is concerned with such issues as whether or not anyone in the room is a prisoner, or has suffered the loss of certain fundamental political rights, or perhaps lacks certain goods which are held to be essential to the fulfillment of basic human needs; the assertion means quite another thing when uttered during a discussion of the free will versus determinism debate, in response to a questioner who is concerned with, say, whether or not everyone in the room has the capacity, in every situation, including that of being behind bars, to choose and to carry out any one of a number of possible actions, so that we could truthfully say, subsequent to the performing of any action by any of the individuals in the room, that he or she "could have done otherwise."[231] That the statement, "everyone in this room is free," means different things in these two different contexts can, I trust, be readily seen from the fact that it would be perfectly *coherent* (though not necessarily *correct*) to affirm the statement in either one of these two contexts while denying it in the other. It follows that it would be a mistake to regard the statement that "everyone in this room is both free and unfree" as a simple contradiction without first investigating in what *sense,* and in answer to what *question,* the people in the room are said to be free, and in what sense and in answer to what question they are said to be unfree. The failure to investigate these matters is, I submit, the error which underlies the inconsistency objection.

The point, in the words of Solomon, is that "even within Sartre's theory of absolute freedom, we must ask *in which ways man is free and which ways he is not.* "[232] Our discussion of Sartre's distinction between "ontological freedom" and "practical freedom," while revealing that Sartre's position is by no means free of difficulties, at least establishes that he uses the word "freedom" in different ways in different contexts, and that he can regard one and the same person in one and the same situation as "free" in one sense and "unfree" in another. This underscores the justice of Solomon's remark, and points out, once again, what is wrong with the inconsistency objection.

It should also be emphasized that the methodological error which we are presently considering—let us call it "the second error"—underlies not only the inconsistency objection but also the omnipotence objection. It underlies the inconsistency objection when Sartre's theory of freedom is held, due to the failure to investigate which sense of freedom is operative in any given statement, to be incompatible with *itself.* It underlies the omnipotence objection when that theory is held, due to the same failure, to be incompatible with *certain facts* with which it is, in fact, perfectly compatible. Let us attempt to clarify the *nature* of "the second error" in connection with the omnipotence objection, before moving on to document that it does *in fact* prop up both the omnipotence objection and the inconsistency objection.

First of all, what I am calling "the second error" is not at all uncommon in the history of philosophy, and can perhaps best be illustrated in connection with what is probably the most famous historical example of it. I refer to Dr. Samuel Johnson's refutation of Berkeley's idealism, which consisted of kicking a stone and exclaiming, "I refute him thus."[233] Johnson's point was that what one kicks is not an "idea of a stone," but a stone, and that if one attempts to reduce stones to ideas of stones, the distinction between real and imaginary stones becomes obliterated. But, as W. T. Jones points out,

> Berkeley had no trouble distinguishing between dream and reality. In a "real" stone, for instance, the visual ideas of such-and-such a colored shape coexist along with the ideas of resistance and pain, when these are accompanied by the muscular sensations called kicking. In an "imaginary" stone, the visual data are accompanied neither by tactile data nor by a sensation of pain.
>
> Moreover, the various data (the color and the shape) making up the real stone are more vivid and more distinct than those making up the imaginary stone. Also, the data in the real stone are independent of one's will (for instance, if I look in the appropriate direction, I cannot but see the stone), whereas the data in the imaginary stone are dependent on one's will. "Dream" stones are to be distinguished from both imaginary stones and real stones, not on the basis of vividness or independence, but on the basis of confusedness and irregularity. Thus the distinctions on which Dr. Johnson rightly insisted can be accounted for in Berkeleian terms.[234]

Thus, the second error, which I maintain is committed not only by Dr. Johnson but also by those who press the omnipotence objection or the inconsistency objection against Sartre, arises when one attempts to refute a theory by exhibiting certain facts or statements with which the theory is alleged to be incompatible, but with which it is in fact perfectly compatible. Characteristically, this error arises from a failure to understand the nature of the claims made by a theory, as when claims of a primarily conceptual nature are confused with straightforwardly empirical claims,[235] or when the precise sense of an ambiguous term like "freedom" is erroneously identified. Berkeleian idealism cannot be refuted by kicking stones, because it is not an empirical theory in the sense of declaring that certain phenomena (those associated with kicking stones) cannot be found, but rather a *conceptual* theory which, *taking these phenomena for its basis,* proposes, on conceptual grounds, new (and allegedly better) ways of thinking about and understanding these phenomena. Thus, this theory is completely compatible with the phenomena cited against it, and the claim that it is incompatible with these phenomena involves a fundamental misunderstanding of the nature of the theory itself.[236]

Similarly, Sartre's theory cannot be refuted, in the manner of the omnipotence objection critics, by citing "everything we know and do" and "the facts of life,"[237] for it too seeks *to understand differently,* rather than *to deny,* the phenomena cited against it. Sartre's theory of "absolute freedom" is not a straightforwardly empirical doctrine which would fly in the face of the facts by claiming, say, that no one is in prison, or that those who are imprisoned are "always free to go out of prison," a claim that Sartre explicitly says "would be absurd."[238] Rather, he attempts, on the basis of such data as that some people are imprisoned, that some of these people cannot escape from imprisonment, and that these people are in some sense, therefore, unfree, to determine, as Solomon suggests, in *which* ways these people are free and in *which* ways they are not.

None of this suggests, of course, that Sartre's theory of freedom is hereby rendered invulnerable to legitimate criticisms. To the contrary, Sartre himself worries extensively about acquitting himself, to give just one example, of the objection that his theory is "an irrelevant truism."[239] But to dismiss Sartre's theory of freedom as "at odds with the facts of life," such as the fact that there are prisoners, by focusing on his "absolute freedom" claims and his insistence that slaves and prisoners are in some sense free, without inquiring into the *nature* of these claims, the *sense* of freedom at issue, or the question of whether the claims are intended as *denials* or *reinterpretations* of the phenomena with which they appear to be at odds, is altogether illegitimate.[240] And, to return to the inconsistency objection, it is equally illegitimate to dismiss a theory as inconsistent without first asking whether the sense of freedom at work in each of the apparently incompatible claims is indeed the same.

Let us take stock. I have identified two objections to Sartre's theory of freedom, and named them "the omnipotence objection" and "the inconsistency objection." I have also claimed that there are two fundamental methodological errors which underlie these two objections: the failure to consider any evidence which runs counter to one's thesis—this is "the first error," which underlies the omnipotence objection—and the failure to inquire into the nature of the question to which a given philosophical assertion is proposed as an answer—this is "the second error," which underlies both the omnipotence objection and the inconsistency objection. I have explained these objections and these errors; I have provided some textual documentation which suggests that Sartre is invulnerable to the objections; and I have outlined some strategies for reading and interpreting Sartre which would not only render him invulnerable to these objections but also reveal the objections to be based upon these errors. What I have not adequately done as yet is to show that Sartre's theory of freedom is *in fact* invulnerable to these objections, and that these objections are *in fact* based upon these errors.

This task is best accomplished in the concrete. Of course, it is not possible to consider every criticism of Sartre's theory of freedom that has ever been offered. It will have to be sufficient, then, to consider the objections of two of Sartre's most influential critics, Wilfrid Desan and Maurice Merleau-Ponty, in some detail.

1.3.2.2.1 *Desan*

Consider the following passage from Desan's widely-read commentary on *BN*, entitled *The Tragic Finale: An Essay on the Philosophy of Jean-Paul Sartre*:

> It may happen, and it does happen, that I am free in deciding an act but not in executing it. I have decided to go from Lille to Paris by bicycle, but while I am on the way, a heavy storm comes up. Obviously, I must either interrupt my trip or go ahead and risk being drenched. No one can claim, however, that I have freely chosen these different hypotheses. The storm was certainly not included in my initial choice. It is true that if I had stayed home, I should not

have been in the storm, but it is also true that what was not foreseen at all cannot be imputed to my free decision. It is not I who choose *this* "situation." The obvious conclusion is that all choice supposes a certain number of *data: I can choose among those data, but the data themselves I have not chosen.* Choice is never unlimited, but rather it happens to be between A or B or C. Even when A, B and C are the result of an anterior choice, they are nevertheless limited and irrevocable. After having spent years preparing myself for the Marines, the result is that I am prepared for the Marines and not for the Air Forces or for a chair of philosophy. Whatever Sartre may say, this is a limitation of my choice. Absolute freedom is a mere illusion.[241]

Before responding to this criticism, it should be pointed out, though Desan fails to do so, that Sartre discusses extensively a very similar example in *BN*. In Sartre's example, I am on my way to see Pierre, when "the abrupt appearance" of something unforeseen "contribute(s) to a radical change in (my) situation":

Let my tire be punctured, and my distance from the next town suddenly changes; now it is a distance to be counted by steps and not by the revolutions of the wheels. From this fact I can acquire the certainty that the person whom I wish to see will have already taken the train when I arrive at his house, and this certainty can involve other decisions on my part (a return to my point of departure, the sending of a telegram, etc.). It is even possible, for example, that sure of not being able to conclude a projected deal with this person, I may return to someone else and sign another contract. Perhaps I shall even give up the whole attempt. And shall I count my project as a total failure? In this case I shall say that I *was not able* to inform Pierre in time, to come to an understanding with him, etc. Is not this explicit recognition of my *powerlessness* the clearest admission of the limits of my freedom? Of course my freedom *to choose,* as we have seen, must not be confused with my freedom *to obtain.*[242]

What, then, is wrong with Desan's criticism?

(1) He urges, as against Sartre, that a distinction must be drawn between freedom "in deciding an act" and freedom "in executing it," and that we are unfree in the latter sense. This, he thinks, shows that Sartre's theory of absolute freedom is "a mere illusion." But, as we have seen, Sartre himself insists upon essentially this same distinction, between what he calls "freedom to choose" and "freedom to obtain," and agrees that, in the example discussed as well as in countless other cases, and indeed *typically,* we are *unfree* in the latter sense. Thus, Desan attempts to refute Sartre's theory of

"absolute" freedom by opposing to it certain distinctions and
claims which he imagines Sartre to be unable to accept, but which,
apparently unbeknownst to him, Sartre has already insisted upon,
and integrated into his theory.

Perhaps part of Desan's problem here is that he attributes to
Sartre, unfortunately without documentation, the opinion that it is
"a false view" of freedom to regard that term as meaning "obtaining what [one] wants, or receiving what [one] desires."[243]
However, what Sartre actually *says* in the section of *BN* which
Desan is here discussing, is that this sense of freedom must not be
confused with "the technical and philosophical concept of freedom, *the only one which we are considering here,* [which] means
only the autonomy of choice."[244] Thus, because Desan thinks that
Sartre *rejects* a certain sense of freedom, which he in fact accepts,
insisting merely that it be *distinguished* from another sense, he
concludes that Sartre cannot acknowledge *in any sense* that I am
unfree if my trip is interrupted by some unforeseen event. But just
as Desan regards me in this circumstance as free in "deciding an
act" but unfree "in executing it," so does Sartre see me as free "to
choose" but not "to obtain." Desan criticizes Sartre for failing to
draw a distinction which, in fact, he does draw. Or at least, if
Sartre's distinction *is* different from Desan's, Desan utterly fails to
indicate *how* it is different, since he ignores Sartre's distinction
altogether.

(2) Another objection to Desan's procedure is that it shows no
awareness of the fact that Sartre has already invented and discussed
in detail an example very similar to the one used against him by
Desan. One would think that Desan's criticism of an example that
Sartre himself discusses would call for an indication of what is
wrong with Sartre's discussion, or at least some hint as to how
Sartre's treatment of the example differs from Desan's own.
Instead, Desan proceeds as if he had dreamed up an example that
Sartre had not anticipated, and which he would be completely
incapable of handling adequately. And his strategy in making this
example count against Sartre consists primarily in the accusation
that Sartre fails to draw a distinction which he does in fact draw,
and the insistence that he does not make a judgment that he does in
fact make (that my freedom can be limited by unforeseen circum-

stances). We must take Desan quite seriously when he remarks, *"whatever Sartre may say,* this is a limitation of my choice": Desan has either never read, or has forgotten, what Sartre *does* say. He *does not know* what Sartre might say.[245]

(3) Desan completely ignores Sartre's discussion of the extent to which I do choose even the unpredictable and the unforeseeable:

> Every free project in projecting itself anticipates a margin of unpredictability due to the independence of things precisely because this independence is that in terms of which a freedom is constituted. As soon as I project going to the nearby village to find Pierre, the punctures, the "headwind," a thousand foreseeable and unforeseeable accidents are given in my very project and constitute its meaning . . . Just as the Romans reserved in their temple a place for unknown gods, so in my project a certain margin of indetermination was created "for the unpredictable" . . .
>
> These observations allow us to bring to light a new characteristic of a free choice: every project of freedom is an *open project* and not a closed project. Although entirely individualized, it contains within it the possibility of its further modifications. Every project implies in its structure the comprehension of the *Selbständigkeit* of the things in the world. This perpetual foreseeing of the unforeseeable as the margin of indetermination of the project which I am enables us to understand how it is that an accident or a catastrophe, instead of surprising me by its unknown or its extraordinary quality, always overwhelms me by a certain quality which it has of "being already seen—already foreseen," by its very obviousness and a kind of fatalistic necessity, which we express by saying, "This was bound to happen."[246]

Now, as we have seen, Desan does not think that I can choose, in any sense or to any degree, that which I do not foresee. Concerning the alternatives presented by the storm (to "interrupt my trip or go ahead and risk being drenched"), Desan insists: "No one can claim . . . that I have freely chosen these different hypotheses. The storm was certainly not included in my initial choice . . . What was not foreseen at all cannot be imputed to my free decision." Of course, we have just seen that Sartre denies all three of these assertions, and Desan gives no reasons whatsoever for rejecting Sartre's denials. Indeed, he proceeds, once again, as if he were completely unaware of the fact that Sartre had ever addressed these issues. In any case, what we need to know, and what Desan neglects to tell us, is precisely *why* "what was not foreseen at all cannot be imputed to my free decision." His failure to address this issue can easily be explained on the assumption that he is oblivious to the existence of Sartre's discussion. After all, Desan's position is clear and straightforward, while Sartre's is paradoxical (e.g., "the perpetual foreseeing of the unforeseeable . . . "), confusing, counterintuitive, and original. Thus, if Desan had been unaware of the fact that anyone had anticipated and challenged his assumptions, he might have thought them sufficiently obvious and uncontroversial as not to require a defense. If, on the other hand, he was aware of Sartre's counterarguments (which seems to me unlikely), he would be vulnerable to charges of dogmatism for rejecting, *without argument,* or discussion, but simply by method of *counter assertion,* the very views of which he claims to be giving a detailed exposition and critique.

(4) Desan says, as against Sartre, that "choice is never unlimited, but rather it happens to be between A or B or C." But Desan presents no documentation to show that this view is opposed to Sartre's, and he completely ignores Sartre's repeated claim that "*being situated* is an essential and necessary characteristic of freedom,"[247] a claim which entails, as we have seen, that freedom always operates within a context in which some things are possible, others are impossible, and still others are merely more or less difficult.[248] *Of course,* "after having spent years preparing myself for the Marines, the result is that I am prepared for the Marines and not for the Air Forces or for a chair of philosophy." But how is this fact supposed to count as an objection to Sartre?

(5) Desan declares "absolute freedom" to be "a mere illusion." His reason for saying this, apparently, is that freedom is not unlimited. But Desan ignores all of Sartre's many affirmations of the restricted and limited nature of freedom[249] (e.g., "freedom can exist *only* as *restricted*"[250]), and he fails to justify his interpretation of "absolute freedom" as something which would be incompatible with the existence of restrictions and limitations. He might as well kick a stone and say, "I refute him thus."

Desan concludes his chapter called "Critique of Sartre's Extreme Form of Freedom" with the following words: "An absolute freedom exists nowhere. It is truly astonishing to find a man like Sartre, who seeks to give us in his phenomenological approach a strictly objective view of what appears in reality, managing nevertheless to build up a conception of freedom which is so thoroughly unrealistic."[251] In this section I have attempted to establish a somewhat different account of what is "truly astonishing."

1.3.2.2.2 *Merleau-Ponty*

Criticisms of a higher quality are raised against Sartre by his colleague and fellow phenomenologist Maurice Merleau-Ponty,[252] a man who is widely regarded, and justly so, as at least Sartre's equal in terms of philosophical ability and importance. These criticisms deserve examination, not only because of Merleau-Ponty's stature, but also because his reading of Sartre is widely believed to be accurate, and seems to serve as a kind of foundation for the severe objections to Sartre which are commonly raised by critics possessing much less understanding of Sartre's philosophy than does Merleau-Ponty. Indeed, as Margaret Whitford points out, "on the whole, critics have accepted more or less uncritically Merleau-Ponty's assessment of Sartre's philosophy."[253] Let us attempt a partial rectification of this situation, then, by turning a critical eye toward Merleau-Ponty's critique of Sartre, focusing especially on his objections to Sartre's theory of freedom which are to be found in the final chapter of his *Phenomenology of Perception* (hereafter cited as *PP*).[254]

Typical of Merleau-Ponty's critique of Sartre's theory of freedom is his complaint that Sartre's concept of "ready-made freedom,"[255] far from guaranteeing the presence of human freedom, seems to "rule it out altogether." As Merleau-Ponty explains,

> If it is indeed the case that our freedom is the same in all our actions, and even in our passions, if it is not to be measured in terms of our conduct, and if the slave displays freedom as much by living in fear as by breaking his chains, then it cannot be held that there is such a thing as *free action,* freedom being anterior to all actions. In any case it will not be possible to declare: 'Here freedom makes its appearance', since free action, in order to be discernible, has to stand out against a background of life from which it is entirely, or almost entirely, absent. We may say in this case that it is everywhere, but equally nowhere.[256]

In other words, "if freedom is always and everywhere present, then the distinction between freedom and unfreedom loses its meaning."[257]

But in the above-quoted passage, and indeed, throughout the chapter on freedom in *PP,* Merleau-Ponty ignores three crucial distinctions in Sartre's theory of freedom. Attention to these three distinctions should, I think, remove most of the bite from Merleau-Ponty's criticism.[258]

First of all, as we have seen, Sartre distinguishes between different senses of freedom, most notably, between "ontological" and "practical" freedom. Consequently, Sartre also draws at least two different distinctions between freedom and unfreedom, namely, between ontological freedom and ontological unfreedom and between practical freedom and practical unfreedom. Thus, Merleau-Ponty's charge that Sartre's theory of freedom obliterates the distinction between freedom and unfreedom is doubly false. In the first place, I am (ontologically) free, while stones are not. In the second place, I am (practically) free to read the *Phenomenology of Perception,* while I am (practically) unfree, or at least very much *less* free,[259] to read top-secret government documents. Merleau-Ponty's objection seems to stem both from ignorance of all of these distinctions, or, more precisely, ignorance of the fact that these distinctions can be found in Sartre's works, and from his conclusion that since Sartre recognizes *one* sense of freedom in which all human beings are free, he must therefore be committed to the view that the distinction between freedom and unfreedom, at least with respect to human beings, is illusory.[260]

(Incidentally, much later on, in an interview, Sartre had this to say about such an interpretation of his thought: "I think that a theory of freedom which does not explain what the forms of alienation are—to what extent freedom can be manipulated, distorted, turned against itself—can cruelly deceive someone who does not understand all it implies *and who thinks that freedom is everywhere.* But I don't think a person who reads what I have written carefully can make a mistake like that."[261])

Another criticism levelled by Merleau-Ponty, one which I have already discussed to some extent,[262] is that Sartre's concept of freedom amounts to nothing more than an "inner," ineffective freedom having nothing to do with acting in the world. As Merleau-Ponty puts it, "the idea of action . . . disappears . . . There are merely intentions immediately followed by their effects, and we are very near to the Kantian idea of an intention which is tantamount to the act, which Scheler countered with the argument that the cripple who would like to be able to save a drowning man and the good swimmer who actually saves him do not have the same experience of autonomy."[263] Or again, in *Adventures of the Dialectic*: "This type of freedom . . . is never a *doing* . . . This freedom . . . is in reality the freedom to judge, which even slaves in chains have."[264] Finally, Merleau-Ponty charges, in the same vein, that the very notion of absolute freedom *guarantees* that the freedom in question must be completely ineffective, since "if freedom is doing, it is necessary that what it does should not be immediately undone by a new freedom."[265] But if I am *absolutely* free, after completing a free act, to undo in every detail what I have done in my previous act, then this previous free act must not have had any real impact— it could not have effected any lasting change. Moreover, if I am truly *absolutely* free, it follows that this analysis will apply to *all* of my actions, so that none of them, even *in principle,* can ever have any lasting effect. Thus, absolute freedom *must* be nothing other than an ineffective inner freedom of judgment.

But we have seen that Sartre explicitly rejects such a conception of "inner freedom," and goes to great lengths to establish that his theory of freedom cannot properly be understood in this manner.[266] We have seen, moreover, that Sartre rejects this inner freedom, not in *reaction* to Merleau-Ponty's criticism, but in *anticipation* of it, since he discusses the point in *BN*, the work which Merleau-Ponty claims to be criticizing. In the light of Sartre's numerous treatments of this issue, which we have examined,[267] but which Merleau-Ponty *completely ignores,* I frankly can find no basis whatsoever for Merleau-Ponty's charge. In order to lend some credence to this judgment, and for its own intrinsic interest, let us ask: where, precisely, does Merleau-Ponty go wrong?

This depends upon how we interpret what he says. If, on the one hand, we take Merleau-Ponty to be charging literally that, for Sartre, my freedom is always capable of undoing anything that I have done, then it would seem that Merleau-Ponty is simply guilty of saddling Sartre with the invalid omnipotence objection.[268] Obviously Sartre does not think, and says nothing to imply, that if I have hurled myself from the top of a skyscraper without a parachute, and am now hurtling toward the ground, I remain free to undo my prior act and to find myself safely at the top of the skyscraper again.

If, on the other hand, Merleau-Ponty is arguing that *since* Sartre cannot possibly mean that I am always free to undo whatever I have done, his claim that I am always free *must therefore* be construed as meaning only that I am always free to think against, or wish against, what has been done, then it would seem that Merleau-Ponty is illegitimately constraining Sartre within a false dilemma. The doctrine that one is always free need not mean, as Merleau-Ponty implies, that one is always free either to succeed completely or else merely to dream of, or long for, success. Rather, it can mean, and for Sartre it *does* mean, that one is always free to *choose a project* and to *attempt to carry it out*.

Finally, it might be the case that Merleau-Ponty is not holding that "freedom," or even "absolute freedom," must be understood either in terms of omnipotence or else as an "inner freedom," but only that *Sartre* has locked himself into this dichotomy. Evidence that this is indeed Merleau-Ponty's view can be found by considering (1) that Merleau-Ponty himself advocates, as against Sartre, a view of freedom which lies between these two extremes; (2) that Merleau-Ponty tends to present Sartre's view of freedom in starkly dichotomous terms, as for example, when he attributes to Sartre the belief that "our freedom . . . is either total or non-existent";[269] and (3) that Merleau-Ponty refers to a passage in which Sartre holds that freedom always is, and always must be, faced with obstacles, in a manner which suggests that he regards this claim as inconsistent with Sartre's general theory of freedom.[270]

Here Merleau-Ponty seems to be guilty of three errors. First, the view that the presence of obstacles is somehow inconsistent with Sartre's theory of freedom, together with Merleau-Ponty's reading of Sartre's claim that freedom is "total," seems to constitute another example of the fallacious omnipotence objection. Secondly, in presenting as Sartre's view the claim that freedom is either total or non-existent, Merleau-Ponty is guilty of ignoring Sartre's distinction between ontological and practical freedom, since the latter freedom is not captured by the total/non-existent dichotomy.

Finally, while it is true that Sartre's *ontological* freedom is either total or non-existent, this does not mean, as Merleau-Ponty apparently thinks, that it amounts either to omnipotence or to a completely ineffective inner freedom.

But this is not all. As a result of Merleau-Ponty's reading of Sartre as advocating this radically dichotomous "either/or" theory of freedom, he accuses him of being a "rationalist" who is incapable of understanding such intermediate phenomena as generality and probability:

> Having built our life upon an inferiority complex which has been operative for twenty years, it is not *probable* that we shall change. It is clear what a summary rationalism might say in reply to such a hybrid notion: there are no degrees of possibility; either the free act is no longer possible, or it is still possible, in which case freedom is complete. In short, 'probable' is meaningless . . . 'It is improbable that Paul will give up writing bad books' means nothing, since Paul may well decide to write no more such books. The probable is everywhere and nowhere, a reified fiction, with only a psychological existence . . . And yet . . . generality and probability are not fictions, but phenomena; we must therefore find a phenomenological basis for statistical thought . . . 'It is improbable' that I should at this moment destroy an inferiority complex in which I have been content to live for twenty years. That means that I have committed myself to inferiority, that I have made it my abode, that this past, though not a fate, has at least a specific weight and is not a set of events over there, at a distance from me, but the atmosphere of my present. The rationalist's dilemma: either the free act is possible, or it is not—either the event originates in me or is imposed on me from outside, does not apply to our relations with the world and with our past.[271]

It is difficult to determine just why Merleau-Ponty thinks that Sartre must embrace the ridiculous position that Merleau-Ponty here attributes to him, and reject the much more sensible position that he himself endorses. He cites just one passage from Sartre, without quoting from it or discussing it in detail, to serve as textual justification for his interpretation,[272] and this passage appears starkly to contradict the interpretation that Merleau-Ponty intends it to justify. Thus, for example, Sartre declares in this passage that my absolute freedom "does not mean that my act can be anything *whatsoever* or even that it is *unforeseeable*,"[273] and argues, in a fashion that is very similar to that of Merleau-Ponty's subsequent discussion, that it would be simplistic to say that a tired hiker must either be simply free or unfree to continue hiking, as if this dichotomy captured all that could be said about the matter. Thus, if I have given in to my fatigue, and have discontinued my hiking, Sartre would reject as overly simplistic both the claims of my friends, who would reproach me for my act, thereby implying that I was free to resist my fatigue longer and could have continued walking as they did, and my own claim that I was *not* free—that I was simply *too tired* to continue. Rather, as Sartre points out,

> There is no doubt that I could have done otherwise, but that is not the problem. It ought to be formulated rather like this: could I have done otherwise without perceptibly modifying the organic totality of the projects which I am; or is the fact of resisting my fatigue such that instead of remaining a purely local and accidental modification of my behavior, it could be effected only by means of a radical transformation of my being-in-the-world—a transformation, moreover, which is *possible*? In other words: I could have done otherwise. Agreed. But *at what price*?[274]

Thus, nothing can be clearer than that Sartre resists falling into the "rationalist's dilemma" that Merleau-Ponty ascribes to him. Plainly, insofar as this example is presented as an illustration of the thesis that free acts can be perfectly *foreseeable,* who can fail to see that Sartre is here acknowledging the legitimacy of the very phenomenon that Merleau-Ponty insists he must refuse at all costs, namely the phenomenon of probability? For Sartre's point, after all, is that if I can "do otherwise" only by radically transforming my being-in-the-world, only by fundamentally altering the nature and order of my projects, only, in short, by surrendering a *very great price,* it is *extremely unlikely*—extremely *improbable,* if you prefer—that I *will* "do otherwise."[275]

Moreover, in an essay published in the same year as Merleau-Ponty's *PP,* we find even more explicit statements from Sartre rejecting the bizarre form of either/or rationalism that Merleau-Ponty ascribes to him. Sartre declares, for example, that "we refuse to let ourselves be torn between thesis and antithesis. We conceive with no difficulty that a man may be a center of irreducible indeterminism, although his situation conditions him totally,"[276] and that "man as we conceive him" is "a total man—totally committed and totally free."[277]

Note how similar this sounds to the view of freedom defended by Merleau-Ponty in *PP:*

> What then is freedom? . . . The world is already constituted, but also never completely constituted; in the first case we are acted upon, in the second we are open to an infinite number of possibilities. But this analysis is still abstract, for we exist in both ways *at once*. There is, therefore, never determinism and never absolute choice, I am never a thing and never bare consciousness . . . The generality of the 'rôle' and of the situation comes to the aid of decision, and in this exchange between the situation and the person who takes it up, it is impossible to determine precisely the 'share contributed by the situation' and the 'share contributed by freedom'.[278]

Nor can this similarity be attributed to changes in Sartre's perspective since the publication of *BN,* for even in that work he had held that "it is impossible to grasp facticity in its brute nudity, since all that we will find of it is already recovered and freely constructed,"[279] and that "it is . . . impossible for me to distinguish the unchangeable brute existence from the variable meaning which it includes."[280] And, more importantly, Sartre had even there made extensive use of that supremely non- rationalistic concept of "the paradox of freedom," which refers to the fact that "there is a freedom only in a *situation,* and there is a situation only through freedom. Human-reality everywhere encounters resistance and obstacles which it has not created, but these resistances and obstacles have meaning only in and through the free choice which human-reality *is.* "[281]

Finally, in addition to the evidence from *BN* that has already been presented establishing Sartre's acceptance of the phenomena of probability and predictability, as well as their consistency with freedom, consider the following three passages from Sartre's subsequent works:

> It is not likely that the worker would have chosen to do *this* work under *these* conditions and within *this* length of time for *these* wages, had it not been forced upon him.[282]

> Since (the anti-Semite), like all men, exists as a free agent within a situation, it is his situation that must be modified from top to bottom. In short, *if we can change the perspective of choice, then the choice itself will change.*[283]

> In a society where everything is bought, the possibilities of culture are practically eliminated for the workers if food absorbs 50 per cent or more of their budget. The freedom of the bourgeois, on the contrary, consists in the possibility of his allotting an always increasing part of his income to a great variety of expenditures.[284]

Of course, it remains to be seen whether or not, or to what extent, such passages as these are consistent with Sartre's early theory of freedom, which Merleau-Ponty is concerned to refute.

Let us now complete our discussion of Merleau-Ponty's critique by taking note of what is perhaps its strangest element, namely the repeated insinuation that Sartre either does not, or is not entitled to, acknowledge the situated nature of freedom. Thus, Merleau-Ponty protests, as against Sartre, that "our freedom does not destroy our situation, but gears itself to it: as long as we are alive, our situation is open,"[285] and that since "we are involved in the world and with others in an inextricable tangle, the idea of situation rules out absolute freedom at the source of our commitments, and equally, indeed, at their terminus."[286]

If we regard these statements as attributing to Sartre the view that freedom is, or *can ever be,* unsituated, the response must be that Merleau-Ponty is simply wrong. As has already been extensively documented above, Sartre holds that freedom *always is,* and *always must be,* situated, that our freedom cannot destroy our situation, that our freedom must *of course* gear itself to its situation, that our situation is always "open" in precisely the sense indicated by Merleau-Ponty, and that our situation presents us with numerous "coefficients of adversity" which arise from our involvement with the world and with other people.[287]

Of course, it is difficult to believe that a man of Merleau-Ponty's undoubted philosophical ability and intimate acquaintance with Sartre could so badly misrepresent his thought.[288] Perhaps it is for this reason that there seem to be many who are willing to take Merleau-Ponty at his word that the difference between Sartre and him is that he, unlike Sartre, regards freedom as always situated.[289] Thus, Remy C. Kwant claims that "the entire chapter about freedom in *Phénoménologie de la perception* is dominated by [Merleau-Ponty's] dispute with Sartre concerning the situated or unsituated character of freedom,"[290] and regards Merleau-Ponty's principal achievement in this chapter to be his demonstration, against Sartre, that "there is no other freedom than situated freedom."[291]

Perhaps a more plausible interpretation of Merleau-Ponty's point here is that, no matter what Sartre may *say* about situated freedom, his doctrine of absolute freedom makes such a notion impossible, and thus, Sartre has no *right* to claim that freedom is situated.[292] But if we ask just *why* Merleau-Ponty might think that Sartre cannot allow for the situated character of freedom, the only answer to be found, and indeed, the answer which is suggested by the context of Merleau-Ponty's remarks about situated freedom, is that Merleau-Ponty regards the notion of situated freedom to be incompatible with the either/or rationalism that he attributes to Sartre. However, since, as we have now seen, there is no basis for attributing such a view to Sartre, Merleau-Ponty would appear to have no remaining reason for denying to Sartre the right to recognize that all freedom is situated freedom.

1.3.3   The Radical Break Objection

The final objection to Sartre's theory of freedom to be considered in this chapter I shall call "the radical break objection." According to this objection there is a radical break between the philosophy of the early Sartre (*BN*) and that of the later Sartre (*CDR*), especially with regard to the subject of freedom. It is claimed that in Sartre's later works he abandons the early theory of absolute freedom, and instead emphasizes freedom's limitations and constraints. While such an interpretation need not in itself be considered a criticism, it is usually presented as one, at least with regard to Sartre's early theory of freedom, in that it is alleged that the *reason* for Sartre's radical break was his recognition that his critics had been right, that the theory of absolute freedom was, indeed, utterly untenable. Thus, the radical break objection holds that the early, "existentialist" theory of "absolute" freedom is indefensible, and is recognized as such by the later Sartre, who abandons it in favor of a "Marxist" theory of "restricted" freedom.[293] But is this interpretation accurate?

1.3.3.1   Sartre's testimony

For what it is worth, Sartre's own testimony reflects considerable ambivalence concerning this interpretation of his thought. On the one hand, in response to an interviewer who asks whether he, in becoming a Marxist, has cast aside his existentialism, Sartre insists,

> I still accept it. I wrote *Critique of Dialectical Reason* to show to what extent I am modifying certain notions in *Being and Nothingness,* and to what extent I stand by the whole of that book. I still uphold the realism of *Being and Nothingness* and its theory of consciousness . . . I still retain absolutely this conception of consciousness.[294]

Or again, in response to another interviewer's question as to whether there is a continuity or a break in his thought, Sartre declares, "there is an evolution, but I don't think there is a break . . . I think that I underwent a continuous evolution beginning with *La Nausée* all the way up to the *Critique de la raison dialectique.*"[295] And in yet another interview, Sartre discusses the "continuity" that he sees in his works, and states bluntly: "I do not believe that there is a break."[296] Finally, in one of Sartre's last interviews, conducted shortly before his death, he remarks: "I think that my contradictions mattered little, that in spite of everything I have always moved in the same direction."[297] Moreover, Sartre's lifelong companion, Simone de Beauvoir, makes the claim, three years after the publication of *CDR,* that Sartre "never has abandoned the concepts of negativity, of interiority, of existence and of freedom elaborated in *Being and Nothingness.*"[298] And it should be noted that even those critics who find little continuity in Sartre's thought concede that, at least as far as the *bulk* of the evidence is concerned, Sartre's own conception of his philosophical output is one which sees his earliest and latest works to be *connected* by a continuous "intellectual development and progress," rather than *separated* by "a radical break."[299]

On the other hand, however, we have Sartre's well-known discussion, in "The Itinerary of a Thought," of the great extent to which he regards his thinking on freedom to have changed over the years—specifically, his increasing realization of the limited nature of freedom and his correspondingly increasing appreciation of "the power of circumstances."[300] The following passage is representative of his comments in this interview:

> The other day, I re-read a prefatory note of mine to a collection of these plays—*Les Mouches, Huis Clos* and others—and was truly scandalized. I

had written: 'Whatever the circumstances, and wherever the site, a man is always free to choose to be a traitor or not . . . ' When I read this, I said to myself: it's incredible, I actually believed that![301]

And, lest we think that the above passage is merely an example of Sartre's penchant for exaggeration, it should be noted that Sartre makes explicit, approving reference to it in a subsequent interview. Moreover, he there takes advantage, once again, of the opportunity to attack the early prefatory note:

> There are things I approve of and others I look upon with a feeling of shame. Among the latter . . . is what I wrote in 1945 or thereabouts to the effect that, no matter what the situation may be, one is always free. And as examples I noted that a worker is always free to join a union or not, as he is free to choose the kind of battle he wants to join, or not join. And all that strikes me as absurd today. There's no question that there is some basic change in the concept of freedom. I still remain faithful to the notion of freedom, but I can see what can modify its results in any given person.[302]

For my part, I am unable to fit these (and other) seemingly inconsistent statements of Sartre's concerning his philosophical development into any kind of coherent pattern. Rather, it seems to me that, on this question, Sartre simply contradicts himself. Perhaps this is unimportant, after all, since ultimately we will have to decide for ourselves, based upon the evidence, whether or to what extent Sartre's later philosophy differs from his earlier views. Thus, I will not bother to enter into a tedious demonstration of what I take to be Sartre's inconsistency on this issue. Instead, I should like now to make two points which I think help to explain Sartre's ambivalent testimony, and which in any case should shed a certain amount of light upon his comments.

The first point is that Sartre's statements in evaluation of his own philosophy almost always sound rather casual and imprecise. One gets the impression that he is not terribly concerned with developing a clear account of his prior thinking, preferring instead always to concern himself with his present endeavors. Indeed, even in the interview which I most recently quoted, Sartre says: "As for the question of unity, I think there is one, *but I can't say I've ever tried to look for it. I've never tried to establish it. I think that's a task for other people.*"[303] Thus, if I am right in thinking that Sartre is inconsistent in his various assessments of his intellectual career, this might in part be explained by the fact that he does not consider it his job to supply such assessments, and thus does not put a great deal of work or thought into them. In any case, this gives us a reason for being wary of taking his comments *too* seriously.[304]

Secondly, there is a danger, in a debate like this one, of absolutizing the issue, of thinking that one must jump either into the "continuity" camp or into the "break" camp, as if there could be no middle ground. And yet, of course, all parties to the dispute must grant both that there are many continuities and many breaks between the thought of the earlier Sartre and that of the later Sartre. Thus, the issue boils down to whether one finds the continuities or the breaks to be, say, more fundamental or more numerous—but both, incontestably, are *there*. And it is my impression, moreover, that the reason why Sartre's own statements on this subject vary so widely is simply that he is sometimes more impressed by the continuities in his thought, and other times by the breaks. Couple this with Sartre's well-known tendency for enthusiastic, overblown rhetoric, and the imprecision on this issue which can be expected from the considerations discussed in the preceding paragraph (not to mention that his comments on this subject almost always appear in interviews, where one cannot expect the same care in organization and in choice of words as can be found in Sartre's composed pieces), and it is not difficult to understand how inconsistencies might find their way into his statements. Be that as it may, the important point to underscore here is that there are both continuities and breaks in Sartre's thought. As Sartre himself puts it, in perhaps his most balanced remark on the subject, "I have changed as everyone changes: within a permanency."[305]

1.3.3.2   Errors of the radical break theorists

This does not mean, however, that it is a completely arbitrary matter whether or not one sees a radical break between Sartre's earlier and later works; nor does it mean that the issue is unimportant. It is not unimportant because, as has been mentioned, the "radical break" theorists tend to wed their interpretation of Sartre with criticism, claiming that Sartre's later, supposedly radically different, philosophy stems from his recognition of the abject untenability of his earlier thought.[306] It is not arbitrary because, while there are both continuities and breaks in Sartre's thought, rendering the issue not clear cut, it is nonetheless possible to interpret Sartre's development in an utterly inaccurate, or at least wildly implausible, manner. In fact, it is my view that the extremely popular "radical break" interpretation of Sartre's philosophy, at least as it is usually presented, rests largely upon certain errors and misunderstandings. Indeed, it is my view that there is no *break* in Sartre's development of his theory of freedom, though there certainly are some minor changes and shifts in emphasis. I shall now try to substantiate these claims.

The first point to be made is that, as has been extensively documented above,[307] Sartre has *always* insisted upon the limited and restricted nature of freedom, even in his earliest works, and even in precisely the same writings in which he simultaneously calls freedom "absolute" and "total." Thus, no matter how much Sartre may have evolved over the years in his thinking on freedom, the fact remains that it is *not* only in his later writings that he acknowledges freedom's restrictions and limitations.

The first interpretive error that typically underlies the radical break theory, then, consists in ignoring the constraints upon freedom that Sartre recognizes even in his earliest works. This, for example, is the problem with Warnock's contention that in *CDR* "we have taken our leave once and for all of the private, compelling myth of the free man, experiencing his freedom in anguish, and faced with no necessity except that of choosing himself."[308]

Concerning Sartre's own (relatively rare) denunciations of his early theory of freedom, as for example his statement, which has already been quoted, that it is "incredible" that he could have "actually believed" that "a man is always free to choose," I think it is difficult to avoid Whitford's conclusion that "he is judging himself rather harshly . . . ; although in *L'Etre et le néant,* the emphasis is on the possibilities of freedom rather than on its limits, nonetheless the limits are clearly defined: freedom is limited by its situation, which includes birth, parentage, body, nationality, other people, intellectual and cultural framework, in short all those factors which impinge on a person and shape him."[309]

A second interpretive error which lends support to the radical break theory, though admittedly much less common than the first error, consists in exaggerating the extent to which Sartre sees freedom as threatened, ineffective, or even non-existent in his later writings. Thus, for example, Desan questions whether freedom "still exists" in *CDR,* and, though he admits that in this work "freedom is nowhere denied—on the contrary, the greater the threat, the more stubborn the defense," he goes on to claim that "there is nonetheless the constant implication that [freedom] is severely handicapped, or what Sartre calls *inert.*"[310]

One suspects that those who, like Desan, see in *CDR* the danger of freedom being swallowed up by its constraints, have failed to take note of the paradoxical, or, if you prefer, the *dialectical* relationship between freedom and facticity that Sartre has insisted upon from the beginning. Thus, in *BN* Sartre claims that

> the resistance which freedom reveals in the existent, far from being a danger to freedom, results only in enabling it to arise as freedom. There can be a free for-itself only as engaged in a resisting world. Outside of this engagement the notions of freedom, of determinism, of necessity lose all meaning.[311]

The bearing of this on the issue at hand is direct. For, as Burkle points out, the fact that "man is continually being made unfree"

> implies that he is also always free . . . The prodigious adversity described in the *Critique* is already evidence of vast human freedom since the very act by which men recognize and articulate their situation is an expression of a kind of freedom. In Sartre's view, limits are not simply there; men posit them by relating to them as limits. The crag does not limit the flower growing at its base, nor is it surpassed by the mountain eagle that soars above it. Only free beings can see themselves as limited: indeed, this is part of what it means to be free. Thus, in Sartre's view every statement showing that society is unfree also shows that men are free.[312]

Or again, consider James Sheridan's reflections on the presence of formidable restrictions to freedom in *CDR*:

> One is immediately reminded that there is no realization of freedom apart from resistance. Only if one encounters the most fierce resistance could one expect to achieve the full revelation of freedom, and, if freedom is to encounter maximum resistance, freedom itself will have to generate that maximum. I suggest that Sartre has knowingly, deliberately thrust his cherished freedom into that aspect of the field in which it is in greatest peril *precisely in order to deepen the awareness that it is* . . . A dialectician could do no less—if he had Sartre's savage courage.[313]

Yet another mistake which seems to underlie the radical break theory is the failure to recognize that Sartre's *interests* in his later writings are somewhat different than what they were in his earlier works, and that this change in interests is generally accompanied by corresponding changes in *subject matter* and in *emphasis*. In fact, it seems clear that it is because of Sartre's change of interests in his later works that he discusses freedom in the context of different subjects in these works, emphasizes different aspects of his theory of freedom in these discussions, and even, for the most part, deals with a different *sense* of freedom altogether from the one that principally concerned him in his earlier writings. The question that must be asked, however, is whether or not these changes in interests, in subject matter, in emphasis, and in senses of freedom dealt with, are sufficient to explain the changes in what Sartre says about freedom from his earlier works to his later works, or whether one must also suppose that Sartre has fundamentally altered his early theory of freedom in his later writings. Let us look at this issue more closely.

That the interests of the later Sartre are somewhat different from those of the early Sartre will, I trust, be granted by everyone. One has only to recall, for example, that in *BN* Sartre is principally concerned with ontology, while in *CDR* he addresses himself much more extensively to anthropological, sociological, historical, and political issues. Consequently, the former work deals primarily with abstract, theoretical questions, while the latter delves directly into the concrete, practical realm. As Sartre himself explains, *"BN* is a general point of view, a fundamental point of view. And *CDR* is a point of view that on the contrary is social and concrete. The one is abstract, studies general truths, and the other is not so concerned with that and places itself upon the plane of the concrete."[314]

Now, Sartre's treatment of freedom in the two books provides us with a perfect test case for evaluating Sartre's analysis of the relationship between the two works. If Sartre is correct, we should expect *BN* to be concerned with such abstract, general questions as whether human beings are *ontologically* free, where freedom is contrasted with, say, determinism, while we would expect *CDR* to be concerned with freedom in the concrete, that is, with what I have been calling *practical* freedom, where freedom is contrasted with, say, slavery. And this, of course, is precisely what we *do* find.

It should also be pointed out that Sartre claims in *BN* to be concerned with ontology to the *exclusion* of ethical matters. Indeed, this is precisely the point of the concluding section of *BN*, called "Ethical Implications,"[315] in which Sartre promises to deal with the ethical questions arising from his ontology in a subsequent work.[316] It is not surprising, then, that in *BN* Sartre issues so many claims for freedom which, from an ethical point of view, sound highly pernicious, such as his famous statement that the slave is as free as his master. One must remember that Sartre is here concerned with ontological issues, such as whether or not the slave has the capacity for free choice, and not with issues pertaining to the range or quality of the choices that are open to the slave, and still less with such ethical issues as whether it is good, or fair, or right, or just for this or that person to be enslaved, or for the institution of slavery to exist. These questions, from an ontological point of view, are simply irrelevant.

It is only natural, however, to expect that as Sartre's interest in concrete, practical issues begins to increase, at the expense of the abstract, theoretical realm, so would he begin to focus more attention on the practical dimension of freedom, rather than on its ontological foundation. Moreover, we would expect to find his increasing preoccupation with ethical and political matters to manifest itself, not only in an ethical concern for those many whose practical freedom is severely limited, but also in a demand that their freedom be expanded, and in a bitter denunciation of those responsible for this situation. Of course, as we have already seen,[317] this is precisely what we *do* find in Sartre's later writings.

The question before us, then, is whether this demand for an increase in practical freedom, which becomes more and more of a preoccupation of Sartre's later works, in some way implies a repudiation of the ontological freedom to which in the earlier writings we are said to be inescapably condemned. The radical break theorists are committed to a positive reply to this question. Sartre, as we have seen, is not. Rather, he holds ontological freedom to be foundational to practical freedom, since, as he never tires of pointing out, we do not even know what "the liberation of a man whose actions were determined [would] mean."[318] Indeed,

Sartre seems to take it as a point of pride that his theory of freedom is able coherently to declare that one can be free and unfree at the same time:

> A revolutionary philosophy ought to account for the plurality of freedoms and show how each one can be an object for the other while being, at the same time, a freedom for itself. Only this double character of freedom and objectivity can explain the complex notions of oppression, conflict, failure and violence. For one never oppresses anything but a freedom.[319]

Why, then, do the radical break theorists persist in believing that Sartre's philosophy undergoes a fundamental transformation in regard to its view of freedom? The radical break theory *appears* to be motivated by an attempt to resolve the contradiction between saying, on the one hand, that, for example, "the slave is as free as his master" (early Sartre), and, on the other hand, that the slave is very much *unfree* and needs to be "liberated" (later Sartre). Now, there is no question that these two statements are *apparently* contradictory. The question, however, is whether they are *really* contradictory, or whether, bearing in mind Sartre's distinctions between different senses of freedom, they are to be taken as mutually consistent statements which merely emphasize different *aspects* of Sartre's analysis of slavery. According to the latter interpretation, the fact that Sartre places much more emphasis on the slave's lack of freedom in his later works than in his earlier ones is to be understood as indicating, not a fundamental change in his view of freedom, but merely a change in interest and in subject matter. Whitford gives a persuasive presentation of this interpretation.

> The slave has two choices, to remain a slave, or to risk everything trying to escape. This is the alternative of which one of the terms may be death. In *L'Etre et le néant,* the emphasis is still on the fact that the slave is *free* to *choose* one or other of the alternatives. Later Sartre shifts the emphasis to the situation and, pointing out how derisory the slave's freedom is in such a situation, goes on to castigate those who create this kind of situation and to espouse the cause of revolution in the hopes of changing it. The situation of the Jew affords another example. In 1943, Sartre wrote that the Jew was free—not to choose whether or not he is a Jew, but to choose whether to be proud or ashamed of his Jewishness. In 1946, Sartre is still writing that the Jew is free, but already the emphasis has changed. Comparing the Jew to a prisoner, he remarks: "The prisoner is always free to run away, if it is clearly

understood that he risks death in crawling under the barbed wire. Is his jailor any less guilty on that account?" The situation in which the Jew finds himself must be changed: "if we can change the perspective of choice, then the choice itself will change."[320]

In the light of the evidence that has already been presented in this section, I think that we are obliged to accept Whitford's conclusion that, "as the examples of the slave and the Jew indicate, his later position is essentially a *development* from the position put forward in *L'Etre et le néant,* not an abandonment of it. It is true that Sartre did modify his views, not by withdrawing his claim that man is free, but by shifting the emphasis away from freedom towards the constraints on that freedom."[321]

1.3.3.3   Radical conversion

Let us now move on to discuss what is perhaps Sartre's most misunderstood concept of all,[322] namely that of "radical conversion." Correcting the misunderstandings which surround this concept should be of crucial help, not only to the understanding of Sartre's philosophical project in general, but also, in particular, for seeing the fundamental flaw in the "radical break" interpretation.

First of all, we must recall those many "pessimistic" elements in Sartre's early philosophy which seemed to leave his thinking at an impasse, necessitating, according to the radical break theorists, the abandonment of that philosophy and the development of a new one. Among these pessimistic elements we might include: (1) Sartre's attribution to all human beings of a futile, utterly unfulfillable desire, that of becoming in-itself-for-itself or God; (2) his apparent view that "the existential condition of life is . . . bad faith";[323] (3) his startling analyses of interpersonal relationships, in which he asserts that "conflict is the original meaning of 'being-for-others,'"[324] that "the essence of the relations between consciousness is . . . conflict,"[325] that (in more literary terms) "Hell is other people,"[326] and that (in an expression of the predominant critical interpretation of Sartre's doctrine) "social action is basically a form of mutual conflict and hatred";[327] (4) his seeming refusal to acknowledge any objective, or even non-arbitrary, value-judgments, claiming instead that "*nothing,* absolutely nothing, justifies me in adopting this or that particular value, this or that particular scale of values";[328] and (5) those two (in)famous, bleak sentences which occur near the end of *BN,* namely, "man is a useless passion,"[329] and "it amounts to the same thing whether one gets drunk alone or is a leader of nations."[330]

On the other hand, however, Sartre was careful, even in *BN,* to indicate that these unpromising judgments did not represent his final words on their respective subjects. Rather, when his analyses would begin to point toward gloomy conclusions, Sartre often inserted brief, somewhat obscure comments to the effect that things need not be this way, provided that there is a "radical conversion" which "cannot be discussed here." As we shall see, these comments have alternatively perplexed and enraged Sartre's critics. But first, in order to facilitate our discussion, let us consider the following four texts, which are probably the most important of Sartre's hints of a radical conversion in *BN.*

First, in a footnote which appears at the close of Sartre's chapter on bad faith, he tells us that, despite the general thrust of the presentation in *BN,* it is possible "radically (to) escape bad faith. But this supposes a self-recovery of being which was previously corrupted. This self-recovery we shall call authenticity, the description of which has no place here."[331]

Secondly, in a footnote which concludes the discussion of "concrete relations with others," Sartre announces that "these considerations do not exclude the possibility of an ethics of deliverance and salvation. But this can be achieved only after a radical conversion which we cannot discuss here."[332]

Thirdly, while Sartre is concerned in *BN* to draw out the implications of the apparently universal project of attempting to become God, he also mentions, in one brief passage to which he calls no particular attention, an act whose function would be "to make manifest and to present to *itself* the absolute freedom which is the very being of the person."[333] But instead of developing this idea in detail, Sartre merely remarks that

> This particular type of project, which has freedom for its foundation and its goal, deserves a special study. It is radically different from all others in that it aims at a radically different type of being. It would be necessary to explain in full detail its relations with the project of being-God, which has appeared to us as the deep-seated structure of human reality. But such a study can not be

made here; it belongs rather to an *Ethics* and it supposes that there has been a preliminary definition of nature and the role of purifying reflection (our descriptions have hitherto aimed only at *accessory* reflection); it supposes in addition taking a position which can be *moral* only in the face of values which haunt the For-itself.[334]

Finally, in the very last section of *BN,* called "Ethical Implications," in which Sartre makes it quite clear that up to that point he has been engaged strictly with ontological issues, and not with ethical ones, he suddenly poses a number of questions concerning the possibility of renouncing the project of being-God, and of replacing it with a project which would take freedom itself as its primary goal. Thus, with regard to the "value of the ideal presence of the *ens causa sui,*" Sartre asks,

What will become of freedom *if it turns its back upon this value*? Will freedom carry this value along with it whatever it does and even in its very turning back upon the in-itself-for-itself? Will freedom be reapprehended from behind by the value which it wishes to contemplate? Or will freedom by the very fact that it apprehends itself as a freedom in relation to itself, *be able to put an end to the reign of this value*? In particular *is it possible for freedom to take itself for a value as the source of all value,* or must it necessarily be defined in relation to a transcendent value which haunts it? And in case it could will itself as its own possible and its determining value, what would this mean? . . . All these questions, which refer us to a pure and not an accessory reflection, can find their reply only on the ethical plane. We shall devote to them a future work.[335]

With these words, *BN* comes to a close. Moreover, to some extent we are forced to guess as to their meaning, since the projected ethical work in which Sartre promised to take them up was never completed. However, I think that an examination of Sartre's subsequent work and activity, and of analyses, scattered throughout his works, of the key terms which appear in these four passages—such as "authenticity," "radical conversion," "accessory reflection," "purifying reflection," etc.—together with a reading of the posthumously published, unfinished fragments of Sartre's proposed ethical work, entitled *Cahiers pour une morale,*[336] yields nearly all of the tools necessary to lay bare the meaning of Sartre's mysterious words.

Before attempting this task, however, it might help to clarify the issues by first looking at a few of the more common critical reactions to these "radical conversion" passages.

Far and away the most common reaction has been silence. Most critics simply do not mention that Sartre anywhere in *BN* tempers the "pessimistic" elements of that work. Now, in some kinds of works—brief expository accounts intended to serve as introductions to the main features of Sartre's early philosophy, for example—this is both understandable and legitimate. One cannot discuss everything, and there is every justification for ignoring brief, obscure footnotes, and passages which point to future works. But it is a highly illegitimate procedure, however understandable, in critical works which take Sartre to task principally for failing to mitigate his gloomier conclusions. After all, if one wishes to hold Sartre to the doctrine that, for example, all human relationships involve mutual hostility, surely fairness dictates that one must at least acknowledge and cite the fact that Sartre himself refuses this interpretation. Moreover, one would then presumably be obligated to produce *arguments* showing that he is wrong in doing so.

The second most common response to the "radical conversion" passages has been to dismiss them as nonsensical. Thus, Warnock answers the second of our four passages, the footnote about an "ethics of deliverance and salvation" which would follow "a radical conversion," by flatly declaring that "within the context of *Being and Nothingness* itself the footnote is impossible to understand."[337] I will argue, to the contrary, that our four passages are perfectly intelligible within the context of *BN,* and even more so when one takes into account Sartre's previous writings.

Yet another common reaction, often linked to the one just mentioned, is to understand the radical conversion "as simply a gratuitous and contradictory move into Marxism."[338] It is difficult to know how to argue with this interpretation, since arguments and evidence are so rarely given in support of it. Rather, the principal argument seems to be simply that the notion of radical conversion is otherwise unintelligible; and this claim, as we shall soon see, is quite false. Otherwise, those who advance this interpretation tend to support it solely through the apodictic tone with which they advance their thesis. Thus, we are told that "*we know* that the radical conversion came and was the conversion to Marxism which is set out in the *Critique of Dialectical Reason,*"[339] and that "we now have the key to these (radical conversion) footnotes—it is Sartre's now famous conversion to Marxism."[340]

For present purposes I shall simply point out that, if the radical conversion *were* a conversion to Marxism (and I do not think that it is), this would completely undermine both the "radical break" theory and all of the criticisms of *BN* which assume that the principal views expressed in that work are endorsed by Sartre. For if Sartre is saying *even in BN* that one must abandon existentialism and instead convert to Marxism, then Sartre's subsequent endorsement of Marxism is surely not a *break,* and one would have to read *BN* as a kind of attempted *reductio ad absurdum* refutation of those very "existentialist" views which Sartre is ordinarily understood to be affirming. Indeed, one would have to suppose that the "gloomy," "pessimistic" elements of *BN* represent Sartre's attempted demonstration of the impasse to which "existentialist" thinking leads—an impasse which can be avoided only by a "radical conversion" to Marxism.

Of course, I am not here endorsing this view; I believe it to be erroneous. My point is only that it is inconsistent to argue *both* that Sartre's early philosophy is untenable, necessitating a radical break in Sartre's thought, *and* that the "conversion" to Marxism is the "radical conversion" discussed in *BN*; and yet it is typically the case that one and the same critic will press both charges.[341] Moreover, I would point out that, while I do reject the interpretation given in the above paragraph, I endorse the idea of recognizing Sartre's use of "dialectical" techniques—for example, appearing to endorse a point of view only so that his readers will entertain it long enough for him to show its weaknesses and reject it. In fact, I think, and will soon argue, that *BN* does attempt a kind of *reductio ad absurdum*—not of his early philosophy, to be sure—but of the pursuit of the desire to be God.[342]

Finally, it should be mentioned that some commentators, while recognizing that the radical conversion involves renouncing the project of being-God at the expense of a project which would take freedom as its highest value, declare that such a project is utterly unintelligible, either because of the nature of Sartre's theory of freedom, or because such a project cannot be reconciled with the general thrust of Sartre's early philosophy. Richard J. Bernstein expresses the latter criticism forcefully in his commentary on the fourth of our "radical conversion" texts:

> This closing passage of *Being and Nothingness* with its rhetorical flourishes, is itself written in bad faith—and I mean this precisely in the sense in which Sartre has characterized bad faith. Sartre is attempting to escape from the stern lesson of his own ontological investigations. If it is true that "all human actions are equivalent," and that none of our choices or acts are justifiable and consequently there is no ultimate sense in saying that one project, choice or act is better than another, then what possible *ethical* significance can be attached to the choice of freedom as "the ideal of being"? Hasn't Sartre—in the main plot of *Being and Nothingness*—already answered the question that there is no other "fundamental attitude" than that of bad faith?"[343]

Clearly, Bernstein is begging the question here. What he evidently fails to notice is that the Sartrean doctrines which he cites—that all human activities are equivalent, that none of our choices or acts are justifiable, that there is no other fundamental attitude than that of bad faith, etc.—are not issued by Sartre *without qualification*. Rather, they appear within a certain context, namely within a discussion of the desire to be God, and are uttered with reference to those who embrace this desire and whose active pursuit of it serves as their fundamental project.[344] And it is this project, of course, which Sartre speaks of renouncing in a "radical conversion," with the implication that such renunciation provides an escape from the rather dire condition that is otherwise, apparently, the inevitable fate of all human beings. The point is that an essential tenet of the *actual* position of Sartre's which Bernstein is here concerned to refute is that it is *false* that all human activities are equivalent, that none of our choices or acts are justifiable, and that there is no other fundamental attitude than that of bad faith. Instead, these pessimistic assertions are offered by Sartre as truths only with the *qualification* that they are applicable exclusively to those engaged in the project of attempting to be God. But Bernstein's *entire argument* against Sartre's position rests on *assuming*, without *argument*, that all of these statements are intended by Sartre to be taken as true without qualification. He is simply assuming the very point at issue, or, if you prefer, begging the question.

Perhaps Bernstein is prevented from taking the notion of radical conversion seriously by his convictions regarding Sartre's motivations in introducing it. He seems to think that the appeal to a radical conversion is something of a cheap, *ad hoc* trick, by which Sartre is desperately "attempting to escape from the stern lesson of his own ontological investigations." Apparently Bernstein thinks that Sartre, having unwittingly found that his ontology led to an impasse, did not have the honesty to admit as much, and tried to cover up the problem by making vague references to a "radical conversion" by which the impasse could be overcome.

This accusation would take on a great deal of plausibility were it the case that Sartre had introduced the notion of radical conversion in *BN,* and only in connection with the gloomier, more distasteful elements of that work. But this notion has been of great concern to Sartre from the very beginning, especially in those early works, such as *TE* and *The Emotions: Outline of a Theory,* which are concerned with describing essential structures of consciousness, and which do not seem to lead to any pessimistic doctrines from which Sartre might be anxious to escape. Our discussion and elaboration of this point will have to wait, however, until I have introduced the crucial distinction between pure and accessory reflection, which Sartre introduces in these works, and which, as we have seen, he connects with the conversion in *BN.* Thus, I am not yet in a position to complete my reply to Bernstein.

In the meantime, let me address those critics who find incoherent the notion of a radical conversion to a project which would take freedom as its highest value, since, as Sartre himself never ceases to proclaim, we are *already* "absolutely free," "condemned to be free," "free in all circumstances," etc. What sense does it make to say that we should value what is already an unalterable state of affairs, especially for someone like Sartre, for whom values are "lacks" to be "*made* real," and for whom valuing is to issue in action?[345]

Of course, the response to this objection consists in pointing out that Sartre distinguishes between different senses of freedom, so that, while *ontological* freedom is always unalterably present, *practical* freedom is not, and is therefore perfectly capable of serving as a value which would issue in actions—actions designed, for example, to *increase* one's own practical freedom as well as the practical freedom of others.

Sartre's critics are often reluctant to accept this, however, seeing the appeal to different senses of freedom as yet another instance of Sartrean sleight-of-hand. The argument seems to be that Sartre's ontological investigations cannot possibly serve as a foundation for the radical conversion, since the sense of freedom involved in such a conversion has *nothing to do with* the ontological sense of freedom discussed in *BN*. Thus, Arthur C. Danto, after admitting to puzzlement over the meaning of the series of questions appearing at the end of *BN*, remarks:

> In any case, there can be no question of generating an ethic on the basis of Sartre's book, for although one might want to say that we should always act so as to maximize and never minimize our freedom and the freedom of others, and take this as a sort of final imperative, the freedom in question would have to be political and *would have nothing to do with* the [ontological] freedom which the book defines. *That* freedom is total and absolute, in and out of gaol.[346]

Surely Danto is right in claiming that ontological freedom is not the same thing as political freedom. For example, as he points out, the former is total and absolute, while the latter is not. But it is surely quite a leap indeed to conclude from this, as Danto apparently does, that the two freedoms must *have nothing to do with one another*. This is simply a *non sequitur*.[347] Nothing that Danto says speaks against the conception of the relationship between the two freedoms which Sartre himself develops, and which we have already studied, namely, that ontological freedom, while not identical with practical freedom, is *foundational* to it.

By now, through the foregoing examination and criticism of rival interpretations, I trust that the interpretation of the radical conversion that I favor has begun to emerge, at least in outline. The radical conversion, I submit, consists of the renunciation of the project of attempting to be God, and the embracing of an alternative project through which freedom would be recognized as the highest value. I have tried to argue that this interpretation is more in keeping with what Sartre says in *BN* than are the alternative interpretations that I have criticized. Two important tasks remain, however. First, more evidence needs to be given to substantiate that my interpretation of the radical conversion is the correct one. Then, much more needs to be said about the *nature* of the conversion itself, as I have interpreted it.

As for the first issue, Sartre's entire life and career subsequent to the publication of *BN* might well be seen as indicating that he regards the pursuit of freedom to be the way out of the impasse to which that work seemed to lead. Indeed, as Joseph P. Fell points out, "the balance of Sartre's career can be seen as the effort to understand what sort of 'situation', and what sort of 'world', would be compatible with the pursuit of freedom as an end and a value."[348]

Consider, for example, the following statement, issued three years after the publication of *BN*:

> I can pronounce a moral judgment. For I declare that freedom, in respect of concrete circumstances, can have no other end and aim but itself; and when once a man has seen that values depend upon himself, in that state of forsakenness he can will only one thing, and that is freedom as the foundation of all values. That does not mean that he wills it in the abstract: it simply means that the actions of men of good faith have, as their ultimate significance, the quest of freedom itself as such . . . We will freedom for freedom's sake, in and through particular circumstances.[349]

Clearly, this passage articulates a point of view which is not found in *BN*, except in those passages which hint of a radical conversion. Indeed, it is scarcely intelligible unless it is understood as referring to those who have undergone the conversion, which places it in contrast with *BN*, which confines its descriptions to those who continue to seek the impossible union of being-in-itself-for-itself. For consider the following three points:

(1) Sartre here says that "freedom *can have no other end and aim but itself,*" while in *BN* it was not only *possible* to have another end and aim, namely that of being God, but this was actually the *predominant* human project—the project which Sartre declared to have "appeared to us as the deep-seated structure of human reality."[350] Thus, it would appear that Sartre is here either (a) contradicting himself, (b) utterly reversing his previous position without giving any indication that he is doing so, or (c) simply

shifting his focus and speaking from the standpoint of the conversion.

(2) Support for (c) can be found by looking at the similarity between Sartre's present language and his language in *BN* when discussing the conversion. Thus, when in the present passage he declares that "freedom can have no other end and aim but itself," and that "freedom is the foundation of all values," he seems to be answering his question, posed in the last section of *BN*, as to whether it is "possible for freedom to take itself for a value as the source of all value."[351] (Incidentally, those who declare that we cannot judge Sartre's intentions in this section of *BN*, since it consists almost exclusively of questions, the meaning of which cannot be ascertained without Sartre's answers,[352] fail to notice that he *does* answer them—clearly and consistently—throughout his subsequent works.)

(3) Finally, notice that, immediately after stating in the present passage that freedom can have no other end and aim than itself, he seems to modify this, claiming only that "*once a man has seen that values depend upon himself, in that state of forsakenness* he can will only one thing, and that is freedom." Even more importantly, Sartre does not here declare that *all* human actions "have, as their ultimate significance, the quest of freedom itself as such." Rather, he says this about "*the actions of men of good faith.*" The significance of this becomes readily apparent when we recall that in *BN* Sartre associates good faith with the radical conversion,[353] and implies that his descriptions in that work are concerned solely with persons in bad faith.[354] Sartre is even more explicit on this point in his subsequent references to *BN*, frequently calling it a work on the "eidetics of bad faith."[355] Moreover, he is consistent, throughout his later works, in maintaining both that the project of attempting to be God is the source of "fundamental alienation,"[356] and that this alienation can be overcome. For example, in one of Sartre's last interviews, conducted very shortly before his death, Sartre is still saying: "I think that there is another modality other than the first modality . . . It is the moral modality. And the moral modality implies that we cease . . . to place being as our goal; we no longer want to be God; we no longer want to be *causa sui*; we seek something else."[357] All of this evidence indicates, I think, that the

present passage, unlike the bulk of *BN,* is concerned with what follows *after* the undergoing of the radical conversion; furthermore, I submit that this evidence tends to support the interpretation of the conversion that I have been advancing, rather than any of those which I have criticized.

Further evidence for this interpretation can be found throughout Sartre's posthumously published *Cahiers pour une morale,* a central theme of which is the radical conversion (here usually called the "moral conversion"). While one must be mindful, in assessing this work, of the fact that Sartre abandoned it and would not permit its publication during his lifetime, it certainly must be accorded great value in helping us to ascertain Sartre's conception of ethics at the time of *BN*—it was, after all, intended as the sequel which was promised at the end of that work, and was written just a few years later.[358] In any case, Sartre's discussion of the conversion in the *Cahiers* is both clear and detailed. There he tells us that "every effort of the For-itself to become In-itself is by definition doomed to failure";[359] and he consequently calls for a "conversion from the project of being-for-itself-in-itself."[360] Only through this "modification of the project" can the "rejection of alienation" be achieved.[361] Following the conversion, the "absolute goal" becomes "human liberty," rather than the for-itself-in-itself, "but this goal is not given it is *willed.*"[362] One must pursue freedom, and abandon the impossible desire to be God, if one is to escape from the gloomy condition in which "all human activities are equivalent" since "all are on principle doomed to failure."[363]

There is one very grave problem with this interpretation, however, and that is that there are many passages in *BN* in which Sartre seems to allow for no possibility of renouncing the project of being God. For example, he bluntly declares that "man is the being whose project is to be God . . . or if you prefer, man fundamentally is the desire to be God."[364] One here gets the impression, not only that there *are* no exceptions, but also that there *can be* no exceptions. Moreover, this impression is strongly reinforced by such declarations as that "my freedom is a choice of being God,"[365] and that "man on coming into the world is borne toward God as toward his limit, . . . (and) *he can choose only to be God.*"[366] Clearly, if these and other similar passages do indeed mean what they *seem* to mean, it cannot be Sartre's position in *BN* that it is possible, through a "radical conversion," to renounce the project of attempting to be God. Rather, we must assume that Sartre's references to a "radical conversion" in that work have some other meaning; and this assumption, in turn, would tend to lend some credence to the "radical break" interpretation. After all, in Sartre's later works he plainly *does* mean by "radical conversion" the renunciation of the project of attempting to be God. Therefore, if this cannot possibly be his meaning in *BN,* it must be that one of the areas in which Sartre has undergone a "radical break" is precisely in his understanding of the "radical conversion"!

Four points need to be made in order to answer this objection. First, it is important to note the distinction which Sartre draws in *BN* between prereflective and reflective values.[367] Sartre's point is that most values are "simply lived"[368] unreflectively, that is, they are not *explicitly* looked upon as values. Rather, I have certain desires (for Sartre, this means that the objects of these desires are "values" for me); these desires lead me to undertake a project which would enable me to satisfy the desires; the adoption of this project leads me to carry out certain actions which must be carried out in order to bring the project to realization; and "my acts," in turn, "cause values to spring up like partridges."[369] Now, according to Sartre, it would be unusual for me to question these values. We tend simply to accept them as given, without inquiring into the nature of their origin or of their justification. Nor do we question the worth or legitimacy of the original desires which underlie these (secondary) values. Finally, we do not consider "renouncing" or "turning our backs" on either our primary values (those which correspond to our most fundamental desires), or our secondary values (those which arise as a result of those acts which are motivated by our most fundamental desires). When, as is usually the case, these values are "simply lived," that is, taken unquestioningly for granted, they are designated by Sartre "pre-reflective values."

However, the fact that these values are *rarely* explicitly taken as objects of our reflective attention does not mean that they *cannot* be. Rather, according to Sartre, we are free to focus upon them directly, at which time they become "reflective values." More importantly, according to Sartre "it is obvious that I remain free in my reflective consciousness to direct my attention on these values *or to neglect them.*"[370]

This brings me to my second point, which is that through reflection one acquires the power, not only to focus upon values, but also to question, neglect, renounce, and abandon them. The bearing of all this on the desire to be God is direct. As Anderson explains,

> I do not by reflection have to reaffirm as valuable any lived values, and this includes both my desire to be God and its unattainable goal. Of course, this goal will still be valuable in the "lived" sense, meaning that it will still in fact be the goal of my fundamental desire. The crucial point to see is that it need not be a value that I deliberately choose to attempt to realize in my life. And I will see this, Sartre suggests, if I realize that the value of God is not an absolute intrinsic value but is one rooted in my very contingency . . . Once I realize the nonabsolute character of this lived value, I see at the same time that there is no necessity for me to choose to value it. I can "neglect" it and confer value on something else. While I will still fundamentally desire to be God, this goal will not be one that I will deliberately attempt to achieve in my life through my actions. (After all, desires do not have to issue into choices and actions.)[371]

This brings me to my third point, namely, that according to Sartre, it is not only *possible* to renounce the project of attempting to be God, it is *necessary* to do so if one is to avoid the hellish condition in which all of one's acts are doomed to failure. This, I take it, is the point of the "radical conversion" passages quoted earlier, as is especially clear in the last of these passages, the concluding section of *BN*. If this interpretation is correct, much of *BN*—for example, the detailed descriptions of bad faith and of concrete relations with others—would have to be read as a kind of moral *reductio ad absurdum* of the project of attempting to be God. It is as if Sartre were holding up these extremely negative and unpleasant descriptions to us and saying, "see what will happen to you if you continue to pursue this impossible project of being in-itself-for-itself? You had better renounce it in favor of another project." Needless to say, if this is indeed what Sartre is doing in *BN,* the standard criticism of that work as being overly pessimistic, and as giving a one-sided analysis which dwells exclusively on the negative side of a number of phenomena, rests largely on a failure to understand Sartre's purpose.

Nor is that purpose particularly difficult to understand. According to the interpretation of *BN* that I am proposing, Sartre is attempting in that work to provide (1) a *description* of the nature of the impasse in which we find ourselves (for example, in his descriptions of bad faith and of hellish interpersonal relationships, and in his declarations that man is a useless passion, that all actions are equivalent, etc.), (2) a *diagnosis* of the cause of this impasse (e.g., the adoption of the project of attempting to be God), (3) a *proposal* for escaping from this impasse (e.g., by abandoning the project of attempting to be God), and (4) an implicit *recommendation* that we adopt this proposal. We should have no more difficulty in understanding this than we would have if, say, an anthropologist were to (1) claim that human beings naturally desire to be aggressive, (2) argue that this fact is the principal cause of contemporary discontents, (3) point out that it is possible, though perhaps very difficult, for human beings to refuse to carry out this desire in action, and (4) urge them so to refuse.[372] After all, as John Stuart Mill pointed out, "that a feeling is bestowed on us by nature does not necessarily legitimate all its promptings."[373] Similarly for Sartre, that a desire is thrust upon us by our ontological condition does not necessarily make it wise for us to embrace that desire.

At this point, however, we should recall the problem with which I am here attempting to deal, namely that the interpretation of the radical conversion which I have been advancing apparently cannot be correct, since Sartre seems unambiguously to preclude the possibility of renouncing the project of attempting to be God. To be sure, we no longer need to be troubled by his declarations that "man fundamentally is the desire to be God," for we have seen that desires need not issue in the undertaking of projects and the carrying out of actions. Moreover, there is no longer any incompatibility between my interpretation of the conversion and Sartre's claim that we must *value* the in-itself-for-itself, since this can be understood to refer to *prereflective* valuing which, again, need not lead to actions which honor that value. Finally, we can understand why Sartre puts so much *emphasis* on the project of attempting to be God—he wants to show us how destructive is the undertaking of this project, and to demonstrate to us the need for renouncing it—and this reason is, of course, perfectly compatible with the possibility of a radical conversion in the sense under discussion. But what on earth are we to do with Sartre's claim that human beings "can choose *only* to be God"?

This brings me to my fourth and final point, namely, that in reading Sartre it is extremely important to be mindful of the specific context in which any given statement appears. In the case of Sartre's statements to the effect that we must *choose* to be God, it is significant that they appear in "Part Four" of *BN,* and precisely not in "Part Two," the part wherein he first elaborates in detail his theory of value and his claim that all human beings have the desire to be God. Let us recall in this connection that in the third of our four "radical conversion" passages, the only one which appears in "Part Four," Sartre tells us that all of his descriptions in that section, with the exception of a brief discussion of "play," refer to those who are actively striving to realize the goal of being God. Thus, as Anderson points out, "in this context Sartre's statements about men's choice to be God can be interpreted to refer not to all men but only to those who have taken God as their goal and value. Such an interpretation would, of course, square with his suggestions in 'Ethical Implications.'"[374]

However one understands Sartre's statements to the effect that we *must* choose to be God (after all, it is *possible* that Sartre contradicts himself on this matter, though I count it as a virtue of the interpretation that I have been presenting that it removes the necessity for concluding this),[375] further evidence in support of my interpretation of the radical conversion can be found by examining Sartre's references, throughout his works, to those concepts which are mentioned in our "radical conversion" passages (e.g., "authenticity," "purifying reflection," "accessory reflection," etc).[376] Examining these concepts will also help me to keep my promise of elaborating more clearly the nature of the conversion as I understand it, and will provide documentation that this notion of the conversion is present even in Sartre's earliest works, and was not suddenly introduced by him as a convenient *ad hoc* escape from the gloomy doctrines of *BN.*

With regard to authenticity, there is no need for extensive commentary. All that needs to be pointed out is that Sartre's definition of authenticity, e.g., "having a true and lucid consciousness of the situation,"[377] fits perfectly with the understanding of "radical conversion" that I have been advancing. Recall, for example, that in the first of our radical conversion passages Sartre links authenticity to the possibility of radically escaping bad faith. Now, if I am right in attributing to Sartre the claim that all human beings pre-reflectively value being-God, as well as the view that the active pursuit of this value is precisely what prevents us from escaping bad faith, nothing could be clearer than that the first step toward such an escape would be the acquiring of "a true and lucid consciousness" of the fact that this pre-reflective value need not be reflectively affirmed as a value and pursued as a goal—that, on the contrary, it is possible to "turn one's back" on this value, and to "put an end to its reign." Further support for such a reading of Sartre, a reading which sees an intimate connection, perhaps even a necessary connection, between, on the one hand, the achievement, through reflection, of a lucid understanding of one's ontological condition and of the possibilities which it presents, and, on the other hand, a "radical conversion" which is profoundly liberating in its effects, can be found in Sartre's distinction between "purifying" and "accessory" reflection. Let us now turn our attention to this distinction.

First of all, let us consider Sartre's concept of "accessory reflection," which

> bears only on the secondary structures of action, as in deliberation over the means to attain a certain end. While engaging in it, one refuses to ask oneself about the existence or significance of a supreme end or of a fundamental choice. Accessory reflection permeates day-to-day living, living which thinks of itself only to justify itself, which finds itself in the wrong only with regard to the use of this or that procedure, which finds one's basic failure not in a choice—which, being fundamental, it prefers to ignore—but in the unavoidable disappointments of "destiny."[378]

Thus, accessory reflection does not call into question one's fundamental project of attempting to be God. Rather, it reinforces the desire to be God, and serves as an accomplice to the naive view that no project is possible other than one which would attempt in some way or another to bring this desire to fulfillment. It takes the project of attempting to be God for granted, and concerns itself only with the question of which of the indefinite number of secondary projects one will pursue as a means for realizing this fundamental project.

"Purifying reflection" (also called "non-accessory reflection"), by contrast, does explicitly focus upon the fundamental project of attempting to be God, and calls into question the supposed necessity of this project. Indeed,

> its role (is) to reveal to man—by giving him access to the moral plane of authenticity—that his quest of being and his wish to appropriate the in-itself *are merely possibilities among other possibilities.* Pure reflection allows him to stop taking as irreducible the basic value that orients all his choices; it ceases to be the ideal presence of the self-caused being. He is then in a position to *choose* this value himself; to imbue it with value or to reject it. [379]

We are now in a position to understand the relationship between the concepts of "accessory reflection," "purifying reflection," "authenticity," and "radical conversion." "Purifying reflection" is the means by which one achieves "authenticity," e.g., "a true and lucid consciousness" of, in this context, the fact that the project of attempting to be God is only one of any number of possible fundamental projects. "Radical conversion," then, consists in the rejection of the project of attempting to be God—a rejection which only becomes possible once one has come to the realization (authenticity) that such rejection is possible—a realization which only becomes possible once one has engaged in purifying reflection. Of course, it is *possible,* following purifying reflection, to *reaffirm* the project of being God, rather than rejecting it. Thus, purifying reflection does not *always* lead to radical conversion. The two concepts are not identical. [380] If one remains at the level of accessory reflection, however, one can neither attain authenticity nor undergo a radical conversion.

Let us now return to Bernstein's charge that the concept of radical conversion is nothing but a convenient, *ad hoc* escape hatch by means of which Sartre dishonestly attempts "to escape from the stern lessons of his own ontological investigations." By way of preliminary reply to Bernstein, it should be pointed out that the possibility of a transition from accessory to purifying reflection, which makes the conversion possible, is discussed even in Sartre's earliest works, such as *TE* and *The Emotions: Outline of a Theory.*

Moreover, in these works, just as in *BN,* purifying reflection is said to "liberate" us from false, and usually self-destructive or self-defeating, beliefs. Clearly, the concepts of "purifying" and "accessory" reflection operate, at least in part, as moral concepts within Sartre's philosophy, as is suggested even by their names. All of this, of course, argues against the notion that these concepts, as well as that of the "radical conversion," represent *ad hoc* attempts by Sartre to escape from the ugly consequences to which his ontology would otherwise commit him. Rather, they illustrate that one of Sartre's principal concerns, from his earliest works to his last, is to describe certain false and destructive beliefs, and to argue that they can and should be overthrown. Let me document this briefly with passages from, first, *The Emotions: Outline of a Theory.*

> Consciousness is caught in its own trap. Precisely because it lives in the new aspect of the world by *believing* in it, it is caught in its own belief, exactly as in dreaming and in hysteria. Consciousness of the emotion is a captive but we do not necessarily mean thereby that anything . . . external to it might have enchained it. It is its own captive in the sense that it does not dominate this belief, that it strives to live, and it does so precisely because it lives it, because it is absorbed in living it . . . Freedom has to come from a *purifying reflection* or a total disappearance of the affecting situation.[381]

> The purifying reflection of the phenomenological reduction can perceive the emotion insofar as it constitutes the world in a magical form. "I find it hateful *because* I am angry." But this reflection is rare and necessitates special motivations. Ordinarily, we direct upon the emotive consciousness an accessory reflection which certainly perceives consciousness as consciousness, but insofar as it is motivated by the object: "I am angry *because* it is hateful." It is on the basis of this reflection that the passion will constitute itself.[382]

Here the belief which is false and destructive, according to Sartre, is that we are nothing but passive victims of our emotions. That is, we refuse to acknowledge the voluntary dimension of our emotional life, and consequently fail to recognize the degree to which we are responsible for it. The only way out of this "trap" which consciousness sets for itself, aside from the total disappearance of the situation which motivates the emotion, is a purifying reflection through which consciousness discloses to itself its responsibility for its emotions. It is significant, moreover, that in the second of these two passages Sartre equates this purifying reflection with "the phenomenological reduction." I will return to this point presently, following our examination of Sartre's use of the concept of "purifying reflection" in *TE*.

> Perhaps, in reality, the essential function of the ego is not so much theoretical as practical . . . Perhaps the essential role of the ego is to mask from consciousness its very spontaneity . . . Everything happens . . . as if consciousness constituted the ego as a false representation of itself, as if consciousness hypnotized itself before the ego which it has constituted, absorbing itself in the ego as if to make the ego its guardian and its law . . .
>
> But it can happen that consciousness suddenly produces itself on the *pure reflective level*. Perhaps not without the ego, yet as escaping from the ego on all sides, as dominating the ego and maintaining the ego outside the consciousness by a continued creation . . . (Then) consciousness suddenly (appears) to itself as infinitely overflowing in its possibilities the *I* which ordinarily serves as its unity.[383]

Here the false and destructive belief, for Sartre, is that we are something solid and almost immutable—a *substance,* or, if you prefer, an *ego*. This ego, according to this (allegedly) false belief, circumscribes our freedom within quite strict limits. To be sure, I retain certain possibilities, but I am really free only to "be myself" in any one of several possible ways. No possibility is admitted for my radical transformation through the adoption of an entirely new fundamental project. Only following a shift from the plane of accessory reflection to that of purifying reflection does it become possible to see that such radical reorientation is indeed possible. Sartre provides an interesting example, which he attributes to Janet, to illustrate this point.

> A young bride was in terror, when her husband left her alone, of sitting at the window and summoning the passers-by like a prostitute. Nothing in her education, in her past, nor in her character could serve as an explanation of such a fear. It seems to us simply that a negligible circumstance (reading, conversation, etc.) had determined in her what one might call a "vertigo of possibility." She found herself monstrously free, and this vertiginous freedom appeared to her *at the opportunity* for this action which she was afraid of doing.[384]

Thus, she was shocked out of what Sartre calls, borrowing from Husserl, "the natural attitude,"[385] through her (perhaps unintentional) use of purifying reflection, which Sartre here, as in the passage quoted from *The Emotions,* equates with "the phenomenological reduction."[386] And Sartre is quite emphatic in *TE* about the practical consequences of this use of the reduction: "No more is needed in the way of a philosophical foundation for an ethics and a politics which are absolutely positive."[387]

Thus, we are now in a position to understand Sartre's curious claim that "purifying reflection" can be equated with the phenomenological reduction. As we have seen, "the phenomenological reduction" is Husserl's name for the procedure of "placing in suspension" the thesis that the experienced world—the realm of intentional objects—really exists. The difficulty in understanding Sartre's endorsement of the reduction in the form of purifying reflection stems, of course, from the fact that, as we have also seen, Sartre *rejects* Husserl's use of the reduction.[388] However, as the several passages quoted from *The Emotions* and from *TE* clearly indicate, Sartre does accept the reduction in the larger sense of calling into question "the natural attitude"—the attitude which accepts uncritically the conventional, habitual views of "common sense."[389]

In order to make sense of this, it is important to see clearly the differences between Husserl's and Sartre's uses of the reduction. There are, I think, at least five fundamental differences.[390] (1) Husserl "brackets" at least some views which he regards as true, or partially true, while Sartre employs the reduction with regard to beliefs which he considers to be both false and dangerous. (2) For Husserl, the bracketed beliefs cannot be *shown* to be either true or false, whereas for Sartre the views in question can be demonstrated to be false. (3) For Husserl, the reduction consists in placing a thesis in suspension, while for Sartre it consists in making the thesis an object of explicit reflection. (4) Husserl's stated motive for using the reduction is his desire to consider questions other than those bracketed (in part because he holds the bracketed questions to be ultimately unanswerable anyway). For Sartre, on the other hand, the motive for the use of the reduction is to show the need for rejecting false and harmful beliefs. (5) Finally, the two men apply the reduction to *different issues.* For Husserl, as we have seen, the phenomenological reduction puts in brackets the question of the actual existence of the objects of experience. For Sartre, on the other hand, this use of the reduction is rejected, but from the passages from his works which we have examined, three different uses of the reduction can be discerned:

> (1) the reduction applied to psychic life resulting in an ontologically free impersonal consciousness; (2) a reduction applied to the life-world, resulting in the distinction between meaning and existence; and (3) a reduction applied to the ideal value of absolute being, which haunts pre-reflective consciousness, resulting in the refusal of that value by moral consciousness. This last use of the reduction is crucial to understanding *BN*.[391]

These admittedly significant differences between Husserl's and Sartre's use of the reduction should not, however, blind us to their important similarities. Thus, both Husserl and Sartre use the reduction as a means for going beyond the uncritical, conventional standpoint of common sense. Similarly, both Husserl and Sartre use the reduction to delineate sharply the boundaries of their respective investigations. For example, just as Husserl's reduction indicates that he is setting aside the question of the world's *existence* so as to focus instead on the *meaning* of the world-as-experienced, so does Sartre's use of the reduction indicate the deliberate incompleteness of his account of human activity in *BN*. Armed with an understanding of Sartre's use of the reduction, one can readily see the incompleteness of that work—that it is concerned, for example, with descriptions of the interpersonal relationships of those who are actively attempting to be God, rather than with descriptions of interpersonal relationships *as such*. Clearly, the failure to recognize the deliberate incompleteness of much of Sartre's work is a major cause of misunderstanding of Sartre's philosophy.[392] As Thomas W. Busch points out, "to sustain an interpretation of (*BN*) as a portrayal of the human condition as hopeless (and perhaps not worth the effort), one must discount certain features of the work which clearly call for a different interpretation."[393] Equally clearly, we can now add Sartre's use of the phenomenological reduction to a list of these features, which would also conclude the "radical conversion" passages, and Sartre's concepts of authenticity and of purifying and accessory reflection.[394]

To all of his, however, the "radical break" theorists have a ready reply. I have been arguing that *BN* is a deliberately incomplete account of human activity, an account which emphasizes the negative consequences of the project of attempting to be God, so as to show the need for the abandonment of this project in a "radical conversion" to a project which would be based upon freedom as the supreme value. This project, I have been contending, was to have been the subject of the ethical work which was promised at the conclusion of *BN* as a sequel to that book. This ethical work was to have supplied descriptions of the "positive" correlates of the "negative" concepts discussed in *BN*. That is, it was to have given us accounts of authenticity, purifying reflection, and of constructive and mutually fulfilling interpersonal relationships,[395] to complement our picture, derived from *BN*, of bad faith, accessory reflection, and the hell of other people.

In reply to this, the "radical break" theorists point to two facts: first, that Sartre never published any such ethical work during his lifetime, and secondly, that the works which did follow *BN*— especially his other major philosophical work, *CDR*—represent an entirely new orientation in Sartre's thinking. He seems to have abandoned his theory of freedom, to have moved from ontology to sociology, and to have rejected "existentialism" in favor of Marxism. According to these radical break theorists, Sartre's works subsequent to *BN* simply do not connect with that book. Thus, these critics conclude that Sartre's later philosophy represents his realization of the failure of his earlier philosophy. They hold that the doctrines of *BN* which lead to failure and hopelessness were Sartre's own, rather than views which he all along held to be disastrous, and from which he wanted to lead us through a radical conversion. After all, if *this* were his intention in *BN*, why did he not subsequently publish a work describing this conversion, and why does his actual subsequent work take the form that it does?

While I have already addressed myself to many points made by the radical break theorists—for example, their claim that Sartre's later work constitutes a rejection of his earlier theory of freedom— I have yet to reply to their objection that my account of the role of radical conversion in Sartre's early work does not square with the actual (non)relationship between Sartre's early and later works. Specifically, I have yet to explain why Sartre's later philosophy takes the direction that it does, and why it seems not to involve an explicit development of the idea of radical conversion.

As with my other replies to the radical break theorists, my strategy here will be to show that while they are correct to focus on a change in Sartre's thinking, the radical break theorists are incorrect in seeing this change in his later philosophy as representing a break from, rather than a modification of, his earlier thought. Moreover, I shall continue my practice of attempting, by focusing on the specific nature of the change in Sartre's thinking, to show that my classification of this change as a "modification" rather than as a "break" is not arbitrary, but is rather the most accurate way of reading what he actually says.

Consider the following statement from *CDR*: "Fundamental alienation does not derive, as *Being and Nothingness* might mislead one into supposing, from some prenatal choice: it derives from the univocal relation of interiority which unites man as a practical organism with his environment."[396] This sentence is indicative of both the continuity and the change in Sartre's philosophy. As we have seen, while Sartre never gives up the idea that human beings are always ontologically free, he also affirms from the very beginning that this freedom is always situated—that it operates against a background of "facticities" which offer varying amounts of "resistance" to it. Now this analysis of freedom and facticity is applicable, of course, both to the choice of the project of being God and to the choice of rejecting this project through a radical conversion. I will argue, then, that the changes in Sartre's thinking about the conversion amount simply to this: In his early works he is concerned to emphasize that these choices are *free* ones, and to encourage individuals to make the correct free choice. In his later works, by contrast, he emphasizes the facticities which render the conversion difficult and/or unlikely, and finds it a more useful and realistic strategy to encourage the alteration of these facticities as a means for facilitating conversions. Thus, we should expect Sartre's later works to be concerned with the alteration of "alienating" situations, and this is precisely what we do find. The radical theorists are quite right, then, to point out that Sartre moves from ontology to a concern with social, political, and economic institutions. They are quite wrong, however, or so I shall argue, to see this shift as discontinuous with Sartre's earlier philosophical enterprise.

Let us look at this more closely. First of all, in what ways can factors external to me make it difficult for me to recognize my freedom, or make it tempting to me either to hide my freedom from myself or to seek to escape my freedom through the pursuit of being?

This can happen, I would suggest, in at least two ways. First, let us recall a point that was developed in our discussion of the "practico-inert," namely, that the meanings which I find already in things, having been inscribed in them by the activities of (usually other) people, function as coefficients of adversity against my (possible) free constitution of other meanings in them. This point, though hardly emphasized in *BN*, is already present there: "I am not only thrown face to face with the brute existent. I am thrown into a worker's world, a French world, a world of Lorraine or the South, *which offers me its meanings without my having done anything to disclose them.*"[397] Or again, "I, by whom meanings come to things, . . . find myself engaged in an *already meaningful* world *which reflects to me meanings which I have not put into it.*"[398] Even more to the point, "in the midst of this world *already* provided with meaning I meet with a meaning which is *mine* and which I have not given to myself, which I discover that I 'possess already.'"[399] And recall the passage quoted above in the section on "my relations with others," to the effect that "the Other's existence brings a factual limit to my freedom" by constituting me as "Jew, or Aryan, handsome or ugly, one-armed, etc."[400]

These passages, especially the last two, illustrate one of Sartre's conceptions of how factors external to me can make it difficult for me to recognize my freedom. Quite simply, the fact that I encounter myself as an "entity" with a fixed meaning serves as a coefficient of adversity against any attempt which I might make to see myself as a freedom capable of transcending that fixed meaning. Moreover, as Sartre increasingly began to realize, there are many individuals who will deliberately attempt to hide my freedom from me, and to impose upon me "the natural attitude" that I simply *am* a certain kind of being with a strictly delineated function.[401] Such individuals are usually aided, furthermore, by the existing economic, social, and political structures, in terms of which my "identity" can easily be framed. Perhaps Sartre's most striking discussion of this point can be found in his biography of Genet:

> Genet is a child who has been convinced that he is, in his very depths, *Another than Self*. . . . In his very depths, Genet is first an object—and an object to others . . . and we shall see that it is simply a matter of progressively internalizing the sentence imposed by adults. . . . This type of alienation is widespread. Most of the time, however, it is a matter of partial or temporary alienation. But when children are subjected from their earliest days, to great social pressure, when their Being-for-Others is the subject of a collective image accompanied by value judgments and social prohibitions, the alienation is sometimes total and definitive. This is the case of most pariahs in caste societies. They internalize the objective and external judgments which the collectivity passes on them, and they view themselves in their subjective individuality on the basis of an 'ethnic character,' a 'nature,' an 'essence' which merely express the contempt in which *others* hold them.[402]

The second way in which external factors can make it difficult for me to recognize my freedom, or can tempt me to hide my freedom from myself, stems from the fact that the attitudes which we adopt are often tools which we use in order to solve specific problems that arise in specific situations. Similarly, the adoption of beliefs which we do not really believe—that is, the practice of lying to oneself, which Sartre calls "bad faith"—is generally a strategy which we adopt in order to achieve a certain end; and it is *more likely* to be adopted by us the more we think it likely—given the nature of our project and of our situation—to be of use to us in *achieving* our ends.

Now Sartre is everywhere concerned to show that bad faith and the flight from one's freedom are strategies which *cannot* succeed—they cannot bring about the results which they are intended to produce. Moreover, in Sartre's later works he points out that these strategies are typically adopted in precisely those situations in which strategies which *would* ordinarily be successful—strategies which include the acknowledgement of one's freedom and a lucid awareness of the structure of one's situation—are closed off. Thus, Sartre's theory of the external origins of the flight from authenticity is in this respect similar to Marx's, as encapsulated in his famous maxim, "(religion) is the *opium* of the people."[403] Quite simply, if one has the *means* (in this case economic) to obtain adequate food, clothing, and health care, one is likely simply to go out and get them. If, on the other hand, one does not have the means for acquiring these goods, one is more likely to attempt to comfort oneself by taking refuge in beliefs which deny the reality of the present situation, or which postulate a future situation which would be vastly different from the present one (e.g., Heaven).

Perhaps the best illustration of this point in Sartre is to be found in his theory of emotions. For Sartre, ordinary (unproblematic) situations do not typically involve emotion. I simply seek to understand the situation as accurately and precisely as I can, and then I take the appropriate steps to utilize the suitable means for bringing about my desired ends. But there are some situations in which I have no instruments whatsoever that could be used as means for achieving my desired result; or at least, there are situations in which such "rational" means-ends strategies are extremely unlikely to succeed, or will succeed only at the cost of great effort or personal danger. It is in precisely these sorts of situations, according to Sartre, that one is likely to attempt to deny the true instrumental structure of the situation, and to alter the situation by means of the "magic" of emotions. Consider the example of what Sartre calls "passive fear."

> I see a wild animal coming toward me. My legs give way, my heart beats more feebly, I turn pale, I fall and faint. Nothing seems less adapted than this behavior which hands me over defenseless to the danger. And yet it is a behavior of *escape*. Here the fainting is a refuge. . . . Lacking power to avoid the danger by the normal methods and the deterministic links, I denied it. I wanted to annihilate it. The urgency of the danger served as motive for an annihilating intention which demanded magical behavior. And, by virtue of this fact, I did annihilate it as far as was in my power. These are the limits of my magical action upon the world; I can eliminate it as an object of consciousness, but I can do so only by eliminating consciousness itself.[404]

Clearly, Sartre does not have a high opinion of this emotional response to the wild animal. To be sure, Sartre is here concerned with showing that this response is a kind of "behavior of escape." Nonetheless, it is plain that this strategy is successful only in the "magical" world in which the obliteration of consciousness brings about the obliteration of the animal. In "the real world," the world which operates in accordance with "normal methods and deterministic links," this behavior simply "hands me over defenseless to the danger." Indeed, one of the central points of Sartre's theory of emotions is undoubtedly that true "liberation is always rooted in unwavering readiness to comprehend what is real and true."[405]

We are now in a position to understand the nature of the change in Sartre's thinking about the radical conversion. Consider the following statement by Sartre concerning emotional consciousness: "Freedom has to come from a purifying reflection or a total disappearance of the affecting situation."[406] A simple formula which captures more or less accurately the nature of Sartre's evolution would be this: Of the two paths to freedom mentioned in the above quotation, the early Sartre emphasizes the former alternative while the later Sartre emphasizes the latter alternative. Consider, then, those who, like Genet, have been conditioned to think of themselves as fixed entities with no freedom to change, or those who lie to themselves, or those who hide their freedom from themselves, in response to difficult situations which seem to admit of no alternative solution. For the early Sartre, the "answer" for these individuals lay primarily in the individual action of undergoing purifying reflection, of "converting" to "authenticity." Thus, Sartre was concerned with showing a Genet that those who tried to "freeze" him in a static definition were wrong—that he was, in fact, free—and with showing those who flee or deny their freedom that these strategies can only lead to failure and futility. For the later Sartre, conversely, the "answer" for these individuals lay in the collective activity of altering the political and economic institutions which foster social conditioning, and which render the flight from authenticity a tempting alternative. After all, "if individual bad faith is grounded in objective structures which we experience together as oppressive, it can in principle be collectively thrown off. Of course this requires a movement beyond the perspective of solitary conversion to a more ample philosophical dimension that also includes social interaction."[407]

This is not to say that there is a break in Sartre's thought. Nowhere in his later writings does he repudiate the value of individual conversion; nor does he deny, in his early writings, that changes in external structures can call forth modifications in individual behavior. After all, even in *BN*, the fact that "each one of my acts, even the most trivial, is entirely free," does not entail "that my act can be anything *whatsoever* or even that it is *unforeseeable*."[408] Or again, Sartre points out, at the outset of his discussion of bad faith, that individual bad faith is grounded in social repression (e.g., the existence of slaveholders, jailers, and others "whose social reality is uniquely that of the No").[409]

But there can be no doubt that Sartre does undergo some changes on these issues: it is only in his later writings that we find him discussing in explicit, voluminous detail, the "external" aspects of bad faith, and his concept of radical conversion undergoes a corresponding modification. No longer can "deliverance and salvation" be brought about solely through individual, "inward" acts of purifying reflection. Rather, present political, economic, and social structures must be altered so as to create an environment in which free human beings, who both recognize their freedom and take it for an end, can thrive and prosper.

Why did Sartre undergo this change? Aside from the fact that he presumably learned something from his critics, at least two reasons can be cited. First, as Sartre himself puts it, life taught him "the power of circumstances."[410] The point in this instance is that life taught him, without refuting his point that authenticity and conversion were always *possible,* that certain prevalent external conditions present "coefficients of adversity" of such magnitude as to render the lucid awareness of one's ontological freedom *highly unlikely*. Thus, from a purely practical standpoint, the most effective way to bring about liberation is to alter these external conditions first, and then to encourage purifying reflection on the individual level, rather than the other way around.

The second reason for Sartre's modification in his understanding of the radical conversion stems, I think, from his increasing interest in practical freedom, as opposed to ontological freedom. Recall that in *BN* Sartre was concerned almost exclusively with ontological freedom. From an ethical standpoint, he was concerned to show the negative consequences of the flight from ontological freedom, and to hint that the answer lay in converting to a project which would take freedom explicitly as a goal. As we have seen, however, in his later works Sartre not only came to see the extent to which the denial of one's ontological freedom is motivated by external conditions, but he also began to concern himself with the fact that these same external conditions seemed to curtail dramatically the *practical* freedom of many individuals. Many people simply did not have enough food to eat, nor did they have sufficient access to many other goods and services which are essential to the living of a healthy and fulfilling life. To this problem Sartre began to devote more and more of his attention, issuing such statements as that "life will be human on the day that everyone can eat his fill and every man can work at a job under suitable working conditions,"[411] that "hunger is an evil: period,"[412] and that there is a "right to have more than one pair of shoes and to eat when hungry."[413]

This increasing concern for practical freedom was incompatible with his early theory of radical conversion for at least two reasons. First, of course, individual private conversion is not likely to prove effective in combatting the problems of poverty and hunger. Secondly, the explicit goal of radical conversion, as originally formulated, was not so much to enhance the practical freedom of others as it was to reconcile oneself with one's own ontological freedom. Indeed, the activity which Sartre in *BN* sets up as the ideal for those who have undergone purifying reflection is "play," which he defines as "an activity of which man is the first origin, for which man himself sets the rules, and which has no consequences except according to the rules posited."[414] As examples of play, Sartre cites, straightforwardly, "sports or pantomime or games,"[415] and provides an extended analysis of skiing.[416] However, as Fell points out,

> Sartre would presumably no longer find the ethics of play, which he had illustrated by skiing, to be a viable option at the present time. Sliding playfully over the surface—as in skiing, yachting, or water-skiing—is the sport of the privileged, indulged in primarily by those who hold a disproportionate share of what is scarce. They play while others labor, and their labor maintains the conditions in which the privileged can play. . . . In retrospect Sartre sees that this is not a time for play, but for work. Conversion is no longer a matter of an instant but of a long labor. . . . Only in a society where all are actually and not just theoretically free, equal, and fraternal can there be an ethics that can justifiably bind each and every individual to the same moral requirements.[417]

Sartre's later writings bear out Fell's contentions:

As soon as their will exist *for everyone* a margin of *real* freedom beyond the production of life, Marxism will have lived out its span; a philosophy of freedom will take its place. But we have no means, no intellectual instrument, no concrete experience which allows us to conceive of this freedom or of this philosophy.[418]

First all men must be able to become men by the improvement of their conditions of existence, so that a universal morality can be created. . . . What matters first is the liberation of man.[419]

1.3.3.4   The radical break objection answered

Thus, the later Sartre agrees with the early Sartre that the fundamental goal is human liberation. A central thread which runs through both *BN* and *CDR* is that the present human condition is neither necessary nor desirable, and that there is a need for a radical conversion to a new way of life which would be directed toward the enhancement of human freedom. The former work develops this thread within an ontological, and largely individualistic, framework, while the latter book develops it from a practical and social perspective. There is some evolution between the two books as regards both the nature of the change that is needed and the strategies that are to be employed in bringing that change about. There is no justification, however, for the view that there is a "radical break" between the two works. Such a view depends for its plausibility upon the incorrect assumption that *BN* is intended as a complete description of an inescapable human condition, rather than as a deliberately incomplete description of precisely those features of the human condition which stand in need of radical alteration.

1.4   Conclusion

Let us review the ground that we have covered in this chapter. We have seen, first of all, that Sartre advances two major arguments in support of the conclusion that human beings are free. Next, in examining Sartre's view of the *nature* of freedom, and in responding to criticisms of his theory of freedom, we have observed that Sartre acknowledges limitations to freedom, that he distinguishes between different senses of freedom, and that his later writings represent a development of, rather than a radical break from, his earlier theory of freedom. Finally, in connection with this latter point, we have begun to witness the tremendous importance of freedom as a *moral* concept within Sartre's thought. We have seen that in his early works he calls freedom "the highest value," "the source of all value," "the foundation of all values," etc., and that in his later works he states repeatedly that the most important ethical task facing human beings at the present time is that of "liberating the oppressed," and, in general, of increasing the practical freedom of all persons. But in assessing Sartre's claim that "freedom is the highest value," there is a need to answer at least three questions: (1) What does Sartre mean by "freedom"?, (2) What does he mean by "value"?, and (3) What does he mean by calling *freedom* a *value,* let alone the *highest* value? We have developed at least a rough answer to the first question in the present chapter; and our ultimate goal is to answer the third question (and then to evaluate the answer given). But first, by way of introduction to the third question, and in order to answer the second question, let us now take up Sartre's theory of values.

CHAPTER 2
Values

2.1 Introduction

We have seen that Sartre considers freedom to be a value, indeed, the "highest" value, the value which serves as the "foundation" and "source" of all other values. But what does Sartre mean by "value"? Consider the following three representative texts:

> Values . . . are demands which lay claim to a foundation.[1]

> Value is always and everywhere the beyond of all surpassings.[2]

> (Value is) the call of something which does not yet exist.[3]

What is to be noticed in all of these definitions is that Sartre seems to think of values as unreal, as "calls" or "demands" which "do not exist." Values, for him, are apparently not the sorts of things that we might encounter regularly in our mundane, day-to-day experience, but are instead granted an exclusive, exotic status all their own. Thus, Sartre says such things as that "the being of value qua value is the being of what does not have being,"[4] and that "value is beyond being."[5]

Consequently, insofar as values are beyond being, they can appear at the level of being only if I "bring them" to being. "I do not have nor can I have recourse to any value against the fact that it is I who sustain values in being."[6] In other words, "my freedom is the unique foundation of values"; and this, according to Sartre, implies the apparently subjectivist conclusion that "*nothing, absolutely nothing, justifies me in adopting this or that particular value, this or that particular scale of values.*"[7]

One of the most interesting features of this theory of value is the degree of its divergence from what might be called the mainstream of the phenomenological tradition, at least as exemplified by Husserl, and by those who have attempted more extensively to apply his insights to the fields of ethics and axiology (the study of values).[8] For example, as against Sartre's assignment to values to the realm of the "beyond being," Husserl had claimed that

> this world is there for me not only as a world of mere things, but also with the same immediacy as a *world of objects with values, a world of goods, a practical world*. I simply find the physical things in front of me furnished not only with merely material determinations but also with value-characteristics, as beautiful and ugly, pleasant and unpleasant, agreeable and disagreeable, and the like.[9]

Similarly, as against Sartre's apparently thoroughgoing subjectivism, Husserl had insisted that "these value-characteristics and practical characteristics . . . belong constitutively to the Objects 'on hand' as Objects, *regardless of whether or not I turn to such characteristics and the Objects.*"[10]

Since Husserl's claims seem, as even Sartre admits (without mentioning Husserl by name),[11] to reflect accurately the nature of our experience, the question arises as to why Sartre, who at least in his early works claims to be a phenomenologist, would want to reject them. We will need to examine briefly, then, some of the reasons that Sartre gives for insisting upon the "unreality" of values and the subjectivity of value-judgments. But first we had better get clear on what we *mean* by "the unreality of values" and "the subjectivity of value-judgments."

2.2   The Subjectivity of Values and the Subjectivity of Value-Judgments

In this section I want to call attention to a distinction between two different doctrines, both of which are defended by Sartre, but which I think he fails to keep adequately distinguished in his thinking. I am referring to the distinction between what I shall call, on the one hand, "the subjectivity of values" or "the unreality of values" (an ontological doctrine), and, on the other hand, "the subjectivity of value-judgments" or "ethical subjectivism" (a meta-ethical doctrine). I will say at the outset that I regard most of Sartre's arguments for ethical subjectivism to be invalid, since they depend upon his failure to distinguish that thesis from "the subjectivity of values," so that, in proving the truth of the latter thesis, he thinks he is also proving the truth of the former, and fails to recognize that his argument for ethical subjectivism depends upon the premise that the subjectivity of values entails ethical subjectivism. This premise is plainly false, however, and its falsity wrecks most of Sartre's arguments for ethical subjectivism, or so I shall argue. But first, let us see what is meant by the Sartrean doctrine that I am calling "the subjectivity of values."

Perhaps the best way to see what Sartre is getting at here is to reflect upon the deep similarities between our experience of values and our experiences of absences, destructions, gaps, etc.[12] As with these phenomena, Sartre regards values as "negativities" which arise only as a consequence of our engagement in projects. We are now in a position to see that values, therefore, occupy precisely the same "subjective" ontological status as do these other negativities.

Consider, once again, Pierre's absence from the café. Clearly, this absence does not "exist" in being. Pierre's absence is not objectively "in" the café. Rather, "the café by itself with its patrons, its tables, its booths, its mirrors, its light, its smoky atmosphere, and the sounds of voices, rattling saucers, and footsteps which fill it," is "a fullness of being."[13] The café is all positivity. It has no "gaps." Pierre's absence appears only after the introduction of my consciousness. It is only as a result of my *project* of looking for Pierre that I encounter his absence. Thus, his absence appears to have only a subjective existence—an existence which is entirely dependent upon my consciousness and my projects.

But notice that, while in one sense Pierre's absence is imposed on the world by my consciousness, in another sense it is *encountered* or *found* in the world. Thus, the existence of the absence seems to depend as much upon the world as upon my consciousness. After all, I might have found Pierre himself, rather than his absence—I *would* have done so had he, in fact, *really been there* in the café to be found.

Now, for Sartre, what is true of absences is also true of values. Thus, my boss's orders reveal to me the value of obeying, not only because I have freely embraced the project of seeking promotion within the company, but also because of certain facts over which I have no control—for example, the fact that my company promotes none but its most obedient workers. Were I to pursue this same project within a different company, say, one which based its promotions more on creativity of thought and stubborn independence of action than on obedience, the values revealed to me by my boss's orders would be of a rather different nature, without my having done anything different to bring forth these different values. So values, like absences, are in some sense *discovered* in the world, even though they originate in acts of consciousness.

Thus, Sartre's theory of values is subjectivist in the sense that it grants values no independent existence in the world apart from consciousness, and holds that values arise only through conscious acts. In other words, Sartre affirms "the subjectivity of values." But at the same time, Sartre's theory is not subjectivist in the straightforward sense of holding that values are simply invented, or are the products of personal feelings and beliefs. Rather, value is granted a rather unique ontological status by Sartre. Like other negativities, value "resides neither in the outside world nor *in* consciousness. *It is a way by which consciousness relates itself to objects of the world.*" [14]

The point to be noticed is that what I am calling "the subjectivity of values" is an ontological thesis, that is, a thesis about what exists and the manner in which it exists. Sartre is arguing that values do *not* exist, or, more precisely, that they owe such existence as they have to human consciousnesses which bring them into being— they have, in other words, only a "subjective" existence. What he is *not* explicitly arguing here is the meta-ethical thesis which I am calling "the subjectivity of value-judgments," which holds, very roughly, that we can have no *knowledge* about values, or that we can have only "subjective" knowledge—that is, knowledge which is dependent upon the nature of the consciousness which judges, or otherwise relates itself to, values, rather than upon the nature of the values themselves that are in question. We shall see, however, that Sartre seems to regard the latter, meta-ethical, thesis as following from the former, ontological, one. As against Sartre, I want to show in the next section that there is no necessary connection between these two theses, that the subjectivity of values (the objective nonexistence of values) is in no way incompatible with the possibility that certain value-judgments are "objectively" true.

2.2.1   The Compatibility of the Subjectivity of Values and the Objectivity of Value-Judgments

One fact which at least mildly suggests the compatibility of the subjectivity of values and the objectivity of value-judgments is that our experience suggests the truth of both of these doctrines. As for the objectivity of value-judgments, I think that James Rachels gives an accurate account of our experience:

> We think that some things *really* are good, and others *really* are bad, in a way that does not depend on how we feel about them. Hitler's concentration camps really were evil, and anyone who thinks otherwise is simply wrong. Therefore we want a theory that will allow for the objectivity of ethics. . . . To say that the concentration camps were evil is to state a fact . . . in much the same way as it is stating a fact to say that people were killed in them. People were killed in those places, no matter what anyone thinks and no matter how anyone feels about it; similarly, on this view, those places were evil no matter what anyone thinks and no matter how anyone feels.[15]

Thus, I would characterize, I trust not too eccentrically,[16] "the objectivity of ethics" which Rachels claims to be well-grounded in our experience, as involving the following four claims: (1) that it is possible, at least in principle, to distinguish between what happens

to be *valued* and what is (really) *valuable,* between what happens to
be *desired* and what is (really) *desirable,* between what anyone
happens to *think* is good or right or valuable, and what *is* good or
right or valuable—in short, that just as in matters of fact it is
possible for anyone, or even *everyone,* to believe mistakenly, so that
there is a difference between what is *believed* to be true (e.g., that
the earth is flat) and what *is* in fact true (e.g., that the earth is not
flat), so is it possible for anyone or everyone to believe mistakenly
about ethical matters, so that what is true in ethics cannot legitimately be reduced to what is *believed* to be true; (2) that our beliefs
or feelings about what is right or wrong, good or bad, are therefore
not always *constitutive* of the rightness or wrongness, goodness or
badness of the things, states of affairs, or acts in question (just as
our beliefs about matters of fact do not make those beliefs true), but
rather that, at least in some instances, our moral beliefs are *founded
in* our experience of the true rightness or wrongness, goodness or
badness, of the things, states of affairs, or acts in question (in a
manner that is similar to the formation of at least some of our
beliefs about matters of fact)—that, for example, it would be false,
as even that confirmed ethical subjectivist Bertrand Russell
admits, to say that "all that is wrong with wanton cruelty is that I
don't like it";[17] (3) that, just as truths about matters of fact are
sometimes founded in experiences of "recognizing," "perceiving," "discovering," etc., as opposed to experiences of "inventing," "creating," "positing," etc., so are moral truths sometimes
recognized rather than invented—just as certain factual states of
affairs coercively press themselves upon me as true no matter how
much I might wish things were otherwise, so that I cannot deny
these truths (or can deny them only through great effort and much
self-deception, and against a tremendous "resistance" which I
experience as acting upon me), so are certain moral truths
coercively and obtrusively present and unyielding in my cognitive
experience; and (4) that, just as there are "good reasons" for
believing certain things rather than others in the realm of matters of
fact, so that differences of opinion as regards such matters need not
lead directly to an impasse or to a fight, since there are legitimate
criteria for evaluating competing claims—logical consistency,
consistency with evidence, explanatory fruitfulness, etc.—and

rational procedures for at least making *progress* toward settling disputes, so are there better and worse reasons for believing one thing rather than another in ethics, and rational criteria and procedures for evaluating and differentiating between competing ethical claims.

But is Rachels *correct* in maintaining that our experience supports this "objectivity of ethics"? It would seem so, at least with regard to such apparently obvious value-judgments as that "love is preferable to hate, peace to war, brotherhood to enmity, joy to sorrow, health to sickness, nourishment to hunger, life to death."[18] Surely it is a powerfully present datum of our experience that these judgments are founded in recognition rather than invention, that their truth does not depend upon our confirming them, that those who disagree with them are simply wrong in the same manner as they would be if they were to insist that the earth is flat, and that there are good reasons for affirming these value-judgments— certainly there are *better* reasons for affirming them than there are for affirming their respective contraries.

Where, then, is the problem? Here we must move to the question of the ontological status of values, for it seems, or at least it has seemed to most people, and to Sartre, that to say that our judgments about values can have objective validity is to imply that values must objectively *exist*. For if values do not exist, we can no more settle disputes about them objectively than we could about such other nonexistent entities as the present King of France—whether or not he is bald, for example.[19] And if values do exist, but only "subjectively," if they are simply the products of human invention, for example, then surely there can be no talk of values being objectively "right" or "wrong"—we can invent whatever we want; there is no such thing as a "right" or "wrong" invention.

The problem, then, is clear. On the one hand, our experience suggests what Rachels calls "the objectivity of ethics." But our experience also suggests the denial of what the objectivity of ethics seems to entail—namely, the objective existence of values. For, as Frederick Copleston points out, "from an ontological or meta-physical point of view . . . it seems absurd, to most people at any rate, to conceive values as existing in some ethereal world of their own."[20] Alternatively, one might suppose that, while values do not exist on their own, in some shadowy world for example, they nonetheless *do* exist as *properties* of objects, states of affairs, and actions. One might say, then, that the objectivity of the judgment that Hitler's concentration camps were bad is founded on the fact that these camps contained the property "bad" and lacked the property "good."[21] But this view faces notorious difficulties.[22] At present, however, it is sufficient to point out, in Rachels' words, that "it is hard to believe, while maintaining one's sense of reality, that goodness and badness are properties in any simple sense."[23] The point is simply that experience does not disclose such properties to us, as it does disclose properties of, say, "redness" and "triangularity." As Hume puts it,

> Take any action allow'd to be vicious: Wilful murder, for instance. Examine it in all lights, and see if you can find that matter of fact, or real existence, which you call *vice*. In which-ever way you take it, you find only certain passions, motives, volitions and thoughts. There is no other matter of fact in the case. The vice entirely escapes you, as long as you consider the object. You never can find it, till you turn your reflection into your own breast, and find a sentiment of disapprobation, which arises in you, towards this action. Here is a matter of fact; but 'tis the object of feeling, not of reason. It lies in yourself, not in the object.[24]

Perhaps the clearest and easiest way to see precisely what is wrong with the view that values are properties of things, in the same way that colors (G. E. Moore's favorite analogy) are properties of things, is by comparing the following four syllogisms:

A. 1. Jupiter is a red planet.
     2. All planets are heavenly bodies.
     Therefore, Jupiter is a red heavenly body.

B. 1. Jupiter is a large planet.
     2. All planets are heavenly bodies.
     Therefore, Jupiter is a large heavenly body.

C. 1. My bicycle is a blue bicycle.
     2. All bicycles are modes of transportation.
     Therefore, my bicycle is a blue mode of transportation.

D. 1. My bicycle is a good bicycle.
     2. All bicycles are modes of transportation.
     Therefore, my bicycle is a good mode of transportation.[25]

Clearly, arguments A and C are valid, while arguments B and D are not. How is this to be explained? Apparently the disparity stems from the difference between such concepts as "red" and "blue" on the one hand, and "large" and "good" on the other. For consider that, while it follows that if something is a blue X, and is also a Y, that it must also be a *blue* Y, such inferences cannot reliably be drawn with regard to *large* X's or *good* X's. When we say that something is blue, we usually do not mean merely that it is blue in comparison to something else, or with respect to other members of its class; rather we are saying something about it which we regard to be true of it irrespective of the particular class as a member of which we might happen to be considering it. Thus, we might appropriately regard "blue," and other terms which are capable of being applied to objects correctly without consideration of either the particular class to which the object belongs or the particular other objects to which the object in question is to be compared, "property" terms. When we say that something is large, however, we usually do mean that it is large in comparison to something else, or with respect to other members of its class. This is why it does not follow from the fact that Jupiter is a large *planet* that it is also a large *heavenly body*. Thus, we might properly regard "large," and other terms which can be correctly applied to objects only relatively, depending upon class membership or upon a particular comparison, "relational" or "comparison" terms.

The question then arises as to whether "good" is more like "blue" or more like "large"; is it a property term or a comparison term. Certainly, syllogism D strongly suggests that it is the latter. After all, a good bicycle might not count as a good mode of transportation when compared with planes, cars, trains, and boats. Thus, as the inventor of these four syllogisms, R. F. Tredwell, concludes,

> In each pair of arguments, the fallacy involved in the second one is the same: 'large planet' means "larger than the run of planets"; 'good bicycle' means "better than most bicycles." But it does not follow that what is large or good in relation to one class is large or good in relation to another. From this argument, . . . we can infer at least that goodness is not a property, for all properties will give valid inferences in this form of argument, and goodness does not.[26]

Now, I want to add a second moral to the one underscored by Tredwell. Surely, just as we can truthfully say that Jupiter is a large planet without thereby committing ourselves to the claim that Jupiter must contain "largeness" as a property, so can we truthfully call certain objects, acts, and states of affairs "good" without thereby committing ourselves to the strange-sounding ontological view that these objects, acts, and states of affairs must contain within themselves the real, existing property of "goodness." On this point I agree with Tredwell, as would, I think, Sartre. But does this argument against the *ontological* objectivity of values in any way undermine, as Sartre apparently thinks it would, what Rachels calls "the objectivity of ethics"? The point that I wish to make is that it does not.

Consider, once again, the claim that Jupiter is a large planet. Could anyone plausibly assert that this claim represents a *purely subjective* judgment? Is there no distinction between someone's *thinking* or *feeling* that Jupiter is a large planet and its *really being* one? Is it impossible to be *mistaken* in one's judgment that Jupiter is or is not a large planet? Are our beliefs and feelings about the size of Jupiter *constitutive* of its size? Do we *invent,* rather than *recognize* or *discover,* the size of Jupiter? Is one's opinion about the size of Jupiter *utterly arbitrary,* or perhaps simply a matter of *feeling* or *taste*? Surely the fact that Jupiter does not contain the objectively existing *property* of largeness does not entail any of these absurd conclusions. Why, then, should we think that a given act's lack of a property of goodness entails that the judgment that it *is* good must be regarded as a "purely subjective" judgment, entailing conclusions about it which would be analogous to the ones which I labelled "absurd" in connection with the judgment that Jupiter is a large planet?[27]

It will no doubt be objected that there is a clear difference between questions about what is large and questions concerning what is good, in that we do have objectively valid, or at least nonarbitrary, (1) criteria for distinguishing large from small, (2) standards concerning what is to count as large and what is to count as small, and (3) procedures for verifying or falsifying claims about size, while no such analogous criteria, standards, or procedures can be found concerning questions about what is good.

But this objection seems to lose its force as soon as we return to an examination of our experience and, in the words of Kurt Baier,

> remind ourselves briefly of how we arrive at our value judgments. When we determine the merits of students, meals, tennis players, bulls, or bathing belles, we do so on the basis of some criteria and some standard or norm. Criteria and standards notoriously vary from field to field and even from case to case. But that does not mean that we have *no* idea about what are the appropriate criteria or standards to use. It would not be fitting to apply the criteria for judging bulls to the judgment of students or bathing belles. They score on quite different points. [28]

Moreover, even when it is reasonable to use the *same* criteria in two different cases, it might not be right to use the same *standards*. For example, even when it is appropriate to use roughly the same criteria (e.g., clarity, cogency, accuracy, etc.) in evaluating the papers of beginning and advanced philosophy students, it would be inappropriate to use the same standards. Thus, a good paper by a beginning student might well be a poor paper when judged by the standards appropriate to advanced students. While it would certainly be difficult to give a precise, definitive account of what the proper criteria and standards should be in any given case, it hardly follows from this that the choice of criteria and standards is arbitrary or subjective—that, as Baier puts it, "we have *no* idea about what are the appropriate criteria or standards to use." Similar considerations apply, I think, to questions pertaining to procedures of verification and falsification.

Doubtless, there are many other arguments for the subjectivity of value-judgments, or against their objectivity, which could be considered. But I am not here concerned to establish the objectivity of ethics. Rather, I have attempted to show in this section only that "the subjectivity of values" does not entail "the subjectivity of value-judgments." At the very least, I hope to have succeeded in showing that the latter does not *obviously* follow from the former, that there is some *doubt* as to whether it does follow, and that it is therefore illegitimate to infer the latter from the former without providing some *argument* which would establish the needed connection between the two clearly distinct doctrines. These conclusions alone, I believe, are sufficient to undermine most of Sartre's arguments for ethical subjectivism, to which we may now turn.

2.3   Sartre's Arguments for Ethical Subjectivism

It is interesting to note that Sartre gives up arguing for ethical subjectivism ("the subjectivity of value-judgments") in his later works, and, as we shall see, occasionally even hints that he has become more sympathetic to ethical objectivism. Thus, the five arguments to be discussed here are all drawn from works published prior to *CDR*. The first three are to be found in *BN*, and are all vulnerable to the objection outlined in the preceding section. The latter two, which are from his famous lecture, "Existentialism is a Humanism" (hereafter cited as *EH*), are not vulnerable to this objection.

2.3.1   *The Experience of Values as "Lacks"*

The fact that, as we recall, Sartre defines values as "demands" and "calls," reflects one of his arguments for "the subjectivity of values." Sartre's claim is that our experience of values differs drastically from our experience of facts. Quite simply, our experience of facts is of that which *is* the case, while our experience of values is of that which is *not* the case, but which *should be* the case. We experience values as lying *beyond* that which is the case, as ideals which make claims upon us, demanding to be acted upon. Thus, Sartre often refers to values as "exigencies," "appeals," "imperatives," "tasks," and "norms." As Anderson explains,

> to experience courage as a value is not for Sartre simply to perceive that courage exists as trees exist, but rather to recognize that courage should be embodied in acts in certain circumstances. Values are not existing facts that in themselves simply are and so can be noted by a disinterested spectator. Values call for, or even command, action; their very being is in being a demand for realization—and as something *to be made real* they must at present be "beyond being." They are something that is "lacked," Sartre says.[29]

Now, insofar as we understand "value" as that on the basis of which I act, it is clear why values must be regarded as "lacks," as "negativities," rather than as entities of some sort which would have an objective existence. The point is that our actions are not merely *sometimes* motivated by that which is "beyond being," that which "is not." Rather, action always "necessarily implies as its condition the recognition of a 'desideratum,'" and this desideratum can never merely be "what is."[30]

The inability of "what is" to serve as a desideratum can be seen in at least two ways. First, whenever I act, it must be that I am trying to bring about some state of affairs that currently "is not." It will doubtless be objected that I sometimes wish merely to sustain present conditions. But such a wish can clearly never be the motive for an *action* unless I regard the present state of affairs as precarious, as in danger of being overturned, as *not* stable and secure, or at least, as *requiring* something that *is not yet,* namely my doing or refraining from doing something in order for the state of affairs to continue. Through my action, then, I desire to bring about a state of affairs that presently is not, namely the *stability* and *security* of the status quo.

Secondly, every act requires not only that I desire to bring about some state of affairs that currently is not, but also that I regard the present state of affairs as *not* the state of affairs that I wish to bring about. Thus, the fact that a worker's salary is, say, fifty dollars a week, is incapable of motivating a revolt. The salary can only become a reason for action when it is regarded as *not enough*. According to Sartre, the worker who revolts "will have to have effected a double nihilation: on the one hand, he must posit an ideal state of affairs as a pure *present* nothingness; on the other hand, he must posit the actual situation as nothingness in relation to this state of affairs."[31]

The subjectivity of values would seem, therefore, to be established. I act only on the basis of what is not. "Value" is that on the basis of which I act. Therefore "value" is not. Value makes its appearance only through the nihilating activities of consciousness. Thus, value has only a subjective, or consciousness-dependent, reality.

And from this ontological conclusion, which I am calling "the subjectivity of values," Sartre does not hesitate to affirm a further conclusion, that the meta-ethical thesis which I am calling "ethical subjectivism" or "the subjectivity of value-judgments" must also be true:

There is ethical anguish when I consider myself in my original relation to values. Values in actuality are demands which lay claim to a foundation. . . . Value derives its being from its exigency and not its exigency from its being. It does not deliver itself to a contemplative intuition. . . . On the contrary, it can be revealed only to an active freedom which makes it exist as value. . . . It follows that my freedom is the unique foundation of values and that *nothing, absolutely nothing, justifies me in adopting this or that particular value, this or that particular scale of values.* As a being by whom values exist, I am unjustifiable. My freedom is anguished at being the foundation of values while itself without foundation.[32]

2.3.1.1 Criticism of the argument from the experience of values as "lacks"

I have two objections to this argument. First, I deny the accuracy, or at least the completeness, of Sartre's phenomenology of value experience. It seems to me that we plainly do, on a regular basis, experience presently existing things, acts, and states of affairs as "good," "bad," "better," "worse," "valuable," "worthless," etc.

In order to illustrate this point, consider the following example. Suppose I am the general manager of a major league baseball team which has just won the world series. As it happens, the contracts of some of the team's best players, those most responsible for the team's recent success, have just expired, leaving the players in question free to negotiate new contracts with new teams. As general manager of the team I wish to do whatever I can to increase the team's chances of continuing to win championships in future years. I sign all of the players in question to long-term contracts.

How would Sartre analyze this? Presumably he would say that the future success of my team (which presently is not) is of value to me, as is the stability and security of the state of affairs in which certain players are members of the team (which, prior to my act of signing them to long-term contracts, was not). Fair enough. But who can fail to see that the *basis* of my valuing the relative permanency of these players' membership in my team is my *recognition of their present value*? I *see* that these are, *here and now, good* players. I fail to see how Sartre could possibly justify the claim that the current value of these players somehow "is not," or is some kind of lack. Nor do I see why he should *want* to say this, except that his theory of value evidently requires it.

Sartre's error, I believe, stems from his adoption of an extraordinarily restricted conception of "value."[33] Clearly, if we insist that "value" can only refer to that which we intend to bring about through an act, and insofar as (intended) consequences of acts are always temporally posterior to the acts themselves, let alone to the decision to undertake the acts, it follows that "value" must always refer to that which is "not yet," and this, of course, is a subset of that which simply "is not." But why should we so restrict our understanding of "value," especially when we consider that there is sanction both in experience and in ordinary language for regarding certain present states of affairs as values?

Nor is this a purely linguistic quibble, for, as we recall, one of Sartre's principal reasons for claiming that "nothing, absolutely nothing, can justify me in adopting this or that particular value, this or that particular scale of values," is that values arise only as a result of my freely chosen projects, and do not "deliver themselves to a (disinterested) contemplative intuition." But we are now in a position to see that these latter two claims are true only on the extremely restricted conception of "value" endorsed by Sartre. Surely, to return to our example, the value of the baseball players *is* accessible to the contemplative intuition of the disinterested observer, without the observer's having engaged in any special project other than that of *looking* to *see* what their value is. *Everyone* is in a position to see, and everyone who has looked *has* seen, that, as an illustration, George Brett is a *better* baseball player than Buddy Biancalana. Nothing could be less plausible— indeed, nothing could be more clearly wrong—than the claim that "nothing, absolutely nothing, justifies me in adopting this particular value-judgment." To the contrary, a veritable mountain of evidence, accessible to all observers irrespective of their idiosyncratic projects, justifies me in adopting the scale of values in which George Brett occupies the position of "better" and Buddy Biancalana that of "worse." The same cannot be said of the contrary scale.

These results can be generalized across the entire range of my experience. For example, I *discover,* in many cases without it in any way depending upon any particular project of mine, that certain people are "courageous," while others are "cowardly," that some acts are "kindly," while others are "cruel," and even that certain objects are "beautiful," while others are "ugly." To be sure, some of these "discoveries" may turn out to be erroneous. There is no reason to expect my value-experience to be always veridical. But at least my value-judgments are *sometimes* founded in experiences of values which do not depend for their appearance upon my engagement in any particular project. Values do appear at least sometimes to deliver themselves to my contemplative intuition and justify my adoption of a particular scale of values. Sartre's denial of this loses all plausibility once we move beyond his extraordinarily restricted conception of "value."

This brings me to my second objection—the one outlined in section 2.2.1, to the effect that the subjectivity of values does not entail ethical subjectivism. The point is that even if we waive my first objection to the present argument, we are still left with the criticism that from the ontological thesis that values do not exist apart from human consciousnesses which make them exist, the meta-ethical thesis that "nothing, absolutely nothing, justifies me in adopting this or that particular value, etc.," simply does not follow. Thus, just as, even if "large" does not exist in the world, apart from human consciousnesses, I am nonetheless *justified* in holding that elephants are larger than rats, and *not* justified in holding the reverse, so does the subjectivity of values fail to preclude my being justified in regarding happiness to be better than misery, or in regarding Albert Schweitzer to be more honest than Richard Nixon, and not justified in holding the contraries of these judgments.

2.3.2   The Distinction Between Facts and Values

At times Sartre seems to imply that the subjectivity of values is guaranteed by a simple logical point—that facts and values are incommensurate because they each belong to their own logical sphere. Thus, Sartre claims that "ontology itself can not formulate ethical precepts. It is concerned solely with what is, and we cannot possibly derive imperatives from ontology's indicatives."[34]

Sartre's conclusion, while identical to that drawn in the preceding section, is more directly arrived at here. The separation of facts and values is not derived through painstaking analyses of the nature of action, of the nihilating capacities of consciousness, or of our actual experience of values, but simply through reflection on the great difference between what it is to say that something is a fact and what it is to say that something is a value. To say that something *is* is not to say that it *ought to be*. Nor can the fact that something *is* in any way *imply* that it ought to be. Sartre even goes so far as to say that "if the values are facts, we maintain that we have no . . . reason to trust ourselves to them."[35] Ontology is one thing: it tells us what is. Ethics is something else: it tells us what ought to be.

2.3.2.1   Criticism of the argument from the distinction between facts and values

Let us grant Sartre's point that conclusions about what is *good* cannot validly be derived from premises solely about what *is*. But surely this does not prove that values and facts are utterly unrelated to one another, so that knowledge of facts could never be in any way helpful in arriving at knowledge of values. Rather, it merely suggests a need (which may or may not be capable of being fulfilled) for true premises which would draw a bridge between facts and values. Thus, while it is true that you cannot infer from the fact that a given state of affairs produces happiness (factual premise) that the state of affairs in question is good (evaluative conclusion) without introducing a premise which would *connect* fact and value (e.g., that happiness, as well as that which produces it, is good), it does not follow from this that the last-named premise cannot legitimately be supplied. The question before us, then, concerns whether or not there *are* any true premises which connect fact and value; but the mere fact that this is the important question is enough to show that the difference between fact and value is insufficient to establish the irrelevance of questions of fact to questions of value.

But *are* there any true premises which connect fact and value? This is too large a question to be dealt with here; but, as we have seen, Sartre's answer is that there clearly are not. Moreover, his negative answer to this question seems to aid his ethical subjectivism. For if we can only have direct knowledge of what is (fact), and never of what is not (value), and if we also cannot have indirect knowledge of value by deriving such knowledge from our knowledge of fact (and Sartre insists that we cannot, since facts and values are utterly unconnected), it does seem to follow that we can have no knowledge whatsoever of value, since no way remains by which we might attain such knowledge. Values are what we *create* or *choose*. They can never deliver themselves to a contemplative intuition.

Now we are in a position to see, however, that the reasons *why* Sartre sees facts and values to be eternally cut off from one another are precisely those which we have already discussed in connection with the previous argument—the business about values being "lacks," "demands," "calls," etc.—and found unsatisfactory. Thus, we must judge Sartre's present argument unsound since it depends upon the previous argument which has already been found wanting. The simple logical point that evaluative conclusions do not validly follow from purely factual premises does not establish that no connection can be found between facts and values. Further justification is required for this point; and the justification which Sartre provides is, as I have already argued, inadequate.

2.3.3   The Hierarchy of Projects

An obvious counterargument to Sartre's strict separation of fact and value could perhaps be constructed from Husserl's insistence that values, far from being radically separate from the realm of what is, are in fact always to be found embedded in the objects of our immediate experience: "I simply find the physical things in front of me furnished . . . with value-characteristics, as beautiful and ugly, pleasant and unpleasant, agreeable and disagreeable, and the like."[36] Or again, as Copleston puts it, "from the phenomenological point of view it is reasonable to use the language of recognition or discovery in regard to truth and beauty considered as values. In other words, our experience of values provides a ground or basis for the idea of values as objective and as transcendent, in the sense that they do not depend simply on one's choice of them."[37] Surprisingly, Sartre at first appears sympathetic to these claims, acknowledging that "in fact I am engaged in a world of values,"[38] and that "values are sown on my path as thousands of little real demands, like the signs which order us to keep off the grass."[39]

But Sartre has an explanation for this experiential datum which undercuts the need to attribute objective existence to the experienced values. His explanation is that it is my *projects* which cause values to "spring up like partridges"[40] in my experience. Thus, to return to a previous example, it is because I have freely chosen the project of being an obedient worker that I immediately experience the ringing of my alarm clock as a demand—as an indication of the value-imperative that I *must* get up and go to work. Similarly, it is only in the context of this project that I experience my boss's commands as imperatives which cannot be ignored. Were I to rearrange my priorities, so that the possibilities of promotion or firing were of little concern to me, the ringing of my alarm clock and the orders of my boss would lose a good deal of their urgency.

Moreover, as soon as I recognize the possibility of changing my project, as soon as I hold my project at a distance from myself in order to analyze it,

> I discover myself suddenly as the one who gives its meaning to the alarm clock, the one who by a signboard forbids himself to walk on a flower bed or on the lawn, the one from whom the boss's order borrows its urgency, the one who decides the interest of the book which he is writing, the one finally who makes the values exist in order to determine his action by their demands.[41]

It is also important to realize that I have many projects, that these projects are hierarchically related to one another, and that values arise from these different projects in different ways. Thus, if I have chosen the project of being an obedient worker, the *value* of this project might appear as a result of my more fundamental project of rising to the top of the company; the value of *this* project, in turn, might be a manifestation of my still *more* fundamental project of acquiring wealth and prestige, etc.

To summarize the argument: values can arise only against the background of a project; and this project can arise only through the free activity of a consciousness. Therefore, values have only a "subjective," in the sense of "consciousness-dependent," reality.

2.3.3.1   Criticism of the argument from the hierarchy of projects

I have three comments. First, it should be noted that the present argument is not really a positive argument *for* the subjectivity of values at all. Rather, it is a defense of the *possibility* of a subjectivist account of value experience against an objection which would seem entirely to rule out all such accounts. But notice that Sartre does not really attempt to *prove* here that his account of our value experience is right, and that the objectivist's account is wrong. He is content merely to show that his theory is *compatible* even with those data of our experience which most strongly suggest an objectivist interpretation. The objectivist's account, however, is of course also compatible with these data. Thus, since Sartre does not here give any reason for supposing that his interpretation of the data, as opposed to that of the objectivist, is *correct,* it must be that he is here depending upon the success of his other arguments for the subjectivity of values. That is, since he is counting on having already made convincing arguments for the view that values have no objective existence, that they are "lacks" which come to being only through consciousness, the present argument is designed solely for those who are already convinced by these arguments, but who need a rebuttal to a particular counterargument. If we are not persuaded by Sartre's previous arguments, however, the present argument is not designed for, and has little chance of, converting us.

My second comment is that even if we grant that Sartre has provided a coherent subjectivist account of our experience of values, and an account which is plausible over a wide range of that experience, it seems to me that his account is not plausible with regard to the *entirety* of our value experience. Thus, while it is almost certainly true that my boss's orders and the ringing of my alarm clock have no objective value, and owe such value as they have to my free projects, which originate and sustain them, such an analysis seems woefully inadequate in explaining my experience of the value of truth, health, beauty, happiness, or, to return to an earlier example, my experience of George Brett being a better baseball player than Buddy Biancalana. At the very least, it is far from *clear* how Sartre's analysis could explain these value experiences.

Finally, even if it were true that all values arise as a result of free projects, this would only prove, and provide a detailed explanation of, the subjectivity of values. It would not establish ethical subjectivism. For, just as it is not a subjective question whether or not Pierre is in the café, or whether or not a given city has been destroyed, even though absence and destruction arise, for Sartre, only as a result of human projects, so might questions about values not be subjective in spite of *their* similar ontological status. After all, it would have been a simple (objective) *mistake* to regard Hiroshima on August 7, 1945 as having *not* been destroyed, even though destruction is (ontologically) subjective. Might it not similarly be a simple mistake to regard truth as having no value, and to regard all value as residing in lies, even if value is subjective?

2.3.4   *The Nonexistence of God*

In *EH*, which has the distinction, which I consider unfortunate, of being the most widely-read of all of Sartre's philosophical works, the principal reason given for the subjective status of values and of value-judgments is the nonexistence of God. On the basis of rather scanty argumentation, Sartre declares his opposition "to a certain type of secular moralism which seeks to suppress God at the least possible expense."[42] According to Sartre, this secular moralism holds that

> it is essential that certain values should be taken seriously; they must have an *à priori* existence ascribed to them. It must be considered obligatory *à priori* to be honest, not to lie, not to beat one's wife, to bring up children and so forth. . . . These values exist all the same, inscribed in an intelligible heaven although, of course, there is no God. In other words . . . nothing will be changed if God does not exist.[43]

Sartre answers that

> the existentialist, on the contrary, finds it extremely embarrassing that God does not exist, for there disappears with Him all possibility of finding values in an intelligible heaven. There can no longer be any good *à priori*, since there is no infinite and perfect consciousness to think it. It is nowhere written that "the good" exists, that one must be honest or must not lie, since we are now upon the plane where there are only men. Dostoevsky once wrote "if

God did not exist, everything would be permitted"; and that, for existential-ism, is the starting point. Everything is indeed permitted if God does not exist.[44]

2.3.4.1   Criticism of the argument from the nonexistence of God

It is difficult to take this argument seriously. For one thing, just a few pages after this stirring declaration that the nonexistence of God entails consequences of the greatest importance—just a few pages subsequent to his denunciation of the judgment that "nothing will be changed if God does not exist"—Sartre suddenly reverses himself and announces that "existentialism is not atheist in the sense that it would exhaust itself in demonstrations of the nonexistence of God. It declares, rather, that *even if God existed that would make no difference from its point of view.*"[45] Moreover, unlike many superficial contradictions in Sartre's work, this one does not, at least as far as I can see, lend itself to any kind of dialectical resolution. Rather, Sartre's incoherence on the subject of the implications of God's nonexistence is apparently real, owing, perhaps, if I may speak bluntly, to the uncharacteristic sloppiness of the work in which it appears.

This brings me to my second worry about this argument that the nonexistence of God entails ethical subjectivism, namely, that it appears only in *EH*, and, more specifically, that it is not mentioned at all in the much more extensive discussion in *BN*. There is every reason to accord less importance to a brief lecture, the aim of which is primarily popularization, and "which in any case is only a transi-tional work,"[46] than to a full-scale philosophic treatise which is intended as a major statement of its author's views. Moreover, in the case of *EH,* Sartre himself is on record as noting its inferior quality. For example, in an interview Sartre states that the lecture "always struck me as a serious error," that its great world-wide sales "bothered me, I have to admit," and that it "articulated ideas that were not quite clearly formulated yet."[47]

Finally, no matter what we take to be Sartre's teaching on the implications of God's nonexistence, it is clear, for essentially the reasons articulated by Socrates in the *Euthyphro,*[48] that no argument that God is required to supply a ground for morality can possibly succeed. Alasdair MacIntyre explains this clearly:

Suppose that a divine being, real or alleged, commands me to do something. I only ought to do what he commands if what he commands is right. But if I am in a position to judge for myself whether what he commands is right or not, then I have no need of the divine being to instruct me in what I ought to do. Inescapably, each of us is his own moral authority.[49]

Interestingly, Sartre himself argued this way in his posthumously published *War Diaries,* which were written prior to *EH,* in 1939 and 1940:

Dostoevsky used to write: 'If God does not exist, all is permitted.' That's the great error of transcendence. Whether God exists or does not exist, morality is an affair 'between men' and God has no right to poke his nose in. On the contrary, the existence of morality, far from proving God, keeps him at a distance.[50]

Thus, I submit that the question of the existence or nonexistence of God is simply irrelevant to the issues concerning the objectivity or subjectivity of values or of ethics. Let us move on, then, to consider one final Sartrean argument in support of ethical subjectivism.

2.3.5   Irresolvable Moral Dilemmas

Sartre's famous argument deserves to be quoted at length:

A pupil of mine . . . sought me out in the following circumstances. His father was quarrelling with his mother and was also inclined to be a "collaborator"; his elder brother had been killed in the German offensive of 1940 and this young man, with a sentiment somewhat primitive but generous, burned to avenge him. His mother was living alone with him, deeply afflicted by the semi-treason of his father and by the death of her eldest son, and her one consolation was in this young man. But he, at this moment, had the choice between going to England to join the Free French Forces or of staying near his mother and helping her to live. He fully realized that this woman lived only for him and that his disappearance—or perhaps his death—would plunge her into despair. He also realized that, concretely and in fact, every action he performed on his mother's behalf would be sure of effect in the sense of aiding her to live, whereas anything he did in order to go and fight would be an ambiguous action which might vanish like water into sand and serve no purpose. For instance, to set out for England he would have to wait indefinitely in a Spanish camp on the way through Spain; or, on arriving in England or in Algiers he might be put into an office to fill up forms. Consequently, he found himself confronted by two very different modes of action; the one concrete, immediate, but directed towards only one individual; and the other an action addressed to an end infinitely greater, a national collectivity, but for that very reason ambiguous—and it might be frustrated on the way. At the same time, he was hesitating between two kinds of morality; on the one side the morality of sympathy, of personal devotion and, on the other side, a morality of wider scope but of more debatable validity. He had to choose between those two. What could help him to choose? Could the Christian doctrine? No. Christian doctrine says: Act with charity, love your neighbour, deny yourself for others, choose the way which is hardest, and so forth. But which is the harder road? To whom does one owe the more brotherly love, the patriot or the mother? Which is the more useful aim, the general one of fighting in and for the whole community, or the precise aim of helping one particular person to live? Who can give an answer to that *à priori*? No one. Nor is it given in any ethical scripture. The Kantian ethic says, Never regard another as a means, but always as an end. Very well; if I remain with my mother, I shall be regarding her as the end and not as a means: but by the same token I am in danger of treating as means those who are fighting on my behalf; and the converse is also true, that if I go to the aid of the combatants I shall be treating them as the end at the risk of treating my mother as a means. . . . I had but one reply to make. You are free, therefore choose—that is to say, invent. No rule of general morality can show what you ought to do.[51]

What is the point of Sartre's story? The standard interpretation, I suppose, is that it represents a straightforward argument for ethical subjectivism based upon considerations of certain features of the phenomenon known as the "moral dilemma." For example, Sartre is apparently claiming that one feature of moral dilemmas is that in such situations *we do not know* what is the right thing to do— indeed that *no* one knows, and no system of ethics can tell us what is the right thing to do. Sartre seems to conclude from this that our lack of knowledge can only be explained on the assumption that there simply is no knowledge to be had; we do not know what is the right thing to do because there *is* no right thing to do, or perhaps, there is no right thing to do until we choose a certain course of action, at which point that action automatically *becomes* right— with moral rightness being understood as a function of individual human choice.

Next, Sartre seems to generalize from his analysis of moral dilemmas to conclusions about morality *per se*. More specifically, he apparently jumps from the (alleged) fact that there are certain situations (moral dilemmas) in which there is no single correct "thing to be done," to the conclusion that there are *no* situations in which there is a single correct thing to be done. Thus, he claims that morality, like art, has to do "with creation and invention," and adds that "we cannot decide *à priori* what it is that should be done."[52] Moreover, Sartre goes so far as to say, in explaining what it means to say that we invent values, that it amounts to "neither more nor less than this; that there is no sense in life *à priori*. Life is nothing until it is lived; but it is yours to make sense of, *and the value of it is nothing else but the sense that you choose.*"[53]

According to this interpretation, it seems to me that Sartre's argument contains two gratuitous and indefensible logical leaps: (1) the jump from the relatively uncontroversial premise that there are situations in which we do not *know* what is right to the conclusion that nothing (or, perhaps more accurately, anything and everything) really *is* right in these situations, and (2) the leap from the already controversial claim that there are situations in which there is no single objectively right thing to do to the even more controversial conclusion that this characterization applies to *all* situations. So far as I can see, Sartre simply does not offer anything in the way of argumentation or justification for these inferences.

Of course, Sartre's text is ambiguous enough to permit alternative interpretations which do not commit him to the drawing of these hasty inferences. For example, there are some indications that Sartre does not, or need not, insist upon (2), since, according to this interpretation, he does seem to regard certain very general moral principles as having objective validity. If so, it is not hard to imagine situations in which such general principles might point quite decisively in a singular direction. Or, even when this is not the case, and we are left with an irresolvable moral dilemma, it still might be the case that these principles could serve to define the situation and to delimit the *range* of possible morally permissible actions.

Textual evidence that this is indeed Sartre's view would include, minimally, the following: (a) his distinction between form and content, together with his apparent claim that it is only because formal principles are too abstract to be decisive in concrete situations that we must resort to choice and invention (e.g., "although the content of morality is variable, a certain form of this morality is universal. . . . Principles that are too abstract break down when we come to defining action. . . . The content is always concrete, and therefore unpredictable; it has always to be invented");[54] (b) his affirmation of the value of freedom (e.g., granted that the content of morality has always to be invented, "the one thing that counts, is to know whether the invention is made in the name of freedom . . .[55] Freedom . . . can have no other end and aim but itself . . . Freedom (is) the foundation of all values");[56] (c) his insistence on the negative value of bad faith or self-deception (e.g., "I define . . . self-deception as an error. Here one cannot avoid pronouncing a judgment of truth");[57] and (d) his endorsement of a peculiar kind of universalizability principle (e.g., "Nothing can be better for us unless it is better for all. . . . Our responsibility . . . concerns mankind as a whole. . . . If . . . I decide to marry and to have children, even though this decision proceeds simply from my situation, from my passion or my desire, I am thereby committing not only myself, but humanity as a whole, to the practice of monogamy").[58]

Similarly, one might be able to interpret Sartre as not even being committed to (1). That is, if one puts enough emphasis on Sartre's form/content distinction, one might be able to argue plausibly that his emphasis upon the need for invention stems, not from any claim that there are situations in which there is no one right act to be performed, but rather from the recognition merely that there are situations in which, for purely practical, technical reasons, it is impossible to determine which act truly is the right one, it being understood that in fact there *is* such a right act. Thus, Sartre might be thought to hold the position that in any situation there is a single act which, say, most promotes freedom, even though we are not always in a position to figure out which act this is. And this lack of knowledge on our part, the interpretation continues, creates a need for us to choose on some other, idiosyncratic and creative, basis.

As against this interpretation, however, it must be pointed out that there are also passages in which Sartre seems unwilling to admit even the most minimal objective foundation for individual moral choice (e.g., "I say that it is . . . a self-deception if I choose to declare that certain values are incumbent upon me; I am in contradiction with myself if I will these values and at the same time say that they impose themselves upon me").[59] Whether such passages are compatible with those quoted two paragraphs ago is, of course, another question, and one which I am content not to pursue here.

Finally, it might be argued that all of the preceding discussion misrepresents Sartre's thought by failing to focus on what is, for him, the most important feature of moral dilemmas. According to this interpretation, Sartre regards the most salient feature of such dilemmas not to be the mere *fact* of our lack of knowledge concerning how to resolve them, but rather the *reason* for this lack of knowledge—namely, that moral dilemmas present us with, in Arthur Danto's words, "equally binding but quite incompatible conclusions"[60] as to what we should do. The argument for ethical subjectivism would then simply be that "truths cannot conflict, but obligations can,"[61] indicating that obligations, and by extension, all the other aspects of morality, have nothing to do with truth. Or, alternatively, the argument might be that "*factual* premises (unlike *ethical* premises) cannot yield true but incompatible conclusions,"[62] indicating, once again, the radical distinction between facts and values which Sartre exploits in his arguments for ethical subjectivism.

At least two objections can be raised against this interpretation. First, concerning its value as an interpretation of Sartre, it must be emphasized that Sartre himself does not describe moral dilemmas as stemming from clashes between incompatible principles. Rather, as we have seen, he speaks of the difficulties in applying abstract moral principles to concrete situations, and of figuring out which of a multiplicity of possible actions would be most in keeping with some moral principle. Thus, while in his discussion of his student's dilemma Sartre considers both Christian and Kantian ethics, he does not attribute the dilemma to a *conflict* between these two ethical systems. Rather, he argues that Christian ethics are too vague to permit a Christian to arrive at the "correct" Christian answer, and that Kantian ethics are too vague to permit a Kantian to arrive at the "correct" Kantian answer. Thus, the interpretation at hand would appear not to be in keeping with what Sartre actually says.

Secondly, considering the interpretation as an argument on its own merits, irrespective of its accuracy as a representation of Sartre's views, I would argue that it is telling only against a certain "absolutist" conception of ethics—that is, against the view that morality consists of a set of commands and prohibitions (do X, do not do Y) which are to be applied rigidly and inflexibly in all situations. Thus, if I conceive of morality as telling me that I must *always* tell the truth and *always* prevent murder, it is possible that I might one day confront a situation which yields to me "equally binding but quite incompatible obligations." That is, I might one day find myself in a situation in which I can prevent a murder only by lying. To be sure, the existence (or perhaps only the possibility) of such a moral dilemma would prove that at least one of my two absolute principles must be wrong. It does not, however, prove that morality is beyond the sphere of truth and falsity, and that moral matters are fundamentally different than matters of fact. It does not, for example, have anything to say against objectivist ethical theories which are based upon *prima facie* moral rules, each of which is accorded a different weight to allow for a resolution of cases in which the rules conflict;[63] nor can it refute objectivist consequentialist ethical theories, that is, theories which hold that the ethical rightness or wrongness of any act is a function of the goodness or badness of the consequences of the act in question, so that "moral dilemmas" can at least in principle be resolved by calculating the consequences of the competing possible acts.[64] In short, the present argument is powerless to undermine any objectivist ethical theory which has built into it a decision procedure for resolving difficult cases. The belief that it does refute any and all allegedly objective ethical theories, and establish the truth of ethical subjectivism, apparently rests, therefore, on a confusion between ethical *objectivism* (defined in section 2.2.1) and ethical *absolutism* (defined above in the present paragraph). There is no evidence, so far as I am aware, that Sartre is guilty of this confusion.

2.3.5.1   Criticism of the argument from irresolvable moral dilemmas

So much for interpretation. Let us now take up the question of whether, or to what extent, Sartre's story really does support ethical subjectivism. More specifically, I want to point out two aspects of Sartre's story which, I think, actually indicate the limitations of ethical subjectivism, and, at the same time, dramatically underscore the difficulty in coherently applying a subjectivist position to situations, like that of Sartre's student, in which a person must make a serious moral choice.

The first aspect of Sartre's story that I want to discuss is the sense of relevance that it exhibits. Notice, first of all, that Sartre mentions certain facts pertaining to the student's situation while neglecting others. For example, "he refers to the relation between father and mother, the fact that the brother was killed, that the petitioner is the only son left, that the mother feels alone and needs him, that he might have difficulties in reaching England, etc."[65] Surely we can all agree that these are *relevant* facts. These are the sorts of facts— unlike, say, facts pertaining to the student's height, his tastes regarding French and English food, his opinions on the subject of architecture, the color of his mother's hair, recent fluctuations in the price of corn, the relative inaccessibility of competent dentists on the weekends, etc., etc.—which one must take note of in order to *understand*, let alone to resolve, the student's dilemma. Similarly, Sartre goes on to provide us with important information about the student's motives in considering various courses of action, and about the possible consequences of these courses of action, without ever bothering to dispense what we would regard as trivial or irrelevant information.

How is this to be explained? Remember that Sartre insists upon the strict adherence to a rigid distinction between facts and values. How, then, does he determine which facts are morally relevant and which are not? Is this determination to be accomplished simply through free invention? Surely this is wildly implausible. We would justifiably dismiss as ridiculous any attempt to describe the student's dilemma in any manner which would make preeminent such considerations as the student's height, the color of his mother's hair, etc., and we would surely reject as unsound any attempt to resolve the dilemma by appealing to the fact that these considerations point in one direction rather than another. Thus, it would seem that Sartre's own example, far from supporting a thoroughgoing ethical subjectivism, instead demonstrates one of the limits to subjectivism, namely, that subjectivism cannot be pushed so far as to make the relative moral relevance of facts solely a function of individual invention or choice.

This in turn at least suggests, moreover, that one's final decision concerning how to act in a given situation is not simply a matter of criterionless, creative invention, since it must, after all, be based upon an accurate assessment of the *relevant* facts. As Frondizi puts it, "it is not a question of deciding blindly, but of supporting (one's) decisions by valid reasons and being able to foresee consequences with due regard to relevant facts, intentions, and motives."[66]

Similar points can be made about the role of moral principles in Sartre's story. Sartre's discussion of the inability of Christian and Kantian ethics to solve the student's dilemma seems almost to imply that he regards the question of whether or not these general ethical theories are essentially correct to be utterly irrelevant. Indeed, this would be consistent with his fundamental subjectivist contention that "what moral principles one has depends on one's choices, and these, being not restricted by criteria of choice, can be of anything at all."[67] And yet, as MacIntyre persuasively argues,

> we are strongly inclined to say that if a man avowedly made it a moral principle that one ought always to walk about with one's hand on one's head we should find what he said unintelligible. If we discovered that he had a belief that doing this prevented some disease, or gave pleasure to himself or others, or was connected with some other recognizable human good, we should begin to understand. And this suggests strongly that the content of moral principles is not open for us to choose, just like that; that we are limited by the character of the concept of a good. . . . To admit this would involve . . . admitting . . . an objective moral order of some sort.[68]

Indeed, the nonarbitrariness of the morally relevant features of the situation and the nonarbitrariness of the moral principles which are relevant to that situation are intimately linked. In order to see this, let us now consider the second aspect of Sartre's story to which I wish to call attention—namely, the fact that only two of the student's many possible courses of action, joining the French resistance or else staying at home to care for his mother, are presented as being worthy of serious consideration. And yet, as A. Phillips Griffiths points out,

> there are plenty of other things he could do. He could learn tightrope walking or set up as an ice cream-vendor or enlarge his earlobes with brass rings. But

these are obviously of no importance, whereas looking after the old mother and joining the resistance are important. Why is Sartre's case serious and dramatic and the other suggestions frivolous and silly? Why does it matter what the young man does, to himself or to anyone? There can surely be no problem at all unless such things as joining the resistance (defending one's country) or looking after the old mother (kindness to a dependent) are morally relevant features of the situation—unless they are things which it is reasonable to consider in deciding what to do. And if there are morally relevant features in the situation, there are corresponding moral principles. If these principles are not correct . . . , then there is no problem, or at least not the same problem.[69]

Or again, consider the following statement by Sartre about his student: "Certainly we cannot say that this man, in choosing to remain with his mother—that is, in taking sentiment, personal devotion and concrete charity as his moral foundations—would be making an irresponsible choice, nor could we do so if he preferred the sacrifice of going away to England."[70] Perhaps so. But might not our judgment to this effect be rooted in our recognition that both of these acts, or perhaps, the different values which are realized by both of them, are *really good*? For, suppose that the student had mentioned as yet another possible course of action that of *murdering* his mother, or of defecting to the Nazis. Does anyone really think that Sartre would have nonetheless given the same reply: "You are free, therefore choose—that is to say, invent"?[71] Thus, even if Sartre is right in insisting that there are situations in which there is no "right" or "wrong" course of action, surely it would be an overstatement to deny that there are any "better" or "worse" choices.[72] Here again we seem to have encountered a limitation to ethical subjectivism. While there may indeed be room for, and even a *need* for, moral creativity and invention, it is not at all clear that we can invent just *anything* without meriting the accusation that we have made, in Sartre's words, "an irresponsible choice."

2.4 General Criticisms of Sartre's Ethical Subjectivism

Let us now conclude the present chapter by briefly discussing some general objections to Sartrean subjectivism—objections which are not tied to any particular one of his arguments for ethical subjectivism.

2.4.1   *The Moral Equivalence of All Free Actions*

A standard criticism of Sartre's ethical position is that it seems to lead to the absurd conclusion that *any* act, so long as it is done on the basis of a free choice, is morally right, or at least, that there can be no moral distinction between acts which are equally the result of free choices. Frondizi formulates the objection this way:

> A simple consideration of obviously immoral cases shows that our free choice or decision cannot turn a bad action into a good one. A man who beats his young children to make them work hard from sunrise to sunset so he can lend their earnings to the poor at high rates of interest, presents a clear case of immorality. Could the man's behavior be seen as good if we could irrefutably prove that he has freely chosen such a course of action? An immoral action might be freely chosen and still be immoral. I am sure Sartre would not deny the immorality of a case such as this; it is the weakness of his moral theory that I am criticizing, not his moral conscience. In other words, if it is sheer choice and not its content that counts, then all possibilities are equivalent and we end up in an ethics of mere chance.[73]

Or again, consider the words of Warnock: "If choosing freely for oneself is the highest value, the free choice to wear red socks is as valuable as the free choice to murder one's father or sacrifice oneself for one's friend. Such a belief is ridiculous."[74]

One possible way of defending Sartre against this objection would be to deny our critics' premise that the freedom with which a choice is made is for Sartre a *sufficient* condition of its moral rightness. That is, even if one concedes to the critics the point that Sartre does not admit to any values external to human choices by which such choices could be objectively judged, that he instead offers a moral theory which is concerned solely with the manner of making decisions, rather than with the specific choices themselves, and that it is a *necessary* condition of a morally right act that it issue from a free choice, it by no means follows that the freedom with which a choice is made is the *only* procedural issue with which Sartre is concerned, or that such freedom is a *sufficient* condition to guarantee the moral rightness of an act. Consider the following passage from *EH*:

> I can form judgments upon those who seek to hide from themselves the wholly voluntary nature of their existence and its complete freedom. Those who hide from this total freedom, in a guise of solemnity or with

deterministic excuses, I shall call cowards. Others, who try to show that their existence is necessary, when it is merely an accident of the appearance of the human race on earth—I shall call scum.[75]

Thus, in this passage, and generally when Sartre is discussing authenticity or purifying reflection, he seems to suggest that in order for a choice to be moral it must not only be a free choice, but it must also be a choice which is founded on a lucid understanding of one's situation, and on an uncowardly acceptance of the responsibility for the consequences of one's actions. Such a criterion of moral rightness is sufficient to distinguish at least *some* free choices from others in terms of their respective moral worth, and thus to refute, or at least to mitigate, the present objection.

2.4.2   *The Authentic Torturer Problem*

For some critics, however, this move creates as many problems as it solves. According to these critics, Sartre must be read as saying that as long as we confront our choices honestly and acknowledge our responsibility for what we choose, and for the consequences of our action, without resorting to deterministic excuses, we are entirely above any possible reproach on the ethical plane.

The obvious difficulty with this ethic is that it leaves us with no legitimate, objective grounds for condemning the actions of, for example, the torturer who offers no excuse for his actions, and who accepts full responsibility for them.[76] A torturer who candidly says, "I have freely chosen to kidnap and torture you, and I take full responsibility for my choice," is apparently above criticism, according to Sartre's theory. To be sure, we can dislike, protest against, impede, punish, or even *kill* such a torturer, and, provided that our choice to do so is free, authentic, lucid, etc., this choice, too, is morally above reproach. The difficulty with Sartre's theory, then, is that it fails to find any moral basis for *distinguishing* between the authentic torturer's pro-torture choices and our anti-torture choices, provided that all of these choices equally meet Sartre's decision-procedural criteria of freedom and authenticity.

A representative statement of this objection, and of the interpretation of Sartre which underlies it, is provided by James Collins:

What authenticates an individual's act of choice, so that it becomes a humane act? Sartre offers two criteria: that it be done with perfect lucidity, and that it involve an acceptance of responsibility. . . .If these conditions are fulfilled, then the act is unconditionally free, value-creative, and authentic or good. . . . But this is no guarantee that the choice will be a good one. . . . Lucidity is . . . not a sufficient condition of good action. Malicious action may . . . be performed on the basis of unblinking honesty. . . . Taken by itself, an awareness of how man stands in existence is too formal a rule to prove useful in resolving particular problems of conduct. It is so hospitable that it is ready to authenticate any act, just as long as the self takes full responsibility for performing the act. Since diametrically opposed plans of action can be espoused by individuals who are equally convinced that no other moral law than their own intention exists, this criterion does not prove adequate for determining concrete choices or settling conflicts.[77]

T. Z. Lavine presents the objection even more forcefully:

A . . . criticism of Sartre's existentialist ethics is that since the only rule it provides me with is the rule to avoid self-deception, and to act authentically, then I have done all that is required of me so long as I follow this rule, and avoid bad faith, and acknowledge that I alone freely choose what I do and am responsible. But then anything that I freely choose to do meets the requirements of authenticity: one freely chosen act is as good as another, and there is no way of discriminating among my freely chosen acts. . . . [Thus] Sartre's French students who joined the underground resistance movement against the Nazis had no more justification than the German students of Heidegger who joined the Nazi Party to fight in Hitler's army for the values of fascism. One is no more justified than the other because neither has any justification; to join the French resistance forces or Nazi army are equivalent acts if freely chosen. "Every time a man chooses his engagement and projects in all sincerity and lucidity, whatever this choice may be, it is impossible to prefer another to it." And if I freely, in all sincerity and lucidity, choose to murder my enemy?[78]

2.4.3 *The Groundlessness of the Value of Authenticity*

But there is worse to follow. Not only does the authenticity with which an action is performed fail to serve as an adequate criterion for ruling out as moral actions certain actions which are in fact (allegedly) obviously *immoral,* but there is also some question as to whether Sartre is entitled, within the confines of his ontological analysis, to insist on even this minimal criterion for distinguishing right and wrong actions. For, as Bernstein argues,

Sartre, who throughout his career has in his actions affirmed the value of reflective lucidity as the highest value, has provided an ontological analysis that undermines this value. If all values are ultimately unjustifiable, then there is no reason to suppose that it is any better or more valuable to be lucid than to be involved in self-deception. The individual in bad faith chooses his being—just as the individual who attempts to escape from bad faith. Both choices are "grounded" in one's nothingness. Both fundamental projects are ultimately gratuitous. There is no reason to value one rather than the other: this is Sartre's own grand conclusion.[79]

2.4.4   The Absurdity of Total Subjectivism

Thus, if Bernstein is right (and his interpretation does indeed appear to be the predominant one), Sartre's theory is unable to find even the most minimal of criteria for distinguishing the greater or lesser moral worth of different human actions. That is, if it is truly Sartre's view that values are *created* by the free choices and free actions of individual human beings, and have no status apart from their being so created, then whatever is freely chosen or brought into being by a free action is valuable, and there are no possible grounds for determining what individuals *should* choose in any given situation. But this entails the absurd conclusion that there is no reason why anyone should not choose hate over love, war over peace, enmity over brotherhood, sorrow over joy, sickness over health, hunger over nourishment, and death over life. To be sure, as a matter of empirical fact, most people do *not* choose hate over love, war over peace, etc., or at least, they do not claim that the first member of each of these pairs is *preferable* to the second member—quite the opposite. Still, the fact remains that on Sartre's view, at least under the present interpretation, *any* choice or preference is as justified as any other; all are equally *groundless*. As Bernstein puts it,

> if we hold fast to Sartre's ontological analysis, we can never justify any criteria, we can never ultimately say that one thing is more valuable than another. . . . If we take Sartre literally, we simply have no ultimate reason for valuing or preferring one [thing] rather than [an] other. . . . The consequence of Sartre's analysis of human reality is not only despair, but nihilism in the coldly technical sense. There never is nor can be any basic reason or justification for one value, end, choice, or action rather than another.[80]

2.4.5   *The Coefficient of Adversity in Our Value Experience*

A related objection to Sartre's subjectivism relies upon his own very fruitful concept of coefficient of adversity. As we recall, Sartre argues that my situation, without ever threatening my ontological freedom, nonetheless never presents itself as *totally* indeterminate with regard to my interpretation of it. Rather, there is a certain coefficient of adversity with regard to the interpretation of *any* situation. Thus, to reprise a point made previously, while my freedom in relation to a particular crag is manifested in my ability to regard it as an obstacle to be cleared away, as an aid to be climbed, or as a beautiful or ugly object, this freedom is not threatened by the fact that I cannot regard it as a poached egg which is singing an aria. If I were able so to regard it, I would be "plunged in a world like that of a dream in which the possible is no longer in any way distinguished from the real."[81] The fact that I cannot so regard it is part of the coefficient of adversity of the crag.

What has all of this to do with ethics? Let us consider another example. Suppose you see some children pour gasoline on a cat and ignite it.[82] Certainly there is a coefficient of adversity concerning your interpretation of "the facts" of the case. You simply are not free, given that you are sane and in possession of a certain minimal amount of knowledge, to see the incident as one in which adults are tossing a rhinoceros into a swimming pool. But is it accurate, or even plausible, to assert that this coefficient of adversity applies only to "the facts" of the case, and not to considerations of value? Does the situation present itself to us indifferently with respect to whether we regard it as "good," "bad," or "neutral" in value? The situation certainly does *not* present itself to us indifferently with respect to whether we consider it as exemplifying kindness or cruelty, benevolence or malevolence, or as to whether or not it is an instance of sadism and torture. To be sure, one might insist that this says nothing about the goodness or badness of the act in question, because one would still have to add such judgments as that kindness is better than cruelty, that benevolence is better than malevolence, and that sadism and torture are bad, in order to yield the judgment that the torching of the cat is bad. But is there no coefficient of adversity with regard to our evaluation of kindness in comparison to cruelty, benevolence in comparison to malevolence, etc.? Such a claim would appear to involve the denial of some of the most fundamental givens of our experience. Moreover, a coefficient of adversity with regard to our experience of values would seem no more to threaten our *freedom* in relation to values than does a coefficient of adversity with regard to "purely factual" matters.[83] Thus, there can be no argument that our *freedom* in relation to values entails that our experience of values must present itself as *totally* indeterminate with regard to our interpretation of, and judgment concerning, that experience.

2.4.6 *Responsibility*

Let us now consider the phenomenon of responsibility, and Sartre's account of it, in order to see if these are compatible with his ethical subjectivism.

Sartre's theory of responsibility is, characteristically, extreme. He speaks of "absolute responsibility,"[84] and argues that "man . . . is responsible for the world and for himself as a way of being . . . [He] carries the weight of the whole world on his shoulders."[85] Leaving aside the many difficulties in understanding what is meant by such an "absolute" responsibility[86]—difficulties which are essentially parallel to those involved in understanding the meaning of an absolute *freedom*—I wish to focus on merely one feature of Sartre's theory, namely the fact that it contains a clearly moralistic dimension. To be sure, in *BN* Sartre is content to define "responsibility" in relatively value-free terms as "consciousness (of) being the incontestable author of an event or of an object."[87] Nonetheless, in that work, and still more in the works following it, Sartre seems to be especially concerned with the ethical aspects of responsibility, with the concept of responsibility being increasingly understood as something like "moral accountability." Thus, when Sartre attempts to refute what he regards as overly narrow conceptions of responsibility, such as those which regard us as responsible only for what we have directly done, rather than for what we have merely allowed to happen, it is quite clear that part of his purpose is to show that when what we allow to happen is *bad,* then not only are we responsible for this badness, but the fact that we are responsible for it also means that we are *guilty* in the face of it, that we are *to blame* for it. Consider, for example, his attack on the pacifist views of Albert Camus concerning the French-Algerian war:

> A fine sight they are too, the believers in non-violence, saying that they are neither executioners nor victims. Very well then; if you're not victims when the government which you've voted for, when the army in which your younger brothers are serving without hesitation or remorse have undertaken race murder, you are, without a shadow of doubt, executioners.[88]

Or again, consider the following passage from Sartre's lecture, "The Responsibility of the Writer":

> If . . . a writer has chosen to be silent on one aspect of the world, we have the right to ask him: why have you spoken of this rather than that? And since you speak in order to make a change, since there is no other way you can speak, why do you want to change this rather than that? Why do you want to alter the way in which postage stamps are made rather than the way in which Jews are treated in an antisemitic country? And the other way around. He must therefore always answer the following questions: What do you want to change? Why this rather than that?[89]

There can be little doubt that in these two passages Sartre is relying upon the moral dimension of the concept of responsibility. Clearly, he is saying that Camus and the pacifists are *morally accountable* for what is done in their name by their government and its army, and that the writer, likewise, is *morally accountable* for his choice of subject matter. But this seems to make sense only on the assumption that there are in each situation better and worse acts which we can choose to perform, and that the betterness and worseness of these acts is not simply determined by actual choice of which act to perform. For if all acts were morally equivalent, or if acts were made right simply by their being chosen, it would make no sense to say that I am morally accountable for my choice of action—I could always justify my choice by pointing out that no other choice could possibly have been better, or that my choice of a given action *made* that action right. We could only say that I did this, and could have done that—we could not say that I *should* have done that, and am *to blame* for not having done so. Surely Sartre admits this, at least implicitly, in the two passages quoted above. Who can doubt that Sartre is saying that Camus and the pacifists are *to blame* for what is done in their name, and that the writer who is more concerned with the manufacturing of postage stamps than with the treatment of Jews in an antisemitic country has the *wrong* priorities (or, if this is too strong, at least that the reverse order of priorities would be *better*)?

But can Sartre, as an ethical subjectivist, possibly claim that in order to be responsible there are certain specific things that we must do—that there are acts which it would be "irresponsible" for us not to do? After all, while in the two passages cited above this seems to be his *intent,* he comes just short of saying it explicitly. He tells us that Camus and the pacifists are "executioners," but he does not add that it is *wrong* to be an executioner; he tells us that whether the writer concerns himself with postage stamps or with the treatment of Jews, we can ask him why he chooses as he does— but Sartre does not tell us what the writer *should* choose, or even that there *is* a "right" choice. Are there, then, any passages in which Sartre does use the word "responsibility" in this sense which entails that one morally *should* do one thing rather than another?

There are. Consider the following passage:

> The responsibility of the writer, today, is very clear: He must construct a positive theory of liberation and freedom. He must put himself in every instance in the position of condemning violence from the point of view of the members of the oppressed classes. And he must establish a true relationship between ends and means. He must refuse forthwith, in the name of freedom—which will not, of course, prevent anything—to sanction any means of violence to establish or sustain an order. He must, finally, give his thoughts without respite, day in, day out, to the problem of the end and the means; or, again, the problem of the relationship of ethics and politics.[90]

But *why* must the writer do these things? Surely the fact that Sartre says so, or that these imperatives reflect Sartre's value-judgments, is insufficient, without some kind of appeal to the *correctness* of what Sartre is saying, and of the value-judgments which underlie it. For otherwise how could Sartre possibly reply to the writer who would say: "I understand what it is that you are urging me to do, Sartre, but I will not do it. While I fully realize that I *could* do as you urge, I choose not to, for I have other value commitments." Surely Sartre does not intend his description of the writer's responsibility to be open to *this* simple kind of rejection. Surely he regards his description as a *true* description of the writer's responsibility, the rejection of which would constitute an *error.*

That Sartre is indeed *serious* in his judgments about responsibility, that he is gripped by "the spirit of seriousness" that he so heartily condemned in *BN*,[91] is evident in nearly all of his statements on the subject, of which the following three will serve as illustrations:

> When the Germans had an oppressive Nazi government, it was obviously the duty of anti-Nazi Germans to protest, to denounce, and to resist.[92]

> This crime (the American war effort in Vietnam), carried out every day before the eyes of the world, renders all who do not denounce it accomplices of those who commit it.[93]

> There is not one of us who is not totally guilty and even criminal; the Jewish blood that the Nazis shed falls on all our heads.[94]

But why should I not be in *favor* of the Nazis, and of the extermination of Vietnamese and Jews? After all, I am free—why should I not, then, "choose—that is to say, invent"? And, if responsibility truly means only "consciousness (of) being the incontestable author of an event or of an object," why cannot I *responsibly* choose to exterminate Vietnamese and Jews, provided that I have the requisite consciousness? Sartre apparently has no adequate answer to this question on the theoretical plane. Rather, I suggest that the evidence indicates, both in regard to his value-judgments concerning responsibility, and in regard to his descriptions of the nature of responsibility, that he is relying upon an implicit appeal to "the objectivity of ethics." As Alvin Plantinga puts it, "Sartre is surreptitiously holding on to the meaning of responsibility appropriate to a world in which there are objective values which I may decide to realize or to reject. But if there is no value exterior to choice, then this notion of responsibility is no longer appropriate or even meaningful."[95] In order to bolster this claim, and to clarify its meaning, let us now take up Sartre's related concept of "anguish."

2.4.7 Anguish

"It is in anguish that man gets the consciousness of his freedom," says Sartre.[96] But does consciousness of one's freedom *always* issue in anguish? And does the phenomenon of anguish reveal to us anything *else* besides our freedom? Let us look at these two questions in turn.

First of all, it is evident that not every consciousness of one's freedom is experienced as anguish. Sartre himself admits this in his response to a questioner following his *EH* lecture: "Obviously I do not mean that whenever I choose between a millefeuille and a chocolate éclair, I choose in anguish."[97] But why not? Is it not because we recognize that there is no *right* or *wrong* choice here, or, at the very least, that insofar as it makes sense at all to speak of the difference between a right or wrong choice here, this difference is *trivial* and *insignificant*? Indeed, why should anyone feel anguish at the prospect of having to make a choice unless it *matters* a good deal whether or not I make the *right* choice, or at least, whether or not I make a relatively *good* choice?

Sartre's subjectivist ethical position, however, seems to undermine the very idea of a "right" choice, or even a "good" choice. He says, for example, that *every* choice is "absurd." "It is absurd in this sense—that the choice is that by which all foundations and all reasons come into being, that by which the very notion of the absurd receives a meaning. It is absurd as being beyond all reasons."[98] As Plantinga points out, however, this seems to imply that

> every choice defines both value and rationality. But if this is so, then it is impossible to make a wrong choice . . . As Sartre constantly repeats, my choice defines reality; prior to my choice there is no right or wrong. But then my choice, in defining the right, can never be mistaken. *Whatever* I choose is right by definition . . . For Sartre, *every* action, *every* choice, is necessarily right. But morality presupposes that there is . . . something morally at stake when I choose or act; there is the possibility of right and wrong, better or worse. For Sartre these distinctions disappear; the notion of a wrong action is for him analytically impossible. And if every actual action is right by definition, there can be no distinction between right and wrong . . . This doctrine makes negative moral judgments impossible and positive ones otiose. And thereby the notions of responsibility and anguish lose their point.[99]

Plantinga illustrates his point by discussing one of Sartre's own examples.

> Sartre tells us of a military commander who has decided to send men on a mission that may cost them their lives. The man is anguished. But why should he be? If we think of the preservation of human life as a value prior to any choice on our part, we can understand his anguish—he is forced to choose a positive disvalue. But if his very choice constitutes value, then no matter what he chooses, he will be right. Why then be anguished?[100]

Thus, it would appear that consciousness of one's freedom is *not* sufficient to bring about anguish; rather, if there is to be anguish, there must also be present the sense that the exercise of that freedom *matters*—that it makes a big difference whether or not I make a *good* choice. This raises our second question. Does the phenomenon of anguish reveal to us anything *else* besides our freedom? Does it, more specifically, reveal to us a lived sense that certain choices are "objectively" better than others, as the preceding discussion would indicate it should?

This question, since it inquires exclusively about what is given in lived experience, needs to be answered on the plane of descriptive phenomenology. Fortunately, Sartre has given us numerous descriptions of anguished persons—the military commander cited by Plantinga, the gambler, the man on the precipice, etc.—in the course of his various discussions of the concept. But all of these examples of anguish, as Jules Gleicher points out,

> seem not only to show the reflective apprehension of freedom, but also to imply an ethical context as a necessary precondition and constitutive element of anguish. The gambler feels anguish not only because he realizes his resolution's fragility, but also because he senses both its importance and its correctness. Without these latter elements, indeed, anguish seems to be absurd, not worth itself . . . Sartre's ethically relativistic account of these anguished moments slights at least half of their phenomenality, and so flies in the face of his general principle, that "appearance lays claim to being."[101]

Thus, the phenomenon of anguish, like that of responsibility, seems to imply the objectivity of ethics.

2.4.8 Repentance

Let us consider one final phenomenon, that of repentance. Suppose that I must choose between two opposed courses of action, and I freely choose one. Later on, when faced with the same choices, and with all relevant facts remaining the same, I choose the other course of action. What, then, is my attitude toward my earlier choice?

Here it seems to me that there are distinctions which Sartre is not able satisfactorily to explain. Suppose, for example, that while I always used to choose vanilla ice cream, I now always choose chocolate. What is my attitude likely to be toward my prior choices? I would probably not regard them as *mistakes*; rather, I would be inclined to think that "I've changed my mind," or that my tastes have changed. Suppose, on the other hand, that while I always used to support the policy of apartheid, I now oppose it. Here it is much more likely that I would regard my prior choice as having been a horrible mistake, and would find myself having to endure a painful experience of repentance.

How is this discrepancy to be explained? The obvious answer, and indeed the one that is suggested by experience, is that the former "conversion" has to do with a simple matter of taste—a "subjective" matter, while the latter conversion is a moral conversion from an objectively wrong position to an objectively right, or at least *better,* one. On Sartre's theory, on the other hand, *all* choices are based upon a "groundless," "unjustifiable," "subjective," fundamental choice, and all criteria for distinguishing right from wrong choices must stem from that fundamental choice. Thus, if I convert from a fundamental project in which it is right to support apartheid to a fundamental project in which it is right to oppose it, this conversion is exactly like the conversion from the choice of vanilla ice cream to the choice of chocolate—in both instances, there are no criteria or standards external to the choices which could legislate between them. But our experience of the apartheid conversion, unlike that of the ice cream conversion, is that the conversion itself is motivated by a *recognition,* rather than by a *choice,* of certain criteria of rightness and wrongness by reference to which I *should* choose one thing rather than another. Sartre, so far as I can see, can neither adequately account for this experience, nor for its difference from the experience involved in changing ice cream preferences. To that extent, his theory flies in the face of the data of experience.

2.5 Conclusion

Let us review the ground that we have covered in this chapter. We have seen, first of all, that Sartre advances a somewhat eccentric conception of values as "lacks" which do not exist, and defends, largely on the basis of this conception, a rather extreme form of ethical subjectivism. In response to Sartre's reasoning, I have drawn a distinction between Sartre's ontological theory concerning the status of values (the subjectivity of values) and his meta-ethical theory concerning the status of value-judgments (ethical subjectivism), and found that the latter, contra Sartre, is in no way entailed by the former. Next we examined five of Sartre's specific arguments for ethical subjectivism, and subjected each of them to criticism. Finally, we attempted to complement our criticism of Sartre's specific arguments for ethical subjectivism by providing eight additional objections to his general position.

Perhaps the reader will be annoyed by the results of this chapter, however, for they would seem to frustrate the overall aim of this work, which is to understand, and to evaluate, Sartre's claim that freedom is the highest value. For if Sartre's theory of value is inadequate, why should we be particularly interested in his analysis of *freedom* as a value? And if Sartre's meta-ethical theory entails that all value-judgments are "absurd," "groundless," "unjustifiable," "subjective," etc., why should we be particularly interested in his judgment that freedom is the highest value? To be sure, if we are fascinated by Sartre the man, we will of course be interested in these matters; but if we are concerned to discover ethical *truths* regarding what is or is not of value, or regarding what is *most* valuable, it would seem that Sartre cannot help us, for it is apparently his view that no such truths can possibly be found. All he can offer us is his *judgment* that freedom is the highest value, but this judgment, according to Sartre's own analysis, is "unjustifiable." Why, then, should it interest us? In the next chapter—the final one—I shall attempt to answer this question.

CHAPTER 3
Freedom As A Value

3.1 Introduction

The goal of this chapter, and of this book as a whole, is to understand, and to evaluate, Sartre's claim that freedom is the highest value. But the results of the preceding chapter, which revealed to us both the radicalism and the untenability of Sartre's ethical subjectivism, now threaten to rob this goal of its interest. How, then, should we proceed?

The first point to be made, as a corrective to the impression left by the preceding chapter, is that Sartre's ethical subjectivism does not represent his only, or even his final, word on the subject of ethics. Rather, as I have hinted, there are many passages, to be found in all periods of Sartre's writing, and usually in connection with the value of freedom, in which he seems to embrace an objectivist position. Thus, we will begin the present chapter with an examination of this objectivist strain in Sartre's thinking.

Following my exposition of Sartre's objectivism, I will consider some objections to it, concentrating especially on criticisms of its foundations. This will lead us to a consideration of intuition, and of its role and legitimacy in ethical reasoning.

Finally, I will ask whether the subjectivist and objectivist strains in Sartre's thinking, particularly in connection with the value of freedom, are reconcilable. In answering this question I will try to show: (1) that they *are* reconcilable, (2) that their reconciliation reveals to us Sartre's most significant contribution to ethics, and (3) that this contribution consists in his explanation of, and his defense of, the thesis that freedom is the highest, or most fundamental, value.

3.2   Sartre's Ethical Objectivism

Let us begin with Sartre's early, "phenomenological," period, in which the objectivity of values is held to be a straightforward consequence of Husserl's doctrine of intentionality:

> All at once hatred, love, fear, sympathy—all these famous "subjective" reactions which were floating in the malodorous brine of the mind—are pulled out. They are merely ways of discovering the world. It is things which abruptly unveil themselves to us as hateful, sympathetic, horrible, lovable. Being dreadful is a *property* of this Japanese mask, an inexhaustible and irreducible property which constitutes its very nature—and not the sum of our subjective reactions to a piece of sculptured wood. Husserl has restored to things their horror and their charm.[1]

Similarly, in a 1939 entry from his posthumously published *War Diaries,* Sartre explicitly expresses his agreement with the value objectivism of the phenomenologist Max Scheler:

> Scheler made me understand that there existed *values* . . . (I) understood that there existed specific natures, equipped with an existence as of right, and called values; . . . (I) understood that these values, whether proclaimed or not, regulated each of my acts and judgments, and that by their nature they 'ought to be'.[2]

The posthumous publication of this passage underscores the legitimacy of Spiegelberg's complaint that "in his apodictic assertions about the subjectivity of all values in *Being and*

Nothingness, [Sartre] ignored (except for a few insignificant references) the phenomenology of value of Max Scheler and Nicolai Hartmann, which must have been accessible to him."[3]

Of course, the value on behalf of which Sartre most often issues objectivist claims is that of freedom. We shall examine these claims shortly. But first, it must be pointed out that freedom is not the only value on behalf of which Sartre is willing to make such claims. Thus, in his essay on "The Historical Process," Sartre exclaims, "I believe precisely that an autonomous morality exists. I think we have definite obligations, including (among others) the obligation to tell . . . the truth."[4] And again, much later, in his "Self- Portrait at Seventy," Sartre insists that he "can *demonstrate* the reasons for refusing this society, I can *show* that it is immoral— that it is made not for people but for profit and that therefore it must be radically changed."[5] Finally, in a revealing autobiographical account of the experiences which led to his dissatisfaction with subjectivism, Sartre comments: "What makes our position original, I believe, is that the war and the occupation, by turning us into a world in a state of fusion, perforce *made us rediscover the absolute at the heart of relativity* itself."[6] Then, in opposition to what Sartre saw as the prevailing view at the time—a view which he characterized as "a sort of moral relativism" in which "Evil was not a very serious matter"—he adds, "We have been taught to take it seriously . . . [since] we lived in a time when torture was a daily fact."[7]

This attack on moral relativism—this insistence that morality is an "absolute at the heart of relativity"—is repeated by Sartre more than twenty years later during a conversation with Simone de Beauvoir. There he remarks, "in the moral field I've retained one . . . thing . . . , and that is Good and Evil as absolutes"; and he proceeds to reject "a certain relativism," which regards "morals as being variable according to the point on the earth's surface at which they are seen."[8] De Beauvoir then quotes as an example of such relativism Dostoevsky's remark, "If God does not exist, everything is allowed," and asks, "You don't think that, do you?" Sartre begins his reply by stating that "in one way I clearly see what he means, and abstractly it's true." But then, without mentioning that he had given Dostoevsky's comment unqualified and enthusiastic support in *EH,* calling it the very "starting point" for existentialism, Sartre quickly adds that "in another [way] I clearly see that killing a man is wrong. Is directly, absolutely wrong . . . It might be said that I look upon man's morals and moral activity as an absolute in the midst of the relative."[9]

Just what is the nature of this "absolute" morality that Sartre is here endorsing? De Beauvoir, too, is interested in this question, and asks Sartre, "broadly speaking, how would you define what you call Good and what you call Evil?" Sartre replies: "Essentially, the Good is that which is useful to human freedom, that which allows it to give their full value to objects it has realized. Evil is that which is harmful to human freedom, that which holds men out as not being free and which, for example, creates the determinism of the sociologists of a certain period."[10]

On this point, the identification of freedom as the good, or at least as the greatest good, Sartre has demonstrated more consistency from his earliest writings to his later ones than he has, perhaps, with respect to any other issue. Thus, in *BN* he urges freedom "to take itself for a value as the source of all value."[11] Again, in *EH* he declares that "freedom, in respect of concrete circumstances, can have no other end and aim but itself"; he asserts that the authentic individual "can will only one thing, and that is freedom as the foundation of all values"; and he urges us to "will freedom for freedom's sake, in and through particular circumstances."[12] Again, in the posthumously published *Cahiers pour une morale,* he calls for an "ordered classification of values" which would lead to freedom as the highest value.[13] Again, in *Search for a Method,* in *CDR,* and in countless smaller works and interviews from the same period and subsequently, Sartre maintains that the highest goal to which human beings can currently aspire is the bringing into existence of a "reign of freedom" in which there would be *"for everyone* a margin of *real* freedom beyond the production of life."[14] Finally, de Beauvoir's *The Ethics of Ambiguity,* which she bases on the ontology of *BN,* abounds in such remarks as "to will oneself moral and to will oneself free are one and the same decision," and "the man who seeks to justify his life must want freedom itself absolutely and above everything else."[15]

3.2.1   *Freedom and Needs*

An obvious objection to this freedom-ethic is that it seems overly vague, formal, and lacking in specific content. Surely the imperative "promote freedom" is insufficient to give us any real guidance in complex or difficult situations. Thus, for example, Frondizi complains of the "emptiness" of Sartre's freedom-value, especially when it is not buttressed by other values which would give it content and meaning: "Freedom for what? one may ask reasonably."[16] Similarly, Frederick A. Olafson sees the difficulty as stemming from Sartre's "downgrading of 'empirical' desires and goals," and instead calls for the recognition of "the quite ordinary needs and desires that we all share."[17]

But is Sartre really all that oblivious to ordinary, "empirical," human needs? It would seem not. Certainly this charge cannot be sustained with regard to his later philosophy, especially *CDR,* in which the concept of "need" is a central and serious concern. And as for Sartre's early philosophy, while it is true that it does not deal directly with the concept of need, the claim that this philosophy is hostile to, or incompatible with, such a concept, can only stem from a failure to appreciate what Sartre has to say in his early works about facticity and the human condition. After all, Sartre in *BN* says such things as that "certain original structures are invariable and in each For-itself constitute human-reality."[18] Why should not some of these structures be, or at least *lead* to, structures of need? Indeed, given Sartre's extensive discussion of facticity, in which he emphasizes the external conditions which prevent me, or at least hinder me, from getting what I want, it is only natural that we would expect Sartre to be sensitive to the fact that these limitations can interfere with the fulfillment of my *needs.* And, in view of his acknowledgement of a "universal human condition," we would expect him to recognize some commonality between *my* needs and those of all other human beings. This is, of course, precisely what we do find, as Sartre repeatedly, even in his relatively early works, explains his notion of the human condition by reference to universal human needs.[19]

It is clear, moreover, that Sartre's concern for human needs is largely moral in character, especially in his later works. Thus, in one passage he explains why "morality is indispensible" by appealing to the simple fact that "indeed men have precise needs and the external situation does not allow them to realize these needs." Sartre presents what he takes to be the ethical implications of this situation with admirable clarity and succinctness: "what I have is yours, and what you have is mine, and if I am in need, you give to me, and if you are in need, I give to you. That is the future of morality."[20]

But now a new problem emerges. How is all of this to be reconciled with Sartre's oft-stated claim that *freedom* is the highest value? Is not Sartre here simply replacing his freedom-ethic with an ethic based upon fulfilling human needs? Or is there perhaps a *connection* between the goal of promoting freedom and that of fulfilling human needs?

Let us take up this last suggestion in some detail, beginning with a consideration of the following passage from Sartre:

> Such is man as we conceive him: a total man. Totally committed and totally free. However, it is this free man who must be *delivered*, by widening his possibilities of choice. In certain situations, there is only room for one alternative, one term of which is death. It must be so that man can choose life, in any circumstances.[21]

Three points must be noted about this passage. First, it contains yet another example of the distinction, which I have so much emphasized, between ontological freedom (man is "totally" free) and practical freedom (human freedom can and should be "widened" by increasing one's "possibilities of choice"). Secondly, it invokes *quantitative* criteria in evaluating one's freedom in a situation (immediately following the reference to the possibility of increasing the possibilities of choice, Sartre speaks disparagingly of situations in which "there is only room for *one* alternative," implying that the presence of a greater number of alternatives would enhance one's freedom). Finally, the passage also invokes *qualitative* criteria in evaluating practical freedom (Sartre speaks disparagingly of situations in which one can only choose *death,* and demands that one must always be able to choose life—implying that it is not only the *number* of alternatives which counts toward enhancing freedom, but also the quality of their content. Thus, Sartre seems to imply that if the quantity of alternatives in two situations is equal, one is freer in that situation which permits qualitatively superior choices. For example, quantity being equal, a situation which includes the choice of life engenders more freedom than does a situation which includes only choices which involve death).

With these three points in mind, I am now in a position to answer the question as to whether or not there is a connection between the goal of promoting freedom and that of fulfilling human needs. First, while such a conclusion is precluded from the outset so long as we are concerned with *ontological* freedom, since *that* freedom is constant in all situations, whether one's needs are being fulfilled or not, there is no such clear, conceptual reason why there cannot be a connection between the fulfillment of human needs and *practical* freedom. But is there such a connection, and if so, what is its nature?

This brings us to the second and third points noted above. It seems to me that, on Sartre's view, there certainly *is* a connection between the fulfillment of human needs and the enhancement of practical freedom in that (1) such fulfillment increases the quantity of one's options, and (2) such fulfillment increases the quality of one's options.

Let us take these in reverse order. First, it is clear that impoverished persons in Chicago during the winter, who must choose between spending their money on food or on heating, face a *qualitatively poor* range of options, especially in comparison to their wealthier neighbors who can have both food *and* heating. Quite simply, going without adequate nutrition and being uncomfortably cold are *both bad*. To the extent that I must choose one or the other, I am, then, comparatively unfree. Similarly, if I am faced with the choice of either working sixteen hours a day at difficult manual labor, or else living (and probably dying) out on the street, I am, once again, practically unfree in comparison to my more affluent neighbors. My choices, in comparison to theirs, are qualitatively inferior.

Secondly, it would seem that extreme poverty and disease, in addition to diminishing the quality of my choices, would also diminish their quantity. If I must choose between expending all of my energies on doing what must be done to remain alive, or else giving in and dying, surely I face a range of choices that is not only poor, but also *narrow.* Or again, to move away from the "basic, animal" needs for food, warmth, shelter, etc., and toward the realm of "distinctively human" needs, to use Mill's familiar distinction,[22] consider that one of the best things to be said on behalf of knowledge is that it opens up opportunities. In order to see this we need only reflect that the more you *know how* to do, the more you can *do*. Therefore, assuming that within a given situation there are no external impediments to the performing of certain actions, one can increase one's range of choices within that situation simply by acquiring the knowledge of *how to* perform these actions. Thus, the fulfillment of fundamental human needs (needs for knowledge and friendship, as well as for food and shelter) enhances human freedom, not only by improving the quality of one's possible choices, but also by increasing their quantity.[23] The fulfillment of fundamental human needs is therefore, for Sartre, not only, and not even *primarily,* an end in itself, but rather a means to the end of enhancing freedom. As he himself puts it, what we want "is not just to have enough to eat but to have enough to eat in order to be able to be free."[24]

Bearing all of this in mind, I am now able to complete the answer to the objection that Sartre's freedom-ethic is too vague and formal to be of any help in concrete circumstances. To be sure, the injunction that we should promote freedom, and eliminate the obstacles which limit it, is formal, but that is because both freedom's needs (and consequently its goals), and also its obstacles, are innumerable. "Need . . . is in fact the lived revelation of a goal to aim at,"[25] says Sartre in *CDR,* and who can deny that there is an uncountable variety of such "lived revelations," owing, perhaps, to the unending novelty of particular situations. And what can be said about freedom's needs can also be said about its obstacles: "what counts in this case is the particular form of the obstacle to surmount, of the resistance to overcome. That is what gives form to freedom in each circumstance."[26] Such, I take it, is Sartre's answer to the objection based on the alleged formalism of his ethic.[27]

Still, a critic might respond that, while the linking of freedom to needs does indeed lend some content to freedom as a value, this value loses its content once the fulfillment of needs has been achieved. In response to this objection, at least two points can be made. First, as far as the "distinctively human" needs are concerned—needs for knowledge, art, science, technology, friendship, and philosophy, to name a few—it is quite clear, as Mill[28] and de Beauvoir[29] both point out, that these needs admit of no final fulfillment, since they correspond to facets of human existence which can be indefinitely expanded and developed. Secondly, once the more "basic" needs have been met—those (typically economic) needs which must be fulfilled in order to permit one to live a non-wretched life—it is *good* that there is no definite content inexorably tied to the promotion of freedom. Indeed, part of the reason for Sartre's valuing of freedom is his recognition that, once certain pressing needs have been taken care of, it is wonderful to be free in the simple sense of being able to do *whatever you want*. This comes across most clearly in Sartre's discussion of his ideal of "play," an activity which "has freedom for its foundation and its goal,[30] an activity "of which man is the first origin, for which man himself sets the rules, and which has no consequences except according to the rules posited."[31] Clearly, "man plays for the sheer joy of playing; he seeks no external goal but simply to exercise and develop his free existence."[32] To be sure, Sartre deemphasizes this ideal of play in his later works, but not, it would appear, from any diminishing of his appreciation for its value. Rather, Sartre's later works neglect play more from an increasing appreciation for the urgency and priority of first improving human living conditions and fulfilling human needs so that there will exist "*for everyone* a margin of *real* freedom beyond the production of life."[33] Only then can we have a "philosophy of freedom" which would develop the ethics of play. The development of this ethic must be delayed, not because it is invalid as an ideal, but rather because oppression is currently so widespread that "we have no means, no intellectual instrument, no concrete experience which allows us to conceive of this freedom or of this philosophy."[34] For now, while seeking to increase the practical freedom of those whose needs are not being met, we can only "dream," as de Beauvoir puts it, "of a future when men will know no other use of their freedom than this free unfurling of itself."[35]

3.3   The Problem of Justification

We have now seen, at least roughly, what Sartre's freedom-ethic, in his "objectivist" phase, amounts to. We have seen, for example, that it finds us obligated to "liberate" the "oppressed," by enabling them to meet their fundamental needs, and to work toward creating a world in which everyone would be free to "play." But what is Sartre's *justification* for this freedom-ethic? One searches in vain through Sartre's writings to find a rigorous, thoroughgoing defense of his fundamental value choices. To be sure, we find that he repeatedly and insistently *expresses* his views and *urges* others to adopt them. But why, in the absence of a convincing, explicit defense of these views, *should* anyone accept Sartre's value preferences?

3.3.1   Intuition

On the rare occasions when Sartre does attempt to advance justifications for his ethical views, they are usually of a casually intuitionist sort. That is, while he implicitly admits that his value choices cannot be supported by an appeal to anything other than themselves, he nonetheless claims that they themselves can be "seen" or "sensed" or in some other way "experienced" as being true—even as being "certainly" or "necessarily" true. Thus,

> I sense in myself certain needs which are not only mine but the needs of every man. To express it another way, it is the experienced certainty of my own freedom, to the extent that it is everyone's freedom, which gives me at the same time the need for a free life and the certainty that this need is felt in a more or less clear, more or less conscious way by everyone.[36]

How one wishes Sartre would have pursued this point! Does he hold that such "sensing" of "experienced certainties" establishes *knowledge* in ethics? If so, what becomes of his expressly-stated ethical subjectivism? If not, *why* not?

An obvious answer to the latter question would be that such intuiting, while adequate as a ground for personal conviction, is inadequate as a ground for genuine *knowledge,* where interpersonally accessible means for verification are held to be required. But this is not Sartre's position, as the following much-neglected passage from *BN* indicates.

There is only intuitive knowledge. Deduction and discursive argument, incorrectly called examples of knowing, are only instruments which lead to intuition. When intuition is reached, methods utilized to attain it are effaced before it; in cases where it is not attained, reason and argument remain as indicating signs which point toward an intuition beyond reach; finally if it has been attained but is not a present mode of my consciousness, the precepts which I use remain as the results of operations formerly effected, like what Descartes called the "memories of ideas."[37]

This passage provokes at least three questions: (1) What does Sartre mean by "intuition"? (2) Are Sartre's claims about intuition true? and (3) Can intuition give us *ethical* knowledge? Let us examine these questions in turn.

3.3.1.1   What does Sartre mean by "intuition"?

Sartre attributes to Husserl, and to "the majority of philosophers," the view that intuition "is the presence of the thing 'in person' to consciousness."[38] Sartre himself, on the basis of ontological considerations which need not concern us here, reverses the terms of this definition, so that it becomes "the presence of consciousness to the thing."[39] On either view, "intuition" refers to the direct apprehension, or, if you prefer, the immediate "seeing" or "grasping" of some point or principle. Thus, to say that we know by intuition that some principle is true is to say that we know this by direct inspection of the principle in question, rather than through the intermediary of reasons. Many philosophers, of course, would deny that there is or can be any such knowledge. Sartre goes to the other extreme and claims that it is the *only* kind of knowledge that there is.

3.3.1.2   Are Sartre's claims about intuition true?

We have seen that Sartre's argument on behalf of intuition is stated extremely briefly. It is not difficult, however, to fill in the outlines of the argument. Let us consider, for example, Sartre's insistence that deduction is not an example of knowing, but is rather an instrument which leads to intuition. The importance of this insistence is that, if it is true, it undercuts the principal argument against the claim that knowledge can be achieved through intuition—the argument, namely, that nothing can be called "knowledge" unless it can be supported by publicly accessible reasons, that we cannot dignify with the title of "knowledge" theses which we claim to "just know" without any reason. Thus, according to this view, we can claim to "know" the truth of a given hypothesis only if we can in some way *demonstrate* that it is true, such as, for example, by showing that its truth is a valid deductive inference from premises which have already been established to be true. But what if the rules of valid deductive inference are themselves things which we "just know" by intuition, without being able to derive them from more fundamental premises? What if *all* reasoning from one step to another involves intuitive insight, and cannot proceed without it? This would seem to indicate that intuition is *necessary* for all knowledge, even if it is not a *sufficient* guarantee of knowledge. But *is* intuition a necessary ingredient in every acquisition of knowledge?

A wonderfully clear argument for the conclusion that it is can be found in Lewis Carroll's paper, "What the Tortoise Said to Achilles."[40] In this paper, Achilles advances an argument in which the proposition Z follows logically from the propositions A and B. The Tortoise then announces that, while he accepts A and B as true, he is not yet ready to accept the truth of Z. Thus, he does not yet accept the truth of the hypothetical proposition C, "If A and B be true, Z must be true." Achilles, in his attempt to convince the Tortoise of the truth of Z, begins by asking him to accept C, which he then does. The new form of the argument, as Achilles represented it in his notebook, was:

A
B
C (If A and B are true, Z must be true)
Therefore, Z.

Achilles then announces to the Tortoise: "If you accept A and B and C, you must accept Z." When the Tortoise asks why, Achilles impatiently replies: "Because it follows *logically* from them. If A and B and C are true, Z *must* be true (D). You don't dispute *that*, I imagine?" The Tortoise agrees to accept D, but only on the condition that Achilles writes it down in his notebook. The conversation between the two then continues as follows. Achilles says:

'Now that you accept A and B and C and D, *of course* you accept Z.'

'Do I?' said the Tortoise innocently. 'Let's make that quite clear. I accept A and B and C and D. Suppose I *still* refuse to accept Z?'

'Then logic would take you by the throat, and *force* you to do it!' Achilles triumphantly replied. 'Logic would tell you "You can't help yourself. Now that you've accepted A and B and C and D, you *must* accept Z". So you've no choice, you see.'

'Whatever *Logic* is good enough to tell me is worth *writing down*,' said the Tortoise. 'So enter it in your book, please. We will call it

(E) If A and B and C and D are true, Z must be true. Until I've granted *that*, of course, I needn't grant Z. So it's quite a *necessary* step, you see?'

'I see,' said Achilles; and there was a touch of sadness in his tone.

The story ends months later when the narrator returns to the same spot to find Achilles and the Tortoise still arguing. Achilles' notebook was nearly full.[41]

Thus, deductive logic without intuition proves nothing. Logic is of no use if it does not help me to *see* that something is so. To be sure, deductive logic can indeed *help* me to see that something is so; therein lies its great value. It is, as Sartre says, "an instrument which leads to intuition." But logic cannot get off the ground unless we directly *see,* without the intermediary of reasons, that, for example, Q follows directly from the truth of premises (P implies Q) and P. Intuition, then, is always *necessary* to knowledge.[42]

Moreover, and perhaps even more radically, Carroll's story also suggests that intuition is *sufficient* for the acquisition of knowledge. For if the purpose of deductive logic is, as Carroll indicates, to bring about intuition, and if such intuition is at least sometimes adequate to give us knowledge, why should we hold in any less esteem an identical intuition which happens not to have been provoked by an acquaintance with a deductive argument? Or again, if *any* instance of knowledge necessarily *involves* intuition, since every inference involves the direct, immediate apprehension of an entailment, we cannot without inconsistency reject out of hand, insofar as we claim to know the truth of certain laws of logic, the possibility that other direct apprehensions of principles might yield knowledge as well. In other words, since we accept as instances of knowledge certain principles which are directly grasped, without the mediation of reasons, it follows that nothing can ever be rejected as an instance of knowledge *solely* on the grounds that it is allegedly grasped in direct intuition.

On the other hand, it must be granted, of course, that since it is clearly the case that not all of our intuitions, or alleged intuitions, yield genuine knowledge, there is obviously a need for criteria which can help us to distinguish knowledge-yielding intuitions from intuitions (or, perhaps, pseudo-intuitions) which do not yield knowledge. But this is inconsistent neither with intuition being necessary for knowledge, nor with the claim that if a statement is supported exclusively by direct intuition it might yet be an instance of knowledge, nor, since the criteria for distinguishing knowledge-yielding intuitions from the non-knowledge-yielding kind might themselves have to be known intuitively,[43] with the claim that intuition, under certain circumstances, is *adequate* for the establishing of knowledge.

But what are the grounds for thinking that intuition can ever be adequate for the establishing of knowledge? We have seen that the standard argument against the possibility of intuition ever being sufficient for the founding of knowledge is untenable. That argument is that "knowledge" refers exclusively to that which can be demonstrated to be true, where "demonstration" is understood as the pointing out of data, other than the conclusion to be established, which collectively point to the truth of this conclusion. But, as we have seen, the invocation of data other than a given conclusion in order to support that conclusion involves inferences from the data to the conclusion, and all inferences rest upon intuition. Thus, there is no difference in principle between "intuitive" knowledge and knowledge which can be demonstrated. *All* knowledge is intuitive, since all demonstrations can proceed only through intuition. Intuition, then, is not only *capable* of serving as the foundation of knowledge, it is the *only* such foundation that can be found. Therefore, insofar as there is any knowledge at all, it is knowledge which is founded on intuition.

This is well expressed by Husserl:

> Immediate *"seeing,"* not merely sensuous, experiential seeing, but *seeing in the universal sense as an originally presentive consciousness of any kind whatever,* is the ultimate legitimizing source of all rational assertions . . . If

we see an object with full clarity, if we have effected an explication and a conceptual apprehension purely on the basis of the seeing and within the limits of what is actually seized upon in seeing, if we then see . . . how the object is, the faithful expressive statement has, as a consequence, its legitimacy. Not to assign any value to "I see it" as an answer to the question, "Why?" would be a countersense.[44]

Thus, Husserl formulates his "principle of all principles" as follows:

> that *every originary presentive intuition is a legitimizing source of cognition,* that *everything originarily* . . . *offered* to us *in "intuition" is to be accepted simply as what it is presented as being,* but also *only within the limits in which it is presented there.*[45]

Why would such a denial of the justificatory function of intuition lead us to absurdity? Suppose that I hold a certain belief A. Someone asks me how I know the truth of A, and I reply that it is supported by consideration B. How, then, do I know the truth of B? Perhaps I can point to C and D, which, taken in conjunction, imply B. But how do I know the truth of C and D? I can appeal to E. How do I know E? Well, I can appeal to F, etc., etc. Clearly, at some point I will run out of further reasons. Thus, I will either have to say that my belief in A is founded on certain premises which I accept arbitrarily, for no reason, in which case it is questionable whether I could legitimately claim to *know* A, since one could with equal justification (or with equally arbitrary justification) affirm the negation of my fundamental premises, with such negations ultimately leading to the denial of A, or else I can claim that my belief in A is justified by a chain of reasoning which begins from premises which are clearly and authoritatively established through intuition. While it is true that this disjunction does not prove that *there is* knowledge which is founded on intuition, it does suggest the hypothetical judgment that *if* we have knowledge at all, it is knowledge which is of necessity founded on intuition.[46]

This suggestion is buttressed, moreover, by Carroll's argument that, not only are our fundamental premises established through intuition, but also the movement from these premises to a conclusion is accomplished through intuition. This argument also provides ammunition against those who would deny the exhaustiveness of our disjunction, and who would point out that, for example, our beliefs and the reasons which justify them could be related to each other as points on the circumference of a circle, rather than as points on a straight line or on a pyramid in which one or a few beliefs would be fundamental to other ones. For even if this new possibility should be the true one, it would seem that intuition would still of necessity form the basis not only of the movement from one point on the circle to another, but also for the adoption of one circle of beliefs rather than another, unless, again, such adoption is attributed to arbitrary choice, in which case it is questionable whether the beliefs in any particular circle can be said to be "known" by us.

Now, what disturbs many people about the suggestion that all knowledge is essentially intuitive is that it blurs, or even obliterates, the important distinction between that which we can *demonstrate* to be true, through rigorous deductive arguments and/ or by appeals to empirical evidence, and that which we claim to "just know" by intuition. As this distinction is normally drawn, only the former kinds of claims can be called "knowledge," since only they can be verified through well-established, publicly accessible tests and procedures. The latter sorts of claims, it is suggested, cannot be accorded the status of "knowledge" at all, since they cannot be publicly verified. Moreover, it is suspected that claims to know by "intuition" are really nothing more than unwarranted attempts to take as authoritative mere hunches and guesswork, or to sanction as "experienced necessities" judgments which merely seem indubitable to us because of the idiosyncracies of our personal psychological constitution, or because we are incapable of taking a critical attitude toward the customs of our nation, class, or other social group.

Two points must be made in response to this objection. First, while it is clear that we do need a distinction between claims with better or worse credentials as candidates for inclusion within the domain of knowledge, and that such a distinction might well be based at least in part upon a distinction between claims which have better or worse grounding, or which lend themselves to a greater or lesser degree to procedures of verification of better or worse kinds, it hardly follows that the only way to draw such distinctions is to begin by separating out intuitive (pseudo) knowledge from knowledge of other kinds. Rather, it might well be that these distinctions can still be drawn even if we claim that all knowledge is intuitive. It might be possible, for example, to distinguish, on the basis of intuition itself, better from worse intuitions. This possibility is grounded in the recognition that clear insight is not

> a matter of a single casual glance. In actual knowing, "seeing" is a matter of looking and looking again, focusing, comparing perspectives; in short, it is a *process* . . . Seeing requires an effort. We can see dimly, obscurely; we can and often do disagree as to what we see and need to look again, carefully, painstakingly, correcting earlier observations, supplementing them with further clarification.[47]

Interestingly, this recognition not only exposes a weakness in the objection which we are presently examining, namely, its uncritical assumption that the distinction between well-grounded and poorly-grounded knowledge-claims can only be accomplished by relegating all claims which are based upon intuition to the latter category, but also underscores a fundamental truth which the present objection emphasizes: that it is often the case that claims which can be amply supported by publicly accessible arguments, empirical evidence, and other means of verification are to be regarded as more reliable and trustworthy than claims which must be grasped all at once, in a single intuition, with no intermediate evidence being available to help guide us in our attempts to focus on the claim. For, as we recall, even Sartre admits that deductive reasoning, for example, is an "instrument which leads to intuition." And if real seeing is indeed typically achieved only as a result of a difficult process, it seems reasonable to assume that we should be much readier to affirm those claims for which many aids can be found to help us to see them clearly, aids which can, so to speak, lead us right up to the claim so that we can get a good, close look at it, than we should those claims which can be seen only through a "long shot," and for which the odds of seeing them clearly are also a "long shot." But none of this implies that such things as deductive arguments and appeals to empirical evidence *replace* intuition; rather, these bring about intuition, or clarify existing intuitions.

Incidentally, the foregoing helps to indicate a line of reply to a related objection, namely, that an understanding of knowledge as being based upon intuition makes it impossible to understand how competing knowledge claims can ever be resolved. You have your claim, based upon your intuition, and I have my counter claim, based upon my quite different intuition. All we can do, so the objection runs, is to ask each other to look again, and, should we each persist in our original claims, to call each other "blind."

But this objection assumes that an appeal to intuition involves the rejection of such instruments as logic and empirical evidence. This, of course, is not so. Intuition is not being proposed as a *replacement* for these instruments. Rather, it is merely that a new understanding of the relationship between these instruments and intuition is being proposed. Thus, if you disagree with me, I am not limited simply to telling you to look again. I can *help* you to look again by drawing distinctions, inventing analogies and examples, citing empirical evidence, focusing on a different, hitherto unexamined aspect of the issue, searching for inconsistencies in your arguments, searching for inconsistencies between your present view and other views that I know that you hold, etc., etc. You, of course, can do the same for me, helping me to see the error of my ways. For "whether we speak of knowing that vitamin C is good for our health or that unprovoked injury demands compensation, we are dealing with claims that must ultimately be based on *seeing*. There is no cognitive court of appeal more basic than that: either you see or you do not."[48] And, while it is strictly speaking true that "if someone claims that he 'just doesn't see that,' there is no recourse but to ask him to look again," it does not follow that we must eschew arguments and evidence. Rather, "all our arguments, examples, elaborations are, at the last instance, devices to *help him see*—or to help us see that we were mistaken."[49]

This brings me to my second point in response to the present objection, namely that, while it is undeniably true that we do tend to confuse the necessary with the merely familiar, or to regard as "intuitively evident" judgments which are in fact contingent upon the idiosyncracies of our psychological make-up, or upon an uncritical acceptance of the dogmas of our society, or of some other social group to which we belong, this unfortunate fact does not constitute a special difficulty for an intuitionist theory of knowledge. For I would argue that it is possible to take steps so as to minimize, though never, of course, to eliminate, the possibility of committing these errors, and that whether or to what extent one takes such steps is in no way connected to the theory of knowledge that one holds, and specifically, that the acceptance of an intuitionist theory of knowledge need not preclude the taking of such steps. To be sure, it is impossible to eliminate the possibility, or even the likelihood when dealing with certain especially difficult or intractable problems, of making mistakes; but this is true no matter what theory of knowledge one holds. In short, while granting that the objection points to an important, permanent obstacle to the obtaining of knowledge, this obstacle is no more one for an intuitionist than for anyone else, and it certainly cannot be eliminated, or even diminished, by the rejection of intuitionism. The belief that the present objection is especially serious for the intuitionist stems, I think, from a failure to appreciate such points as those which I have tried to establish in the immediately preceding paragraphs, namely, that intuition is not appealed to as a *replacement* for the more public methods of verification, such as logic and scientific experimentation, but rather, as an *explanation* of how it is that such procedures yield knowledge (and as a justification for the claim that we can know certain things without the mediation of logic or science).

Let us look at this more closely. The danger of confusing the necessary with the merely familiar, and the individually or culturally relative with the universal, *would* be particularly acute for dogmatic intuitionists who would claim infallibility for all of their intuitions, and who would refuse to investigate any possible procedures for verifying or clarifying their intuitions, and who would reject, without careful consideration, the claims of those with competing intuitions. But this is not so for intuitionists who would agree with my claims in the immediately preceding paragraphs that clear intuition is usually achieved only as the result of a difficult process, that even clear intuitions are fallible, that such tools as logic and empirical investigations are valuable aids to intuition, rather than its competitors, and that one can avoid a great number of errors in one's intuiting by exploiting the valuable resource of discussion and argument with those who disagree. These are the sorts of procedures, moreover, that *anyone,* it would seem, should follow in order to minimize error, whether one is an intuitionist or not. Those who think that the present situation is especially serious to intuitionists have in mind, I think, the kind of intuitionists who would insist that all of their intuitions were absolutely veridical and beyond the pale of intelligent and responsible disagreement. But intuitionists need not behave this way or think this way.

3.3.1.3   Can intuition give us ethical knowledge?

If *all* knowledge is intuitive, and if there *is* such a thing as ethical knowledge, it follows that all *ethical* knowledge is intuitive. But *is* there such a thing as ethical knowledge? What does our intuition reveal with regard to this question? Consider the following three quotations:

> We are *not* in fact free to choose absolutely anything . . . For instance, we do not *choose* to prefer pleasure to pain.[50]

> It is not possible to contemplate and compare dead matter and life, brutality and reason, misery and happiness, virtue and vice, ignorance and knowledge, impotence and power, . . . without acquiring the ideas of better and worse, perfect and imperfect, noble and ignoble, excellent and base.[51]

> The experiences of millions of lives over centuries of time, relived by each of us in those aspects common to all men, *prove* to us that love is preferable to hate, peace to war, brotherhood to enmity, joy to sorrow, health to sickness, nourishment to hunger, life to death.[52]

Surely these experiences, these "intuitions," lay claim to knowledge. Thus, just as we *know, because we can see,* that the giraffe is taller than the ant, so that we cannot simply *decide* to regard the ant as taller than the giraffe (or at least, we can do so only after overcoming a tremendously powerful coefficient of resistance which hinders such a judgment), so too do we know because we can see (find, discover, etc.) that happiness is better than misery, that knowledge is better than ignorance, that freedom is better than slavery, etc. And this seeing is likewise of such a nature as to place a tremendous coefficient of adversity in the path of any attempt to hold the contraries of these judgments.

It will immediately be objected that the preceding claims certainly do not apply to *all* experienced values, or to *all* of the value-judgments which we formulate in our lives. At least *some* of the values which we encounter in our experience we recognize as having arisen as a direct result of our own free choices, and still others, while unquestionably experienced as involuntarily imposed upon us, we recognize both as not imposing themselves upon others, and as being of such a nature that even we need not consider ourselves bound by them.

But recognition of such experienced values only underscores our awareness of other experienced values which, by contrast, *do* have something of the binding and necessary character outlined above. There is, then, a difference, founded in experience, between values in regard to their perceived necessity and degree of intersubjective bindingness. J. N. Findlay explains this clearly:

> 'Values' and 'valuations' must . . . , it is plain, permit of a distinction, not always wholly clear, but certainly always felt even by moderately sophisticated persons, between such values and valuations as are freely allowed to be 'personal', peculiar to the individual, and neither expected nor required to hold for other persons, and other valuations and values which are felt to impose themselves with a certain necessity or ineluctability, which it is felt must impress itself on *anyone,* or at least on anyone who reflects at all carefully on the matter. Thus the valuation of sitting on beaches or eating meals in the open or wearing flowers in one's hair are obviously by their very nature and structure matters on which no agreement can be expected or demanded, whereas the valuation of being happy, of enjoying freedom and power, . . . of being truly informed as to the state of things, etc., are obviously, in varying degrees, values disagreement with which tends to seem absurd, unfeasible, perverse, mistaken, wrong . . . Our impression may be mistaken, but the utterances 'I like bondage, I rejoice in being discriminated against, I value a state of deep unhappiness' seem to involve a certain deep absurdity . . . a certain vein of deep nonsense of which philosophy must take account . . . Between these extreme limits of values and valuations which seem to have a cogent and mandatory quality and others which have no such character, lies a whole spectrum of intermediate cases, those which in a vague manner impress us as mandatory and cogent but in whose case we can readily be brought to doubt their cogent or mandatory character. All these distinctions are genuinely 'part of the phenomena', whether or not we decide that they can ultimately be sustained.[53]

Now, what is here said about values can also be said about human actions. That is, there are at least *some* actions which seem powerfully to resist our attempt to applaud them. There is a coefficient of adversity which exerts a force against our desire to approve of such actions, and this force is of sufficient power as to be able, all by itself, to obliterate any moral theory which would attempt to oppose it.

Consider the following little story, invented by William Gass:

> Imagine I approach a stranger on the street and say to him, "If you please, sir, I desire to perform an experiment with your aid." The stranger is obliging, and I lead him away. In a dark place conveniently by, I strike his head with the broad of an axe and cart him home. I place him, buttered and trussed, in an ample electric oven. The thermostat reads 450° F. Thereupon I go off to play poker with friends and forget all about the obliging stranger in the stove. When I return, I realize I have overbaked my specimen, and the experiment, alas, is ruined . . . Something wrong has been done. Any ethic that does not roundly condemn my action is vicious . . . No more convincing refutation of any ethic could be given than by showing that it approved of my baking the obliging stranger.[54]

It is important to note, moreover, that this is so even if we cannot give a satisfactory theoretical account of precisely *why* the baking of the obliging stranger is wrong. For, as Gass points out, even then our judgment that the baking is wrong "is not inexplicable; it is transparent."[55]

It would seem, then, that a strong *prima facie* case can be made for the claim that we can, and indeed *do,* have ethical knowledge. We find, moreover, that this (alleged) knowledge seems to be based upon intuition. However, if the arguments of the preceding section are sound, this fact, far from constituting an objection to our claim that there is ethical knowledge, is precisely what we should expect to find. Thus, our current (tentative) conclusion that there is ethical knowledge, coupled with the conclusion of the preceding section that all knowledge is intuitive, yields the conclusion that there is intuitive ethical knowledge. All that remains to be done before we give our wholehearted support to this conclusion is to refute the most important and prevalent objections to it. I have selected six such objections. Let us now conclude the present section with a brief evaluation of each of them.

Perhaps the most prominent objection, and one which we have already examined in the preceding section, is simply that "intuition" or "seeing" cannot constitute knowledge—knowledge requires proof. We have seen, however, that it is difficult, or even impossible, to achieve *any* knowledge in *any* field which is not ultimately founded on intuition. Moreover, we have seen that there are some value-judgments (e.g., that happiness is better than unhappiness, that health is better than sickness, that knowledge is better than ignorance, etc.) which give themselves with every bit as much obviousness, certainty, universality, and necessity, as do judgments in any other areas, including logic and mathematics.

To be sure, one must concede, with Barnes, that "if one argues purely abstractly that honesty, consistency, feelings of pleasure, and the sense of being happy with one's life are not self-evident goods which one ought to seek, I agree—abstractly—that there is no external, impersonal proof that they are."[56] But the fact that we cannot *prove* the truth of certain value-judgments does not undermine their self-evident obviousness. For it must be remembered that precisely the same point as Barnes' can be made with respect to fundamental judgments in fields other than ethics. Thus, while it is admittedly difficult to refute the sceptic in ethics, it is no more difficult than it is to refute the general sceptic, since, as A. C. Ewing points out, "if he is a complete sceptic he will refuse to accept the premises of any argument against himself or the logical principles underlying the argument in question."[57] But this does not mean that there is no ethical knowledge, any more than it means that there is no knowledge of *any* kind.

A second objection is that *since* we cannot prove our fundamental value-judgments, and must instead rely on intuition, it follows that no way can be found to legislate between conflicting opinions on ethical matters. As Bertrand Russell puts it, "in a question as to whether this or that is the ultimate Good, there is no evidence either way . . . Since no way can be even imagined for deciding a difference as to values, the conclusion is forced upon us that the difference is one of tastes, not one as to any objective truth."[58]

We have seen in the preceding section, however, that an intuitionist account of knowledge leaves plenty of scope for non-arbitrary argumentation, and even demonstration. There is no need to resort to throwing up one's hands and saying "you have your intuition and I have mine." It is simply not true that "no way can be even imagined for deciding a difference as to values." Rather, we can "imagine" plenty of ways. Thus, we can appeal to principles of consistency; we can draw distinctions; we can point to analogies and parallels; we can expose lapses of logic; we can point out hitherto unnoticed consequences and implications, etc., in a common effort to reach a sound common ground.

True, these methods will not always produce agreement. But this is the case in all fields of inquiry, including not only history, sociology, psychology, and anthropology, but also the physical sciences, and even logic and mathematics. Why, then, should we single out ethics as a "subjective" discipline?

To conclude, then, far from there being no conceivable way to reconcile ethical differences, there are, in fact, an indefinitely large number of ways, all of which, on my view, involving getting the opposing parties to "turn toward" and thus to "see," what they did not before. To be sure, as Husserl admits, "under some circumstances, one seeing conflicts with another."[59] But this implies neither that no resolution of the conflict is possible, nor that such a resolution must involve a movement beyond intuition, nor that this situation implies the illegitimacy of intuition as a source of knowledge. What it does tell us, says Husserl, is

> that perhaps in a certain category of intuitions . . . seeing is, according to its essence, "imperfect," that of essential necessity it can become strengthened or weakened, that consequently an assertion having an immediate, and therefore genuine, legitimizing ground in experience nevertheless may have to be abandoned in the further course of experience because of a counter legitimacy outweighing and annulling it.[60]

A third objection is that the mere fact of moral disagreement is enough to show the falsity of, or at least to embarrass, objectivist ethical intuitionism.[61] I trust that enough has already been said to refute this objection. I will here point out only that this criticism rests on at least three errors: first, it rests on the false assumption that an intuitionist must regard all intuitions as equally accurate, as equally worthy of being considered "knowledge," an assumption which would indeed be falsified by the existence of moral disagreement; secondly, it rests on the false assumption that nothing can be done to legislate between conflicting intuitions; and finally, it being conceded that there is no universally accepted decision-procedure for resolving ethical disputes, the objection rests on the inconsistent application to ethics, but not to other fields of inquiry, of a standard of knowledge by which no field of inquiry could be considered to yield knowledge unless all of the disputes within it were resolvable in terms of a universally accepted decision-procedure. Such a standard would, incidentally, if consistently applied, render all of the sciences "non-cognitive."

Another objection to intuitionism concerns the psychological doctrine which is held to be essential to it. Specifically, it is objected that there is no evidence for the existence of any special psychological faculties, such as the infamous "moral sense," which must be postulated to give a causal explanation of our gaining access to ethical knowledge. Still less can intuitionism be defended if that position is understood as conveying the "suggestion that the truth of a proposition alleged to be intuited is guaranteed by the nature of our psychological state in apprehending it or can be *inferred* from the nature of this state."[62]

But intuitionism need not be understood in this way, and I am not advocating such an intuitionism. By "intuitionism" I mean only the doctrine that we can know some things by directly grasping them, without the intermediary of reasons, and that all knowledge is ultimately rooted in such direct grasping. To affirm these claims it is certainly not necessary to postulate a special moral faculty to explain ethical intuitions any more than it would be to postulate special logical, mathematical, scientific, historical, aesthetic, etc., faculties to explain intuitions in these spheres. To be sure, it might well be true that veridical ethical intuitions come more easily to people with certain psychological constitutions than with others, but this is also true, of course, of, for example, mathematical intuitions.[63] We do not on this account feel the need to postulate a mathematical faculty. Why should we do so in ethics?

As for the notion that the truth of a proposition can be guaranteed by the nature of the psychological state through which one apprehends it, this is, of course, in no way required by intuitionism as I have described it.

A fifth objection to intuitionism concerns the ontology which is allegedly essential to the theory. Specifically, the objection is directed against the claim, which is indeed advanced by some of the most important of the intuitionists in ethics,[64] that our knowledge that a given action or state of affairs is right or good depends upon our intuitive seeing in that action or state of affairs the *property* of "rightness" or "goodness." Similarly, an intuitionist might claim that our knowledge that a given action ought to be done is founded on an intuitive apprehension of the property of "oughtness." Aside from pointing to the ontological queerness of such a view, critics have also put forth the straightforwardly empirical objection that they, along with nearly everyone else, including those who apparently can competently discriminate between "good" and "bad" states of affairs, or "right" or "wrong" actions, confess to having never apprehended such properties.

My answer to this objection consists in the rejection of the claim that "rightness," "goodness," oughtness," etc., are properties, and also of the claim that the positing of such properties is essential to intuitionism. As proof, I offer that in order to intuit that A is better than B it is no more necessary to suppose that A has more of the property "goodness" in it than does B than it would be to insist that I can only perceive that C is larger than D if C does, in fact, have more of the property "largeness" in it than does D.

A final objection to intuitionism is that it allegedly is an inherently intolerant theory, in that it engenders a spirit of dogmatism in its adherents. Leaving aside the empirical question of whether or not intuitionists in fact tend to be intolerant and dogmatic, the objection is mitigated by the realization that an intuitionist need not, as I do not, hold that ethical intuitions are invariably, or even typically, accurate, or that it is inappropriate to discuss or to argue with those whose intuitions disagree with our own. Since our intuitions might well be wrong, we need not, and I think should not, dismiss those who disagree with us as morally blind or wicked. Nor should we expect them to take our claim to intuit the truth of something as evidence that it is in fact true. Rather, the procedure should be to attempt, through the use of arguments, illustrations, distinctions, etc., to lead our interlocutors to the point from which they will be able to see what we see, as they, too, attempt to point us toward their own counterclaims.

3.4   Subjectivism and Objectivism in Sartre

Let us now return to Sartre. We have seen, in the preceding chapter, that the early Sartre defends a rather extreme form of ethical subjectivism. However, we have also seen, in the present chapter, that there are objectivist strains running through Sartre's writings in all stages of his career, becoming increasingly prominent in his later writings. Moreover, we have seen that Sartre's phenomenological orientation in philosophy, and especially his intuitionist theory of knowledge, are both more consistent with objectivism than with subjectivism, a circumstance which has the possible further advantage of enabling him to escape from the objections raised against him in the preceding chapter. But how are we to make sense of the presence of both subjectivist and objectivist strands in Sartre's thought? Can the two strands be reconciled?

Perhaps the best way to focus this discussion is by concentrating on Sartre's claim, stated implicitly and explicitly throughout his works, that freedom is the "highest" or most important value. Is this to be taken in the "subjectivist" sense in which choices are foundational to values, or in the "objectivist" sense in which values are foundational to choices? In Sartre's early works, the claim that freedom is the highest value is usually intended in the subjective sense in which it means only that all values are constituted in the free choices of individual persons. In his later works, however, Sartre seems to mean by this claim that we are morally *obliged* to choose freedom, and to make our subsidiary choices on the basis of their tendency to promote or diminish freedom. Thus, according to this "objectivist" reading of Sartre's claim, it is perfectly intelligible to speak of free choices which are "erroneous," "mistaken," or "wrong."

Let us begin, then, with the subjectivist interpretation of the claim that freedom is the highest value. According to this interpretation, freedom is the most important value because it is the value which uniquely underlies, and is entailed by, all other values. That is, "since freedom is ontologically entailed in all values as their source, the choice of any and all values logically entails the prior valuing of freedom."[65] It is significant that in the series of questions which Sartre poses at the conclusion of *BN*— one of the first passages in which he suggests that freedom, rather than the impossible God, might be taken as the highest value—he asks whether it is "possible for freedom to take itself for a value *as the source of all value.*"[66] Similarly, de Beauvoir argues that since freedom is both "the source from which all significations and all values spring" and "the original condition of all justification of existence," it follows that "the man who seeks to justify his life must want freedom itself absolutely and above everything else."[67]

I call this the "subjectivist" interpretation of the claim that freedom is the highest value because, on this interpretation, the claim is *not* "that freedom should be chosen because it possesses some intrinsic objective value. Quite the contrary, the argument is that it is precisely because nothing, including freedom, has objective value, because values come only from freedom, that freedom should be chosen above all."[68] This can be clearly seen from the fact that Sartre's (and de Beauvoir's) claims on behalf of the value of freedom are conditional in the sense that they presuppose the prior evaluations of individuals. That is, Sartre does not simply say, "You should value freedom." Rather, he says, "*since* you value X, Y, and Z, you should value freedom." Sartre does not really attempt to *prove* that freedom should be valued above all other values. Instead, he thinks that once people *recognize* the relationship between freedom and other values, they will *want* freedom above all other values. Indeed, he explicitly states that "*once a man sees that values depend upon himself,* . . . he can will only one thing and that is freedom as the foundation of all values."[69]

So much for the subjectivism of the early Sartre. Is this subjectivism maintained in Sartre's later writings? Is the claim that freedom is the highest value to be understood in the same way as it is in the earlier works? It would seem not. For here we no longer find the language of "I define," "I reply," and "I declare," in connection with value-judgments. Rather, Sartre now claims to "discover" that, for example, "hunger is an evil: period." Gone too is the emphasis on "desire" and "choice." In its place, we find the much more "serious" language of "rights," "requirements," and "needs."

How are we to account for this change? To a large extent it seems to stem from a shift in Sartre's conception of the relationship between consciousness and that which it lacks. While in *BN* consciousness is said to experience itself as *desire* for what it lacks, in *CDR* this experience is held to be one of *need*. Thus, while not explicitly announcing the fact, Sartre appears to move from an ethic in which the free consciousness simply *invents* values, to one in which this consciousness also *recognizes* or *discovers* at least some values. For, as Barnes points out,

> *Desire* suggests the possibility of unrestricted movement, of a freedom which may change the objects of its desire at will. *Need* brings in something from the outside, a necessity which man cannot ultimately escape, no matter how much he may vary his reaction to it.[70]

It is little wonder, then, that the ethical messages of the earlier and later Sartre differ from one another. For the early Sartre, with his emphasis on desire, the point is to renounce "the spirit of seriousness," and to invent values through the activity known as "play." This is the ethic of "You are free, therefore choose—that is to say, invent." For the later Sartre, on the other hand, with his emphasis on need, there is little call for the invention of values. Rather what is needed is the bringing to realization of such discovered values as food and clothing. This is the ethic of "hunger is an evil: period."

Of course, Sartre himself sees this later ethic as a development of, rather than an abandonment of, his earlier ethic. "It is not a question of giving up freedom, . . . but of giving [it] a content."[71] This content is supplied by the connection which Sartre sees between freedom and the satisfaction of human needs. On his view, I cannot be (practically) free if I am hungry, diseased, or poor. My valuing of freedom, then, immediately attaches a *discoverable* value to food, medicine, and money, without my having to "invent" these values. Thus, once one accepts the value of freedom, one must abandon, or at least postpone in this world of scarcity, contra the early Sartre, an ethic of "play." There is, then, a definite drift from the subjective to the objective in the later Sartre, given that one values freedom most of all, for while in the early Sartre this seems to result in a morality in which we have no obligations other than those which we freely invent or choose, in the later Sartre it clearly issues in specific, stringent duties toward others—helping them to meet "the most elementary requirements of everyday life," for example.[72]

How, then, are we to understand this shift in Sartre's thinking? I would argue that Sartre's shift is intelligible in the light of the corresponding shift in his understanding of the radical conversion. Recall that Sartre first conceived of the conversion as a private decision, accessible to all individuals, to give up the project of being-God and to adopt instead a project based upon freedom as the highest value. Once enough people had undergone such conversions, Sartre apparently thought, there would follow a gradual elimination of the social structures which lead to poverty, ignorance, disease, etc.—structures which, on Sartre's view, are sustained by the desperate behavior of those trying vainly to be God. Later, however, Sartre de-emphasizes the idea of individual conversion. Given the nature of the present social order, it is highly unlikely that very many people are going to undergo a Sartrean conversion. Thus, this social order must first be changed— poverty, ignorance, and disease must be diminished greatly—and *then* it will be possible for individual conversions to take place on a grand scale.

With this change in his understanding of the conversion comes a corresponding shift in his understanding of what "valuing freedom" calls for. For the early Sartre, the individual conversion to the valuing of freedom leads to "play"—the free unfurling of freedom in its baseless creation of values. For the later Sartre, the conversion is a social one in which we all fight together to enhance practical freedom by eliminating its barriers, so that the day might eventually come in which we can all enjoy "play."

Understood this way, Sartre's freedom-ethic would appear to contain both objectivist and subjectivist elements. The claim that freedom is the highest value entails, under present circumstances, that we should do more than merely *invent* values freely. Rather, it calls for the *recognition* on our part of certain stringent duties toward others. Thus, from the claim that freedom is the highest value, it follows that, no matter what I might think or feel about it, I am *wrong* if I do not act so as to help others to fulfill their needs. This ethic is, therefore, objectivist in the sense which I have defined.

On the other hand, at least a major part of Sartre's concern for the fulfillment of fundamental human needs seems to be rooted in his subjectivist view that freedom is the source of all value, and that the ideal human situation—one which can be reached only through the fulfillment of these needs—would be that of "play," in which freedom can blissfully go about its business of creating values, unburdened by the stringent obligations toward others which the present situation dictates. Here we are reminded of Sartre's longing for that world in which "there will exist *for everyone* a margin of *real* freedom beyond the production of life." "But we have no means, no intellectual instrument, no concrete experience," Sartre immediately adds, "which allows us to conceive of this freedom"[73] or of this world. Thus, insofar as Sartre's freedom-ethic is based upon the value of *this* unknowable freedom, it is based upon a value which currently is not, and which we value because it *would* be the source of all those values which would be created by freedom through the activity of play.

3.5   Sartre's Contribution to Ethics

At last we are in a position, then, to assess Sartre's claim that freedom is the highest value, and, in so doing, to summarize his considerable contribution to ethics.

The most important of these contributions consists, I believe, in the wealth of tools which he has provided us for resolving the conflict between subjectivism and objectivism. As we have seen, Sartre himself tends to oscillate between the two positions, without ever really reaching a stable conclusion, and without ever seriously attempting to reconcile the two strains in his thought. Nonetheless, there are many features of Sartre's thought which remain constant throughout this oscillation, and it is instructive to examine the conflict between subjectivism and objectivism with these features prominently in mind. I submit that when we do this we find (1) that Sartre, in his respective subjectivist and objectivist moods, has pointed out some of the most compelling components of each position, and (2) that these compelling components of subjectivism and objectivism are consistent with the features of Sartre's philosophy which remain constant throughout his development.

(1) What, then, are the attractive features of subjectivism to which Sartre has called attention? Principally, Sartre has shown that ethics has much to do with, or at least *should* have much to do with, human invention and creativity. Sartre the subjectivist points to a real truth in insisting that, so to speak, "morality is made for man, not man for morality," that moral rules are not "written in stone," that it is up to us to *choose* and to *decide* what is best for us and how we should live. Sartre the subjectivist celebrates, and rightly so, the fact that there is a legitimate place for elasticity, for non-conformity and non-rigidity in ethics, for a certain looseness and playfulness and individuality that is lacking in traditional, "serious," objectivist moralities. Sartre the subjectivist argues convincingly that there is more than one way to lead a good life, and that objectivist moralities which teach that there is only one right answer to every ethical question—moralities which claim that there is only one "true way"—are intolerably intolerant. Lastly, Sartre the subjectivist has done an admirable job of showing that many traditional objectivist moralities, both religious and secular, tend to be irrational, arbitrary, harmful, and motivated by a desire more to maintain the status quo, no matter how unjust it might be, than to promote human welfare.

On the other hand, in his "objectivist" moods Sartre has done much to underscore the weaknesses, or at least the limitations, of subjectivism, and the strengths of objectivism. Sartre the objectivist realizes that there is a place for *seriousness* in ethics, as well as a place for reason and for truth. While play, choice, invention, creation, nonrigidity, etc., definitely have their place, there is also a point at which one must call a halt. Sartre the objectivist recognizes that it is simply and uncompromisingly wrong to "play" with other people's lives without their consent, to "choose" a role for them as my slaves, to "invent" a world in which I enjoy fantastic wealth while they starve, etc. In his stinging criticisms of "right-wing oppressors," Sartre the objectivist seems implicitly to recognize a place in ethics for strictness, rigidity, and intolerance.[74] In short, while Sartre the subjectivist speaks of moral truths which are *created* by human freedom, Sartre the objectivist balances this with an appeal to moral truths which are *recognized* by human *reason* or *intuition*. Both of these apparently incompatible positions seem to have their strengths.

(2) What features of Sartre's work remain constant throughout his work, and throughout his oscillation between subjectivism and objectivism? Obviously the unifying thread running through all of Sartre's work is his preoccupation with, and his distinctive theory of, freedom. "Everything that I have tried to write or do in my life was meant to stress the importance of freedom," says Sartre.[75] We have seen that Sartre's theory of freedom remains substantially the same throughout his works. We have also seen that Sartre tends to assimilate his theory of freedom into both his subjectivism and his objectivism. Thus, in his subjectivist phase he emphasizes the importance of the freedom to *choose* and to *create* values. Similarly, in his objectivist phase he claims to *see* that freedom is the highest value, that it has this status even if I choose not to value it, and that such valuing on my part would simply be mistaken. It is my view that it is possible to reconcile these two phases in a synthesis, in which ethics would be understood as a dialectic of invention and discovery, or, if you prefer, of volition and intuition, with freedom being central to the understanding of both phases of the dialectic. We shall take a closer look at this dialectic presently; but first, let us examine its two phases and point out their connection with freedom.

First, with regard to the "objective" phase of the value of freedom—the discovery or intuition that freedom is a uniquely valuable value, I would like to buttress Sartre's claims by quoting at length the corroborating, though considerably calmer and more sober, testimony of Erazim Kohák:

> We can focus not only on the way we have in fact structured our world but on the way that a subject, any subject, necessarily structures a world.
> Here examples are not hard to come by, even on the most ordinary level. Take the universally human significance of freedom, understood as the possibility of voluntary action. We cannot justify the recognition of freedom as a basic human need in terms of cultural conditioning. Most societies, at most times, considered slavery natural and legitimate, and all societies at all

times concern themselves, legitimately and necessarily, with the regulation rather than the fostering of freedom. On uncritically empirical grounds, we could at most conclude that freedom is a luxury indulged in by some members of some societies at some times, or that it is a fleeting moment in the periodic exchange of roles between master and slave, not a human need.

Yet our lived experience as subjects contradicts such a conclusion. We need but imagine the difference between performing a task, even one we regard as intrinsically pleasurable, voluntarily and under coercion. The metaphor of love and rape is trite but apt. We experience voluntary action as self-constitution, and the same act under coercion as self-destruction. In lived experience, freedom presents itself as crucial to the constitution of human identity . . . Deprivation of freedom is equivalent to destruction of subjectivity.[76]

Secondly, with regard to the "subjective" phase of the value of freedom—the phase in which the unique value of freedom consists in its being foundational to all other values which we choose or invent—I would like, once again, to buttress Sartre's claims by quoting from a similar argument by Olafson, from his book on the ethical aspects of existentialism:

If a man thinks of himself as a morally autonomous being, the very nature of this character that he imputes to himself is such as to absorb any other feature of his nature which he might designate as the basis for his relationships with other human beings . . . Let us suppose, for example, that a man proposes to make the fact that he is a proletarian—or a white man—or a Buddhist—the primary basis of his association with other human beings. Since he is at the same time . . . committed to the doctrine of moral autonomy, he will be forced to admit that his being a proletarian, or a white man, assumes the criterial function he assigns to it only as the result of a choice on his part. In fact, *being* a proletarian or a Buddhist or even a white man in any sense which implies the imposition of priorities by which, e.g., being a white man takes precedence for purposes of action over being something else, inescapably turn out to involve an exercise of the same autonomy that presides over the whole moral life . . . If he is an autonomous moral being, then in every subordinate goal he sets himself, and in every principle he adopts, he is also bringing into play that fundamental capacity for self-determination. He cannot repudiate or remain indifferent to the latter without, at the same time, withdrawing the claim he makes for the subordinate goals that are its expression.[77]

Thus, we are now in a position to see how ethics can be conceived as a dialectic of discovery and invention, of intuition and volition, with freedom being central to both phases of the dialectic. We discover (with Kohák) that freedom is a value of unique importance, and (with Olafson) that its unique importance consists largely in the fact that it is a source of all those values which we choose or invent. These two insights strongly suggest, even if they do not strictly entail, certain important ethical implications. For example, if we couple them with the rejection of ethical egoism, it seems to follow that our freedom to choose or to invent values is circumscribed within certain strict limits which are set in place by our recognition of the value of the freedom of others. Moreover, what I see or recognize *depends* to a great extent upon what I choose or invent; and conversely, what I choose or invent depends to a great extent upon what I see or recognize. Sartre's strength is that he recognizes, and articulates with admirable clarity, the dialectic of the voluntary and the involuntary with regard to both perception and action. His weakness is that he apparently fails to see the application of this dialectic to ethics.

Sartre's clearest illustration of this dialectic, which we have already examined at length, is that of the crag. Recall that Sartre argues that how I *see* the crag is largely a function of my freedom— of my voluntarily chosen projects. Thus, the crag appears as a valuable aid if my project is to find a vantage point from which to view the countryside; it appears as an obstacle if my project is to prepare the field on which the crag appears for farming; it will appear as beautiful or ugly if my interest is purely aesthetic, etc. But Sartre also shows that my freedom in relation to the crag is greatly limited by the nature of the crag itself. Thus, my freedom in choosing to attempt to climb the crag cannot render an unclimbable crag climbable—this is part of the "brute being" of the crag. Similarly, it is clear that the crag places strict limits on my freedom to formulate projects with respect to it. I cannot see the crag as a refreshing liquid to drink, as an interesting artifact to put in my pocket and carry home, or as a vehicle in which to fly to the moon. Less strictly, the nature of the crag serves to *suggest* certain projects to me. Thus, a tall crag with a slight incline is much more likely to suggest to me the project of climbing it so as to get a good look at the countryside than is a short crag with a steep incline; a light crag which is loosely stuck in the ground is more likely to suggest to me the project of clearing it away than is a heavy crag which is firmly entrenched, etc.

Let us now apply this to ethics. In his subjectivist moods Sartre has argued, quite convincingly I think, that many of our value-judgments stem from our free choices, not in the crude subjectivist sense in which thinking something to be good is completely reducible to liking it or approving of it, but rather in the sense that what I *see* as good or bad, and what I fail to see in evaluative terms at all, are each largely determined by my many freely chosen projects in life, which are themselves largely determined by the more fundamental of my freely chosen projects, or even by a single freely chosen fundamental project. Thus, if my fundamental project is to be a teacher, I am more likely to see knowledge as a great positive value and ignorance as a great disvalue than I would if my fundamental project were to be the world's greatest public relations man.

On the other hand, in his objectivist moods, Sartre implies that my freedom to choose projects and thereby to make values emerge is limited by an involuntary dimension—the dimension of what I see to be so, to be irreducibly true irrespective of my freedom or its choices. Thus, my need for food is something I find, rather than invent, and so it is a matter of discovery rather than creation that vegetables, fruits, grains, and cheeses will meet this need, but that plastic, glass, sawdust, and television sets will not. Similarly, I find that the world suggests certain choices and values to me, and that these suggestions carry varying degrees of coercive force. Indeed, *some* value-judgments, e.g., that pleasure is better than pain, that health is better than sickness, that cruelty for its own sake is wrong, etc., present themselves as true apart from my freely choosing to accept or reject them, and as so irreducibly true and important as to place limits on which choices I may legitimately make. Thus, just as there is a dialectic of the voluntary and the involuntary in the perception of objects, so is there this dialectic in the constitution of values. Moreover, an appreciation of the role of freedom in both phases of the dialectic helps us to understand just how dizzying this dialectic is: Values are recognized and created through freedom; but we are not free not to recognize freedom as a value, partially because it is in virtue of our freedom that we choose what we value;

but our choice of what we value is not entirely free; there are involuntary elements which suggest certain choices to us, and which limit the possibilities of choice; but we are free to take up or not these suggestions, to choose from within the area circumscribed by these limitations, etc., etc. Just as Sartre has said of the situation in general that it "is an ambiguous phenomenon in which it is impossible for the for-itself to distinguish the contribution of freedom from that of the brute existent,"[78] so it is in the *ethical* situation.

Let us explore this in more detail by reintroducing another of Sartre's contributions to moral philosophy, namely, his analysis of moral dilemmas. Recall that Sartre's most famous example of a moral dilemma is that of a young student who must choose between fighting for France against the Nazis and staying at home to care for his aged mother. Sartre points out that the traditional "objective" moral systems are incapable of determining what the young man should do, and concludes, rather hastily, that there is nothing to ethics but personal choice, that *whatever* the young man would choose, he would be right—that his chioce would be *constitutive* of right. Thus, Sartre arrives at radical subjectivism. But notice that this dilemma can be much more plausibly analyzed in terms of the dialectic which I have outlined, in which there is an involuntary dimension, an "objective" dimension within which the realm of free choice is circumscribed by our recognition of ethical truths. Two advantages of this analysis over Sartre's are: (1) that it explains, while Sartre's does not, why not just *any* choice would be defensible—surely even Sartre would be unwilling to condone as a legitimate third alternative choice that of fighting *for* the Nazis, and (2) that it explains, while Sartre does not, why *this* situation, unlike others, is a genuine moral dilemma—quite simply, it is a situation in which a person must choose between two incompatible courses of action both of which are very good. For the subjectivist, of course, either *no* situations are moral dilemmas (since nothing is "really" good or bad) or else *all* situations are moral dilemmas (since all situations present choices between incompatible courses of action, all of which, were they to be chosen, would be good). What Sartre's form of subjectivism cannot explain is why some situations are moral dilemmas and others are not.

At the same time, there is some point to Sartre's subjectivism, but this point is consistent with the conception of ethics being here advocated. The point is that there *is* considerable room for choice and invention in ethics, that the truths of ethics are *not* determinate enough to dictate what should be done in every concrete circumstance, that there are *different kinds* of good lives, and thus, that there is *not* one and only one right act to be performed in every situation.

This brings us to yet another of Sartre's contributions to moral philosophy, namely, his ideal of play. Recall that, in play, there are no "rules" except for the ones which we, the players, freely invent. All of the values which arise in play are those which we freely choose or create. In play, we are subjected to no external constraints of any kind. For the early Sartre, this is what ethics, once the foolish project of attempting to be God has been overthrown, is all about.

The later Sartre, however, is far more serious. People are starving to death. The world is at the mercy of ruthless dictators. These are the evils which must be addressed and remedied. Now is a time for *work,* not play.

And yet, these two positions are not incompatible, and their resolution underscores, once again, the conception of ethics being here advocated. For, in the first place, if play is indeed the ideal, then it is clear why seriousness and an attitude of urgency are appropriate in our world. After all, people who are hungry and oppressed are *not* able to play. And, in the second place, seeing what is wrong with hunger and poverty points us in the direction of play as an ideal, for a major part of what is wrong with hunger and poverty, aside from the considerable pain which they cause, is that they close off play. The poor have to expend so much time and energy struggling to stay alive that it is impossible for them to engage in the creative, self-expressive exercise of their freedom that is play.

Here again we have an ethics of invention and discovery. The most satisfying and fulfilling values are those which emerge from the free creative expression of our own unique personalities. These are the values of *invention.* But such free creative expression is only possible if we are first *free*—free in the sense of being relatively unconstrained, including being unconstrained by the need to scramble for food, medical care, warmth in the winter, etc. The value of freedom in this sense is something we *discover.*

Such a conception of ethics captures, it seems to me, both the serious and the playful sides of morality. It accounts for the fact that we have certain strict duties, from which we cannot in good conscience escape, no matter what our choices, and for the fact that much of what is deeply good and valuable to us is not in any sense obligatorily so, but arises instead solely from our free choices, without being in any way dictated by any true "objective" ethical theory. The importance of freedom in this conception of ethics is manifest. Many, perhaps most, of our strict duties are derivable from our duty to protect and to promote freedom, both our own and that of others. And the importance of freedom in "play" is too obvious to require elaboration.

This brings to mind yet another of Sartre's contributions to ethics—namely, his teleological (some would say utopian) notion of judging current actions in accordance with their tendency to bring about a certain kind of improved society and world—a world in which there would be no poverty, hunger, and exploitation, a world in which people would be truly free to play. This again suggests seriousness and playfulness, discovery and invention. We have now a serious, discovered obligation to promote freedom, so that, once we have achieved this freedom, we can playfully invent.

Such a conception of ethics is, to my knowledge, unique in the history of western philosophy, though it shares obvious affinities with such different moral and political philosophies as, for example, those of Karl Marx and John Stuart Mill. Sartre's is *not,* contrary to popular belief, a totally relativistic, solipsistic, anarchistic, nihilistic, or pessimistic ethic.[79] Rather, it is an ethic which implores us both to *recognize* the great *value* of our freedom, and to *use* that freedom to *invent* values. No adequate ethical theory can fail to recognize either of these two fundamental dimensions of our moral experience. It is the chief virtue of Sartre's ethical theory that it recognizes, and, with admirable clarity and insight articulates, both of them.

Notes

Introduction

1. Thomas W. Busch, "Sartre: The Phenomenological Reduction and Human Relationships." *Journal of the British Society for Phenomenology* 6, No. 1 (January 1975), p. 55.

2. Thomas C. Anderson, *The Foundation and Structure of Sartrean Ethics* (Lawrence: The Regents Press of Kansas, 1979), p. 5.

3. Jean-Paul Sartre, *Being and Nothingness,* trans. Hazel E. Barnes (New York: Philosophical Library, 1956), p. 628. (This work will hereafter be cited as *BN*.) Though Sartre did not publish any specifically ethical works during his lifetime, his *Cahiers pour une morale* (Paris: Gallimard, 1983), has been published posthumously.

Chapter One: Freedom

1. Hazel E. Barnes, *Sartre* (Philadelphia J.B. Lippincott, 1973), p. 187.

2. In referring to Sartre's "early" philosophy, I have in mind primarily, aside from *BN*, such works as: *Imagination: A Psychological Critique,* trans. Forrest Williams (Ann Arbor: Ann Arbor Paperbacks, 1972); *The Transcendence of the Ego,* trans. Forrest Williams and Robert Kirkpatrick (New York: The Noonday Press, 1957), hereafter cited as *TE*; "Intentionality: A Fundamental Idea of Husserl's Phenomenology," trans. Joseph P. Fell. *Journal of the British Society for Phenomenology* 1, No. 2 (May 1970): 4–5; *The Psychology of Imagination,* trans. Bernard Frechtman (New York: Washington Square Press, 1968), as well as many lesser works written and published during this same period (roughly, from the early 1930s through the middle of the 1940s).

3. Cf. Mary Warnock, *The Philosophy of Sartre* (New York: Barnes & Noble, 1967), especially pp. 130, 135, 150; her *Ethics Since 1900* (New York: Oxford

University Press, 1966), p. 139; her *Existentialist Ethics* (New York: St Martin's Press, 1967), pp. 50–52; and her *Existentialism* (New York: Oxford University Press, 1970), p. 126. See also Richard J. Bernstein, *Praxis and Action* (Philadelphia: University of Pennsylvania Press, 1971), pp. 155–156; and Thomas Molnar, *Sartre: Ideologue of Our Time* (New York: Funk & Wagnalls, 1968), p. 122.

4. Cf. *BN,* p. 67.

5. Cf. Edmund Husserl, *Ideas Pertaining to a Pure Phenomenology and to a Phenomenological Philosophy: First Book,* trans. F. Kersten (The Hague: Martinus Nijhoff, 1982), #84, pp. 199–202. (This work will hereafter be cited as *I*); his *Cartesian Meditations,* trans. Dorion Cairns (The Hague: Martinus Nijhoff, 1977), #14, pp. 32–33. (This work will hereafter be cited as *CM*); and his "Phenomenology," trans. Richard E. Palmer in *Husserl: Shorter Works,* ed. Peter McCormick and Frederick A. Elliston (Notre Dame: University of Notre Dame Press, 1981), p. 23.

6. "Intentionality," *op. cit.,* p. 5, emphasis added.

7. *Ibid.,* p. 4.

8. *Ibid.*

9. *Ibid.*

10. *Ibid.*

11. *Ibid.,* pp. 4–5.

12. Herbert Spiegelberg, *The Phenomenological Movement* (The Hague: Martinus Nijhoff, 1982), p. 508.

13. *BN,* p. lx.

14. I do not mean to suggest that this is a disreputable interpretation. To the contrary, there is an abundance of textual documentation to support it. Cf. *Husserliana* III, pp. 360–465 (cited by Spiegelberg, *op. cit.,* p. 126) for a list of all the passages which characterize Husserl's "idealistic" position. On the other hand, for an anthology of quotations which exemplify a "realistic" interpretation of Husserl's philosophy, see Jean Wahl, "Note sur quelques aspects empiristes de la pensée de Husserl," in his *Phénoménologie-Existence* (Paris: Arthaud, 1947), pp. 107–135.

15. *I,* #46, p. 102.

16. Sartre, *Nausea,* trans. Lloyd Alexander (New York: New Directions, 1964), pp. 170–182. A superior translation of parts of this passage is that of Robert Denoon Cumming in his anthology, *The Philosophy of Jean-Paul Sartre* (New York: Vintage Books, 1972), pp. 59–68. For a detailed discussion of *Nausea* as an argument against the phenomenological reduction see Thomas W. Busch, "La Nausée": A Lover's Quarrel with Husserl." *Research in Phenomenology* XI (1981): 1–24.

17. Maurice Merleau-Ponty, *Phenomenology of Perception,* trans. Colin Smith (New Jersey: The Humanities Press, 1962), p. xiv. (This work will hereafter be cited as *PP.*) Throughout the preface to *PP,* Merleau-Ponty presents this opposition to a thoroughgoing reduction as Husserl's own teaching. For example,

he claims that Husserl's philosophy is one in which "the world is 'already there' before reflection begins—as an *inalienable presence*," and states that all of phenomenology's efforts are "concentrated upon reachieving a direct and primitive contact with the world" (*PP*, p. vii, emphasis added). While this interpretation might well be disputed, some justification for it can be found in those Husserlian texts which seem to indicate that the reasons for imposing the brackets are primarily methodological, and are not inspired by any real doubt about the external existence of the world (Cf. *I*, #49, pp. 109–112; *CM*, #7–8, pp. 17–21; "Phenomenology," *op. cit.*, p. 28; and *Formal and Transcendental Logic*, trans. Dorion Cairns [The Hague: Martinus Nijhoff, 1969], #94–98, pp. 232–250.)

18. *BN*, p. xlvi.

19. *I*, #67—70, pp. 153–160.

20. Cf. Erazim Kohák, *Idea and Experience: Edmund Husserl's Project of Phenomenology in "Ideas I"* (Chicago: The University of Chicago Press, 1978), pp. 251–252.

21. Cf. Robert C. Solomon, *From Rationalism to Existentialism* (New Jersey: Humanities Press, 1978), pp. 251–252.

22. *PP*, p. xvi.

23. *BN*, p. lxii.

24. See works by Husserl cited in note 17.

25. Frederick A. Olafson, "Sartre, Jean-Paul" in *The Encyclopedia of Philosophy, Vol. 7*, ed. Paul Edwards (New York: Macmillan, 1967), p. 290.

26. *The Psychology of Imagination, op. cit.*, p. 234.

27. *Imagination, op. cit.*, Chapter IX, pp. 127–143.

28. For purposes of brevity, I have grossly simplified Sartre's argument, which includes a critique of Husserl's notion of "*hyle*."

29. *The Psychology of Imagination, op. cit.*, p. 233.

30. *TE*, p. 31, emphasis added.

31. *I*, #57, 80, pp. 132–133, 190–192.

32. *TE*, p. 31.

33. *TE*, p. 37.

34. *TE*, p. 34.

35. *TE*, pp. 38–40.

36. Husserl, *Logical Investigations, Vol. Two*, trans. J. N. Findlay (New York: Humanities Press, 1970), Investigation V, #4, pp. 541–542. A bit later on in the same work (#8, p. 549) Husserl bluntly declares: "I must frankly confess, however, that I am quite unable to find this ego, this primitive, necessary centre of relations."

37. *TE*, p. 40.

38. Spiegelberg, *op. cit.*, p. 502. See also his "Husserl's Phenomenology and Sartre's Existentialism" in his *The Context of the Phenomenological Movement* (The Hague: Martinus Nijhoff, 1981), pp. 51–61, especially p. 58.

39. *I*, #57, p. 132.

40. René Descartes, *Meditations on the First Philosophy,* especially Meditation II. Cf. John Veitch's translation in the anthology *The Rationalists* (Garden City, New York: Anchor Books, 1974), p. 119.

41. *TE,* p. 45.

42. *Logical Investigations, Vol. Two, op. cit.,* Investigation V, #12, pp. 561–562.

43. *TE,* pp. 48–49. Aron Gurwitsch claims (in his "A Nonegological Conception of Consciousness" in his *Studies in Phenomenology and Psychology* [Evanston: Northwestern University Press, 1966], p. 290, note 8) that, on the descriptive level, there is complete agreement on this issue between Sartre and Gestalt psychology.

44. I have borrowed this phrase from the title of Gurwitsch's article, cited in the preceding note.

45. *TE,* pp. 53–54.

46. *TE,* p. 40.

47. *TE,* pp. 41–42.

48. *TE,* p. 41.

49. There is some question as to whether Sartre is correct in interpreting Husserl's transcendental ego as a substantival entity. See Kohák, *op. cit.,* pp. 44, 181–182, and 202, note 21; and Pratima Bowes, *Consciousness and Freedom: Three Views* (London: Methuen, 1971), pp. 145–146.

50. Compare with *I,* #77, pp. 174–177.

51. *BN,* p. lii, translation modified (See the original text, *L'être et le néant* [Paris: Gallimard, 1943], p. 18.) (This work will hereafter be cited as *EN.*)

52. This way of phrasing the point was suggested to me by David Michael Levin.

53. *BN,* p. liii.

54. W. T. Jones, *A History of Western Philosophy: Vol. V, The Twentieth Century to Wittgenstein and Sartre* (New York: Harcourt Brace Jovanovich, 1975), p. 345.

55. *TE,* pp. 43–44.

56. Sartre is not the only philosopher to claim a connection between "the systematic elusiveness of 'I'" and the experience of freedom. See Gilbert Ryle, *The Concept of Mind* (New York: Barnes and Noble, 1949), pp. 195–198.

57. James M. Edie, "Sartre as Phenomenologist and as Existential Psychoanalyst" in *Phenomenology and Existentialism,* ed. Edward N. Lee and Maurice Mandelbaum (Baltimore: The Johns Hopkins Press, 1969), p. 150.

58. *Ibid.,* p. 152.

59. *BN,* p. 33. See also Sartre's *Saint Genet,* trans. Bernard Frechtman (New York: Mentor, 1964), p. 49.

60. *BN,* p. 509.

61. *BN,* p. 29.

62. Sartre's reasons for saying this in *BN* may stem from the particular concerns of that work. Sartre himself later described *BN* as an "eidetic of bad

faith," as quoted by Michel Contat and Michel Rybalka in their *The Writings of Jean-Paul Sartre: Vol. 1, A Bibliographical Life,* trans. Richard C. McCleary (Evanston: Northwestern University Press, 1974), p. 84. (See also the documents cited by Anderson, *op. cit.,* p. 155, note 32, which support this interpretation of *BN*.) This issue will be discussed in some detail subsequently in this chapter, during the discussion of Sartre's notion of "radical conversion." For now, it is sufficient to point out that Sartre has not always claimed that freedom can be known only through anguish. For example, in *What is Literature?,* trans. Bernard Frechtman (London: Methuen, 1978), p. 42, he states that "the recognition of freedom by itself is joy." And in one of his last interviews, conducted shortly before his death (Benny Lévy, "Today's Hope: Conversations with Sartre," trans. Lilliam Hernandez, George Waterston, and Claire Hubert. *Telos* 44 [Summer 1980]: 155–181), Sartre attributes his preoccupation with despair and anguish in *BN* to such factors as the social and political climate in which that work was written, the prevailing intellectual fashions, and the fact that these notions were crucial to his philosophical forebears, Kierkegaard and Heidegger. He even adds that he has never personally experienced anguish (p. 156). On the other hand, Simone de Beauvoir protests, in *Adieux: A Farewell to Sartre,* trans. Patrick O'Brian (New York: Pantheon Books, 1984), p. 119, that Sartre had been bullied into these statements by his young interlocutor, and that Sartre's treatment by him during the interview had amounted to an "abduction of an old man."

63. *BN,* p. 29. For an excellent literary anticipation of Sartre's theory of anguish, see Edgar Allan Poe, "The Imp of the Perverse" in *Collected Works of Edgar Allan Poe, Vol. 3,* ed. Thomas Ollive Mabbott (Cambridge, Massachusetts: The Belknap Press of Harvard University Press, 1978), pp. 1217–1227.

64. *BN,* p. 29.

65. *BN,* pp. 29–30.

66. *BN,* p. 33.

67. Sartre, "Cartesian Freedom" in *Literary and Philosophical Essays,* trans. Annette Michelson (New York: Collier Books, 1962), p. 196. (This book will hereafter be cited as *LPE.*)

68. *BN,* p. 23.

69. *BN,* p. 47, trans. modified (see *EN,* p. 85.).

70. *BN,* p. 443.

71. *BN,* p. 24, emphasis added.

72. *The Psychology of Imagination, op. cit.,* p. 238.

73. *Ibid.,* p. 16.

74. Cf. Fernando Molina, *Existentialism as Philosophy* (Englewood Cliffs, N.J.: Prentice-Hall, 1962), p. 86.

75. *The Psychology of Imagination, op. cit.,* p. 234.

76. *Ibid.,* p. 240.

77. *Ibid.,* p. 243.

78. *LPE,* p. 189.

79. *LPE,* p. 190.

80. *LPE*, p. 191.

81. *BN*, pp. 8–9.

82. Cf. Arthur C. Danto, *Sartre* (London: Fontana, 1979), p. 68.

83. It is perhaps worth pointing out that, despite his rhetoric, Sartre is not here advocating a radically "subjectivistic" or "idealistic" account of destruction. To be sure, there is no destruction without my nihilating act. Indeed, my precious vase would not even be *destructible* were I not capable of envisioning it as it is *not*, but as it *could be*, namely, destroyed. But my nihilating act does not *itself* destroy the vase. Moreover, were it to be destroyed, this would be "an irreversible event which I could only verify" (*BN*, p. 9). Finally, were my vase made of certain materials which it is in fact *not* made of, it would be *in*destructible, *in spite of* my ability to envision it as destroyed. In short, nihilating acts of consciousness are necessary but not sufficient conditions of the appearance of destruction. A part must also be played by forces and arrangements of matter which exist in the world, apart from any consciousness.

84. Sartre points out that even questions which on the surface do not permit a negative reply—for example, "What does this attitude reveal to us?"—can in fact always be met with such replies as "nothing," or "nobody," or "never" (*BN*, p. 5).

85. *BN*, p. 5, trans. modified (see *EN*, p. 39).

86. *BN*, p. 5.

87. *BN*, p. 5, trans. modified (see *EN*, p. 39).

88. *BN*, p. 5, emphasis added.

89. *BN*, p. 5.

90. *BN*, p. 23.

91. Ian Craib, *Existentialism and Sociology: A Study of Jean-Paul Sartre* (Cambridge: Cambridge University Press, 1976), pp. 17–18.

92. Cf. *I*, #35, pp. 69–73.

93. Cf. Dagfinn Føllesdal, "Sartre on Freedom" in *The Philosophy of Jean-Paul Sartre*, ed. Paul Arthur Schilpp (La Salle, Illinois: Open Court, 1981), pp. 392–407.

94. The example is Sartre's (*BN*, pp. 9–11). For a similar example, see Sartre's *The Words*, trans. Bernard Frechtman (Greenwich, Conn.: Fawcett, 1966), pp. 57–58.

95. *BN*, p. 9.

96. *BN*, pp. 9–10.

97. *BN*, p. 10.

98. A. J. Ayer, "Novelist-Philosophers V—Jean-Paul Sartre." *Horizon* XII, No. 67 (July 1945), pp. 18–19.

99. *BN*, pp. 10–11.

100. Similar considerations can, I think, be brought to bear against Ayer's "suspicion that what is called existentialist philosophy has become very largely an exercise in the art of misusing the verb 'to be'" (Ayer, *op. cit.*, p. 25). It is also perhaps worth pointing out that Ayer's critique of Sartre's doctrine of negativity gains a specious plausibility through his decision to translate *"le néant"* as

"nothing" rather than as "nothingness." "To say that two objects are separated by nothing is to say that they are *not* separated" is perhaps a plausible judgment; but suspicion is cast upon it when "nothingness" replaces "nothing" in this translation, for the former term, unlike the latter, suggests a technical usage in which some kind of negative *entity* is being named.

101. Barnes points out that, while Sartre often uses the two terms "consciousness" and "being-for-itself" as if they were interchangable, they are in fact "inseparable but not the same" (Barnes, *op. cit.,* p. 54). Nonetheless, I shall follow Sartre in using the two terms more or less interchangably, since the difference between them does not, I think, significantly bear upon the issues discussed in this study.

102. Recall the discussion of the transcendence of the ego above.

103. As we have seen in the discussion of the phenomenological reduction, Sartre does not subscribe to a *Kantian* notion of a thing-in-itself; that is, he does not believe in any "noumenal" reality which Being *really* is, apart from its appearances.

104. *BN*, p. lxvi.

105. *BN*, p. 509.

106. *BN*, p. 555.

107. *BN*, p. 509.

108. *Sartre on Theater,* ed. Michel Contat and Michel Rybalka, trans. Frank Jellinek (New York: Pantheon Books, 1976), p. 205.

109. Sartre, in *Pour et contre l'existentialisme,* ed. C. Audry (Paris, 1948), p. 188, as cited in Mark Poster, *Existential Marxism in Postwar France: From Sartre to Althusser* (Princeton: Princeton University Press, 1975), p. 126.

110. *BN*, p. 441.

111. *BN*, p. 550.

112. Cf. *PP*, pp. 436–442; Warnock, *The Philosophy of Sartre, op. cit.,* p. 112; Føllesdal, *op. cit.,* pp. 400–404; Risieri Frondizi, "Sartre's Early Ethics: A Critique," in Schilpp, *op. cit.,* pp. 383, 385–388; Maurice Cranston, *Jean-Paul Sartre* (New York: Grove Press, 1962), p. 83; Wilfrid Desan, *The Tragic Finale: An Essay on the Philosophy of Jean-Paul Sartre* (New York: Harper Torchbooks, 1960), pp. 170, 173; Remy C. Kwant, *The Phenomenological Philosophy of Merleau-Ponty* (Pittsburgh: Duquesne University Press, 1963), pp. 205–211; and Herbert Marcuse, "Sartre's Existentialism" in his *Studies in Critical Philosophy* (Boston: Beacon Press, 1973), pp. 172–177.

113. Cf. the previously cited works of Warnock and Ayer.

114. *BN*, p. 481.

115. Cf. the four quoted passages which are featured later in this section.

116. Reinhold Grossmann, *Phenomenology and Existentialism* (London: Routledge and Kegan Paul, 1984), pp. 262–263.

117. *Ibid.,* p. 167.

118. Walter Kaufmann, *Without Guilt and Justice* (New York: Delta, 1973), p. 144.

119. Frondizi, *op. cit.*, p. 383.

120. Sartre, "The Itinerary of a Thought" in *Between Existentialism and Marxism*, trans. John Mathews (New York: William Morrow, 1976), p. 35.

121. Sartre, speaking in a film which has been transcribed as *Sartre By Himself*, trans. Richard Seaver (New York: Outback Press, 1978), p. 58.

122. *Ibid.*, p. 59.

123. Sartre, *Critique of Dialectic Reason*, trans. Alan Sheridan-Smith (London: Verso, 1982). (This work will hereafter be cited as *CDR*.) I have here quoted the translation of Starr and Jim Atkinson in Cumming, *op. cit.*, p. 463.

124. *CDR*, p. 331.

125. Sartre, "On 'The Idiot of the Family'" in *Life/Situations: Essays Written and Spoken*, trans. Paul Auster and Lydia Davis (New York: Pantheon Books, 1977), p. 116.

126. Cf. the works cited in note 3 above.

127. *BN*, p. 489, emphasis added.

128. *BN*, pp. 495–496.

129. *BN*, p. 328, emphasis added.

130. *BN*, p. 497.

131. *BN*, p. 83.

132. *BN*, p. 498.

133. *BN*, p. 495. This passage should give pause to those who equate "absolute freedom" with "unrestricted freedom."

134. *BN*, p. 507.

135. *BN*, p. 481, emphasis added.

136. Howard R. Burkle, "Jean-Paul Sartre: Social Freedom in 'Critique de la raison dialectique'." *Review of Metaphysics* 19, No. 4 (June 1966), pp. 751–752.

137. *Ibid.*, p. 756.

138. *BN*, p. 481.

139. *BN*, p. 482.

140. *BN*, p. 488.

141. *BN*, pp. 488–489.

142. It is true that Sartre says on p. 482 of *BN* that "the coefficient of adversity in things can not be an argument against our freedom." But it is clear from the context in which this passage occurs, and from his distinction (on pp. 483–484) between two different senses of freedom, that this applies to only *one* sense of freedom, the one with which he is principally concerned in that particular passage.

143. *BN*, p. 488.

144. *BN*, p. 482.

145. *BN*, p. 549.

146. *BN*, p. 551.

147. *BN*, p. 488.

148. Cf. the previously cited works of Warnock, Desan, Kwant, and Marcuse.

149. *BN*, p. 509.

150. *BN*, p. 309.

151. *BN*, p. 548. See also *BN*, p. 549, where Sartre says that "being-in-situation defines human reality."

152. *What is Literature?*, *op. cit.*, p. 112.

153. *BN*, p. 489.

154. Solomon, *op. cit.*, p. 280, emphasis added.

155. *Ibid.*

156. Sartre, *Anti-Semite and Jew*, trans. George J. Becker (New York: Schocken Books, 1974), p. 60, emphasis added.

157. Sartre, *Existentialism and Humanism*, trans. Philip Mairet (Brooklyn: Haskell House, 1977), p. 46.

158. Sartre, "Introduction to 'Les Temps Modernes'," trans. Françoise Ehrmann, in *Paths to the Present: Aspects of European Thought from Romanticism to Existentialism*, ed. Eugen Weber (New York: Dodd, Mead & Company, 1962), p. 438. All of this is often missed by commentators. For example, Sonia Kruks asserts, without referring to any of the "human condition" passages: "For Sartre, since situations are each uniquely brought into being by individual free projects, we [can] not talk of a *general* situation" ("Simone de Beauvoir and the limits to Freedom." *Social Text* 17 [Fall 1987], p. 118).

159. *CDR*, p. 67.

160. "Glossary" to *CDR*, p. 829.

161. For the benefit of those who tend to exaggerate the extent of Sartre's evolution, consider the following two passages from *BN:* "I find myself engaged in an *already meaningful* world which reflects to me meanings which I have not put into it" (p. 510). "I am not only thrown face to face with the brute existent. I am thrown into a worker's world, a French world, a world of Lorraine or the South, which offers me its meanings without my having done anything to disclose them" (p. 514).

162. *CDR*, p. 193.

163. *CDR*, p. 162.

164. *CDR*, p. 162.

165. Barnes, *op. cit.*, pp. 159–160.

166. Cf. the chapter on "Concrete Relations With Others" in *BN*, pp. 361–430.

167. Solomon, *op. cit.*, p. 310, emphasis added.

168. Joseph S. Catalano, *A Commentary on Jean-Paul Sartre's "Being and Nothingness"* (Chicago: The University of Chicago Press, 1980), p. 209.

169. *BN*, pp 523–524. Such passages are often ignored by Sartre's critics. To give just one recent example, Kruks criticizes Sartre for allegedly not recognizing the extent to which others limit my freedom. She writes: "in *Being and Nothingness* other people are commonly presented as only a peripheral or indirect structure of 'my' situation, (and not as) *directly* involved in my own constitution of the meaning of . . . a free project" (*op. cit.*, p. 116).

170. Recall, for example, the passages cited in notes 116–119 above.

171. Recall, for example, the passages cited in notes 105–111 above.

172. Grossmann, *op. cit.*, p. 262.

173. *BN*, p. 495.

174. Frondizi, *op. cit.*, p. 383.
175. *BN*, pp 523–524.
176. *EH*, p. 46.
177. Grossmann, *op. cit.*, p. 167.
178. *BN*, p. 482.
179. Frondizi, *op. cit.*, p. 383.
180. Maurice Cranston, *Freedom: A New Analysis* (New York: Longmans, Green and Co., 1953), p. 3.
181. For a detailed analysis of the different but related senses of freedom which have appeared throughout the history of western philosophy see Mortimer J. Adler, *The Idea of Freedom* (Garden City, N.Y.: Doubleday, 1958 and 1961, 2 Vols.)
182. *What is Literature?, op. cit.*, p. 231, note 24.
183. *LPE*, pp. 184–185. See also de Beauvoir's discussion in *The Ethics of Ambiguity*, trans. Bernard Frechtman (New York: The Citadel Press, 1970), pp. 28–30, which, because of her close personal and philosophical relationship with Sartre, can perhaps be considered authoritative.
184. *BN*, pp. 483–484.
185. Sartre, "Self-Portrait at Seventy," in *Life/Situations, op. cit.*, p. 88; and his "Reply to Albert Camus," trans. Benita Eisler, in *Situations* (Greenwich, Conn.: Fawcett Crest, 1969), pp. 67–68. See also Francis Jeanson's discussion in *Sartre and the Problem of Morality*, trans. Robert V. Stone (Bloomington: Indiana University Press, 1980), pp. 14–15, a work which can be considered authoritative, since Sartre has explicitly endorsed it "as interpreting my views to my complete satisfaction" (interview with Jacques L. Salvan, quoted in Salvan's *The Scandalous Ghost* [Detroit: Wayne State University Press, 1967], p. 14). (See also Sartre's glowing recommendation of Jeanson's book in his "Letter-Foreword" to that work, on pp. xxxix–xl.)
186. *The Writings of Jean-Paul Sartre, Vol. 1, op. cit.*, p. 200.
187. *Ibid.*, p. 387.
188. *Ibid.*, p. 453; and Sartre, "The Responsibility of the Writer," trans. Betty Askwith, in *The Creative Vision: Modern European Writers on their Art*, ed. Haskell M. Block and Herman Salinger (New York: Grove Press, 1960), pp. 174–175.
189. "The Responsibility of the Writer," *op. cit.*, p. 180.
190. Interview with Desan, quoted in Desan, *op. cit.*, p. xvi.
191. John Deigh called this to my attention.
192. *The Writings of Jean-Paul Sartre, Vol. 1, op. cit.*, p. 200, emphasis added.
193. *BN*, p. 481.
194. *BN*, pp. 481–482.
195. *BN*, pp. 483–484.
196. *BN*, p. 550.
197. Marcuse, *op. cit.*, p. 174. Similarly, Calvin O. Schrag cites the "slave in chains" passage and states that "in Sartre's radical view of freedom, the question remains whether freedom does not cancel itself" (*Existence and Freedom:*

Towards an Ontology of Human Finitude [Evanston, Illinois: Northwestern University Press, 1961], p. 196).

198. Sartre, "A More Precise Characterization of Existentialism," trans. Richard C. McCleary, in *The Writings of Jean-Paul Sartre, Vol. 2: Selected Prose,* ed. Michel Contat and Michel Rybalka (Evanston: Northwestern University Press, 1974), p. 159.

199. Sartre, "Materialism and Revolution," in *LPE,* p. 244, emphasis added.

200. *Ibid.,* p. 245, emphasis added.

201. *Anti-Semite and Jew, op. cit.,* p. 136, emphasis added.

202. Sartre, interview with Jean Duché, quoted in Føllesdal, *op. cit.,* pp. 404–405, emphasis added. See also de Beauvoir's response to this criticism in *The Ethics of Ambiguity, op. cit.,* pp. 24–26.

203. *BN,* p. 488. Thus, Kruks' comment that, for Sartre, we cannot "judge one situation to be more free than another" (*op. cit.,* p. 118) is true in one sense of "freedom," but not in another.

204. *LPE,* p. 244.

205. Anderson, "Is a Sartrean Ethics Possible?" *Philosophy Today* 14, No. 2 (Summer 1970), p. 123.

206. Anderson, *The Foundation and Structure of Sartrean Ethics, op. cit.,* p. 56. See also Margaret Whitford, *Merleau-Ponty's Critique of Sartre's Philosophy* (Lexington, Kentucky: French Forum, 1982), pp. 55–56.

207. Herbert J. Muller, *Issues of Freedom* (New York: Harper and Brothers, 1960), especially Chapter I: "The Meanings of Freedom," pp. 3–20.

208. *Ibid.,* p. 5.

209. *Ibid.*

210. *Ibid.,* p. 8.

211. Warnock, *The Philosophy of Sartre, op. cit.,* p. 118. For incisive criticism of Warnock on this point see Burkle, *op. cit.,* p. 754, and James F. Sheridan, Jr., *Sartre: The Radical Conversion* (Athens, Ohio: Ohio University Press, 1969), p. 5.

212. Cf. *PP,* p. 437 and Merleau-Ponty's *Adventures of the Dialectic,* trans. Joseph Bien (Evanston: Northwestern University Press, 1973), p. 196. The objection is also raised by Schrag, (*op. cit.,* p. 196): "When Sartre writes that even the individual who is subject to the executioner's tools is free, it would seem that the freedom of which he speaks is no more than a freedom to accept one's fate, which, to be sure, still has the earmarks of freedom but can hardly be understood as total and infinite."

213. *BN,* p. 550.

214. Sartre, "Introduction to 'Les Temps Modernes'," *op. cit.,* p. 441.

215. Many commentators, however, seem to think that Sartre *would* make this absurd claim. Indeed, this is the interpretation given in all of the works cited in note 112, with the single exception of Føllesdal's.

216. *BN,* pp. 483–484, emphasis added. Notice that there are two distinct senses of freedom operating in this passage.

217. Anderson, "Is a Sartrean Ethics Possible?", *op. cit.,* p. 123.

218. De Beauvoir seems to embrace such an idea when she suggests "establishing an order of precedence among various 'situations.' Though, subjectively speaking, salvation [is] always possible, one should still choose knowledge rather than ignorance, health rather than disease, and prefer prosperity to penury" (*The Prime of Life,* trans. Peter Green [New York: Lancer Books, 1966], p. 661).

219. *BN,* p. 550.

220. Isaiah Berlin, "Two Concepts of Liberty," in his *Four Essays on Liberty* (New York: Oxford University Press, 1969), p. 130, note 1.

221. This argument does not show that it is *impossible* to distinguish between situations in terms of the quantity of choices permitted within each. But it does show that such a quantitative differentiation would have to be reconciled with the fact that there are an infinite number of possibilities open to one in *every* situation.

222. P. H. Partridge, "Freedom," in Edwards, ed., *The Encyclopedia of Philosophy, Vol. 3., op. cit.,* p. 223.

223. Cf. Muller, *op. cit.,* pp. 10–12.

224. *The Writings of Jean-Paul Sartre, Vol. 1, op. cit.,* p. 387. Note the distinction between two senses of freedom.

225. *Ibid.,* p. 453. Again, note the distinction between different senses of freedom.

226. Sartre, "A Long, Bitter, Sweet Madness," trans. Anthony Hartley. *Encounter* 22, No. 6 (June 1964), p. 61, emphasis added.

227. Howard Zinn, *The Politics of History* (Boston: Beacon Press, 1971), p. 23.

228. Cf. Bertrand Russell, *Religion and Science* (New York: Oxford University Press, 1968), pp. 223–243; Ayer, *Language, Truth and Logic* (New York: Dover Publications, 1952), pp. 20–22, 102–113; and Charles L. Stevenson, *Ethics and Language* (New Haven: Yale University Press, 1960).

229. Peter Caws, *Sartre* (Boston: Routledge & Kegan Paul, 1979), p. 113.

230. See Chapters Two and Three of the present work.

231. I do not necessarily mean to imply that this is an adequate account of the meaning of "free will." Rather, I am here concerned only to show how different questions concerning free will are from questions concerning political freedom.

232. Solomon, *op. cit.,* p. 273, emphasis added.

233. Cf. Frederick Copleston, *A History of Philosophy, Vol. 5: Modern Philosophy: The British Philosophers, Part II: Berkeley to Hume* (Garden City, N.Y.: Image Books, 1964), p. 12.

234. Jones, *A History of Western Philosophy: Vol. III, Hobbes to Hume* (New York: Harcourt Brace Jovanovich, 1969), p. 289.

235. Cf. section 1.2.2.3 above.

236. This is not to say, of course, that this theory is not vulnerable to other perfectly legitimate objections.

237. Cf. those passages cited in notes 116–119 above.

238. *BN,* p. 483.

239. *BN,* p. 483.

240. It is interesting, for example, that Walter Kaufmann, who refers to "Sartre's extravagant emphasis on man's complete freedom," and calls this "at odds with the facts of life (Kaufmann, *op. cit.,* p. 144), elsewhere in the same work (p. 5) agrees with Sartre that "the freedom to make fateful decisions is inalienable. Even a prisoner condemned to death retains this freedom." And yet, in repudiating Sartre's doctrine of "complete freedom," he fails to say how that freedom differs from the "inalienable" freedom which he endorses.

241. Desan, *op. cit.,* p. 170.

242. *BN,* p. 505.

243. Desan, *op. cit.,* p. 108.

244. *BN,* p. 483.

245. Even without consulting Sartre's discussion of this specific example, one would have only to consider his treatment of "the coefficient of adversity" to see that he would regard the situation described by Desan as a limitation to freedom.

246. *BN,* p. 507.

247. *What is Literature?, op. cit.,* p. 112.

248. See the discussion of "Limitations to Freedom" above.

249. See the quotations sprinkled throughout the discussion mentioned in the preceding note.

250. *BN,* p. 495.

251. Desan, *op. cit.,* p. 173.

252. For a lengthy list of "the principal statements of Merleau-Ponty's views on Sartre," consult Whitford, *op. cit.,* p. 149, note 6.

253. Whitford, *op. cit.,* p. 10. On p. 150, note 7, of the same work, she provides a list of authors whom she deems guilty of this charge. On the other hand, the following authors *do* question the validity of Merleau-Ponty's critique: De Beauvoir, "Merleau-Ponty et le pseudo-sartrisme," in her *Privilèges* (Paris: Gallimard, 1955), pp. 201–272; Sheridan, "On Ontology and Politics: A Polemic." *Dialogue* 7, No. 3 (December 1968), pp. 449–460, who claims, in agreement with De Beauvoir, that "Merleau-Ponty either did not or would not understand Sartre" (p. 458); Monika Langer, "Sartre and Merleau-Ponty: A Reappraisal," in Schilpp, *op. cit.,* pp. 300–325: who states: "I am in agreement with de Beauvoir's contention that the Sartrism which Merleau submitted to such scathing criticism in the *Adventures of the Dialectic* is a 'pseudo-Sartrism' " (p. 300); Whitford, *op. cit.,* who argues that Merleau-Ponty's "own preoccupations lead him to do less than justice to the most positive aspects of Sartre's philosophy because he tends to discard all those elements which he cannot make use of for his own purposes (p. 10), and that he "presents a one-sided and selective account of Sartre's thought as a whole" (p. 12); Mikel Dufrenne, "Sartre and Merleau-Ponty," in Hugh Silverman and Frederick Elliston, eds., *Jean-Paul Sartre: Contemporary Approaches to His Philosophy* (Pittsburgh: Duquesne University Press, 1980), pp. 209–218, who argues that Merleau-Ponty pushed his objections to Sartre's theory of freedom "to the point of caricature" (p. 211); and Jeanson, *op.*

cit., especially pp. 187–194. Moreover, Sartre himself, in an interview (in Schilpp, *op. cit.*, pp. 5–51) explicitly endorses an interlocutor's claim that "Merleau-Ponty took from you a pseudo-Sartre" (p. 25).

254. *PP*, pp. 434–456.

255. *PP*, p. 439.

256. *PP*, pp. 436–437.

257. Kwant, *op. cit.*, p. 207.

258. Compare on this point Jeanson, who, in his commentary on the above-quoted passage from Merleau-Ponty, accuses the latter of "a misunderstanding," which "consists in conflating two senses of freedom which Sartre keeps distinct" (*op. cit.*, p. 191), and Whitford who, commentating on the same passage, remarks, "Here it sounds as though Merleau-Ponty is confusing ontological freedom with (practical freedom). One wants to reply that it is not a question of distinguishing between actions which are free and actions which are not, but between men who are free and stones which are not" (*op. cit.*, p. 63).

259. I am not, strictly speaking, *completely* unfree, since I could after all engage myself in the project of obtaining and reading certain top secret government documents. But certainly I am (practically) *less* free, since to do so would involve great risks, and would yield a very low probability of success.

260. It is true that later on, in *Signs* (Evantson: Northwestern University Press, 1964), Merleau-Ponty acknowledges that Sartre distinguishes between different senses of freedom, but he then goes on to call these two senses "different and really antagonistic idea(s) of freedom" (p. 155), without, in my judgment, satisfactorily explaining the basis for this claim.

261. *Life/Situations, op. cit.*, p. 89.

262. See section 1.3.2.1.5 above.

263. *PP*, p. 437.

264. *Adventures of the Dialectic, op. cit.*, p. 196.

265. *PP*, p. 437.

266. See section 1.3.2.1.5 above.

267. Cf. the passages cited in the course of the discussion in section 1.3.2.1.5 above.

268. See sections 1.3.1 through 1.3.1.2 above.

269. PP, p. 454.

270. *PP*, p. 438. Whitford, *op. cit.*, p. 155, note 12, also points this out.

271. *PP*, p. 442.

272. *PP*, p. 441. The passage cited by Merleau-Ponty is *BN*, p. 453f.

273. *BN*, p. 453.

274. *BN*, p. 454.

275. See also Jeanson's very helpful commentary on this point, *op. cit.*, pp. 191–192.

276. "Introduction to 'Les Temps Modernes'," *op. cit.*, p. 441.

277. *Ibid.*, punctuation altered slightly.

278. *PP*, p. 453.

279. *BN*, p. 83.

280. *BN*, p. 498.

281. *BN*, p. 489.

282. *LPE*, p. 237.

283. *Anti-Semite and Jew, op. cit.*, emphasis added.

284. Sartre, *Search For a Method*, trans. Hazel E. Barnes (New York: Vintage Books, 1968), p. 93. (This work will hereafter be cited as *SFM*.) Sartre adds that "the field of possibles, however reduced it may be, always exists, and we must not think of it as a zone of indetermination, but rather as a strongly structured region which depends upon all of History and which includes its own contradictions" (p. 93).

285. *PP*, p. 442.

286. *PP*, p. 454, punctuation altered slightly.

287. In addition to the documentation for this point already presented above in the present work, see Langer, *op. cit.*, pp. 319–320.

288. Perhaps this is why de Beauvoir, Sheridan, and Whitford, in the works cited in note 253 above, each provide a hypothesis to explain just why Merleau-Ponty got things so very wrong. Interestingly, there is little agreement among their hypotheses.

289. For a list of authors who do take Merleau-Ponty at his word, see Whitford, *op. cit.*, p. 150, note 7, and Langer, *op. cit.*, p. 322, note 5.

290. Kwant, *op. cit.*, p. 208.

291. *Ibid.* Note also that the title of the section in Kwant's book which is concerned with Merleau-Ponty's critique of Sartre's theory of freedom is called "Absolute or Situated Freedom?", (p. 205).

292. Aside from its superior plausibility, this interpretation is also supported by the observation, noted by Whitford, *op. cit.*, pp. 62–63, that Merleau-Ponty is generally less concerned with the details of what Sartre actually says than with what Merleau-Ponty takes to be the consequences of Sartre's fundamental theoretical framework—the consequences of the in-itself/for-itself model, for example.

293. Cf. the works cited in note 3 above. See also Walter Odajnyk, *Marxism and Existentialism* (New York: Doubleday, 1965), p. xxii; T. Z. Lavine, *From Socrates to Sartre* (New York: Bantam Books, 1984), pp. 386–387; Colin Wilson, *Introduction to the New Existentialism* (Boston: Houghton Mifflin, 1966), p. 30; and Desan, *The Marxism of Jean-Paul Sartre* (Garden City, N.Y.: Doubleday, 1965), pp. 107–108. Sartre himself seems to endorse this interpretation in a famous passage from *SFM* (p. 8). But see Barnes' argument in her introduction to *SFM*, pp. viii ff., that this passage may not mean what it seems (out of context) to mean. In any case, Sartre himself repudiates the interpretation in an interview printed in Schilpp, *op. cit.*, pp. 20, 24.

294. Sartre, speaking in an interview printed in Max Charlesworth, *The Existentialists and Jean-Paul Sartre* (London: George Prior, 1976), pp. 106–107.

295. "An Interview with Jean-Paul Sartre," in Schilpp, *op. cit.*, p. 12.

296. Sartre, in Leo Fretz, "An Interview with Jean-Paul Sartre," in Silverman and Elliston, *op. cit.,* p. 225.

297. "Today's Hope," *op. cit.,* p. 157.

298. De Beauvoir, *Force of Circumstance,* trans. Richard Howard (New York: G.P. Putnam, 1964), p. 7. See also the following two works, both of which are primarily concerned with demonstrating the continuity in Sartre's philosophical development: Sheridan, *Sartre: The Radical Conversion, op. cit.;* Norman McLeod, "Existential Freedom in the Marxism of Jean-Paul Sartre." *Dialogue* 7 (June-July 1968): 26–44.

299. Cf. Bernstein, *op. cit.,* pp. 155–156, note 48, from which quoted passages were taken. On the other hand, see Robert Champigny, *Humanism and Human Racism: A Critical Study of Essays by Sartre and Camus* (The Hague: Mouton, 1972), p. 43, note 4, who argues that Sartre tends to exaggerate the extent of his evolution.

300. "The Itinerary of a Thought," *op. cit.,* p. 33.

301. *Ibid.,* pp. 33–34. A translation of the prefatory note to which Sartre here refers can be found in *Sartre on Theater, op. cit.,* pp. 205–206.

302. *Sartre By Himself, op. cit.,* p. 58.

303. *Ibid.,* p. 57, emphasis added.

304. I do not mean to imply, of course, that we should *ignore* Sartre's views on this subject, or ascribe *no* value whatsoever to them.

305. "A Long, Bitter, Sweet Madness," *op. cit.,* p. 63.

306. Cf. Odajnyk, *op cit.,* p. xxiii; Bernstein, *op. cit.,* p. 156, note 48; Lavine, *op. cit.,* p. 390; Warnock, *The Philosophy of Sartre, op. cit.,* pp. 178–179; and Warnock, *Existentialism, op. cit.,* p. 126.

307. See the discussion of "Limitations to Freedom" above.

308. Warnock, *The Philosophy of Sartre, op. cit.,* p. 181.

309. Whitford, *op. cit.,* p. 59.

310. Desan, *The Marxism of Jean-Paul Sartre, op. cit.,* p. 108.

311. *BN,* p. 483.

312. Burkle, *op. cit.,* p. 753.

313. Sheridan, *Sartre: The Radical Conversion, op. cit.,* p. 164.

314. Sartre, in Fretz, *op. cit.,* p. 225. See also the "Conclusion" to *SFM,* where Sartre suggests that *BN* is *foundational* to *CDR,* (pp. 167ff.).

315. *BN,* pp. 625–628.

316. As is well known, Sartre published no such work during his lifetime, though his *Cahiers pour une morale, op. cit.,* has been published posthumously. For a useful discussion of possible reasons *why* Sartre abandoned his ethical treatise, see Anderson, *The Foundation and Structure of Sartrean Ethics, op. cit.,* Chapter One, pp. 3–14.

317. Cf. those passages cited in notes 224–226 above.

318. See note 202 above.

319. *LPE,* p. 251. See also McLeod, *op. cit.,* pp. 35–36 on this point.

320. Whitford, *op. cit.,* pp. 59–60. I have inserted translations for the quotations from Sartre which Whitford gives in the original French. The translations are from *Anti-Semite and Jew, op. cit.,* pp. 136 and 148, in that order.

321. Whitford, *op. cit.,* p. 60.

322. This will be documented later in the present section.

323. Bernstein, *op. cit.,* p. 142.

324. *BN,* p. 364.

325. *BN,* p. 429.

326. Sartre, "No Exit," trans. Stuart Gilbert, in *No Exit and Three Other Plays* (New York: Vintage, 1949), p. 127.

327. James Collins, *The Existentialists* (Chicago: Gateway, 1968), p. 84.

328. *BN,* p. 38.

329. *BN,* p. 615.

330. *BN,* p. 627.

331. *BN,* p. 70, note 9.

332. *BN,* p. 412, note 14.

333. *BN,* p. 581.

334. *BN,* p. 581.

335. *BN,* pp. 627–628, emphasis added.

336. For bibliographical data on this book, see note 3 to the "Introduction" above.

337. Warnock, *The Philosophy of Sartre, op. cit.,* p. 130.

338. Busch, "Sartre: The Phenomenological Reduction and Human Relationships," *op. cit.,* p. 60. Busch is highly critical of this interpretation.

339. Warnock, *Existentialist Ethics, op. cit.,* pp. 50–51, emphasis added. See also her *Existentialism, op. cit.,* p. 126, and her *Ethics Since 1900, op. cit.,* p. 139.

340. Lavine, *op. cit.,* p. 386.

341. Cf. the works cited in note 306 above.

342. Other, rather more eccentric interpretations of the radical conversion, which I have chosen, for reasons of space, not to discuss, can be found in: Jules Gleicher, *The Accidental Revolutionary: Essays on the Political Teaching of Jean-Paul Sartre* (Washington, D.C.: University Press of America, 1982), p. 27; Barnes, *Sartre, op. cit.,* pp. 73–74; Kurt F. Reinhardt, *The Existentialist Revolt* (New York: Frederick Ungar, 1972), p. 165; and Molnar, *op. cit.,* p. 122.

343. Bernstein, *op. cit.,* pp. 150–151.

344. Cf. *BN,* p. 627.

345. Cf. *BN,* pp. 84–95.

346. Danto, *op. cit.,* pp. 145–146, emphasis added. I have changed Danto's reference to "metaphysical" freedom to read "ontological" freedom, so as to maintain terminological consistency.

347. Bernstein, *op cit.,* p. 152, echoes this *non sequitur.*

348. Joseph P. Fell, *Heidegger and Sartre* (New York: Columbia University Press, 1979), p. 150.

349. *Existentialism and Humanism, op. cit.,* p. 51. (This work will hereafter be cited as *EH*).

350. *BN,* p. 581.

351. *BN,* p. 627.

352. Cf. Danto, *op. cit.,* p. 145.

353. *BN,* p. 70, note 9.

354. See the documents cited by Anderson, *The Foundation and Structure of Sartrean Ethics, op. cit.,* p. 155, note 32.

355. *Ibid.* This view of *BN* is also shared by the two most authoritative commentators on Sartre. See de Beauvoir, *The Ethics of Ambiguity, op. cit.,* pp. 11, 13–14, 46, and Jeanson, *op. cit.,* pp. 180–184, 208–209.

356. Cf. *CDR,* pp. 227–228, note 68.

357. "Today's Hope," *op. cit.,* p. 157.

358. *BN* was published in 1943. *Cahiers pour une morale* was written in 1947 and 1948.

359. *Cahiers pour une morale, op. cit.,* p. 488.

360. *Ibid.,* p. 499.

361. *Ibid.,* p. 486.

362. *Ibid.*

363. *BN,* p. 627. Cf. *Cahiers pour une morale, op. cit.,* pp 486–570.

364. *BN,* p. 566.

365. *BN,* p. 599.

366. *BN,* p. 566, emphasis added.

367. *BN,* pp. 93–95. This distinction was brought to my attention by Anderson, *The Foundation and Structure of Sartrean Ethics, op. cit.,* p. 30.

368. *BN,* p. 95.

369. *BN,* p. 38.

370. *BN,* p. 95, emphasis added.

371. Anderson, *The Foundation and Structure of Sartrean Ethics, op. cit.,* p. 31.

372. I owe this example of aggression to Anderson, *The Foundation and Structure of Sartrean Ethics, op. cit.,* pp. 34–35, though he may not approve of my extension of it. The considerations presented here are sufficient, I think, to refute Leslie Stevenson's complaint that "there is an apparent contradiction between Sartre's constant insistence on our freedom, and his analysis of the human condition as necessarily determined in certain respects. For he holds that as conscious beings we are always wanting to fill the 'nothingness' which is the essence of our being conscious; we want to become things rather than remain perpetually in the state of having possibilities unfulfilled" (*Seven Theories of Human Nature* [Oxford: Clarendon Press, 1974], p. 88). Here Stevenson commits three errors: (1) he fails to distinguish between necessary *wants,* which would not undermine our freedom—think of the necessity of wanting food, and necessary *choices of action,* which would; (2) he fails to distinguish between different senses of freedom, and thus fails to see that constraints which limit freedom in one sense, do not do so in another; and (3) he ignores the radical conversion passages. The latter failing is particularly evident in the following passage: "[Sartre] analyses human life as a perpetual attempt to achieve the logically impossible. But why *must* it be so? . . . Cannot someone *choose* not to want to become an object . . . ?" Of course, it is precisely Sartre's point that *all* of us can and *should* so choose. But Stevenson misses this, and concludes, "It is hard to see whether Sartre even tries to resolve these contradictions at the heart of his theory" (Ibid).

373. John Stuart Mill, *Utilitarianism* (Indianapolis: Hackett, 1979), p. 41.

374. Anderson, *The Foundation and Structure of Sartrean Ethics, op. cit.,* p. 32.

375. Further discussion of the difficulties in Sartre's concept of "choice" are beyond the scope of this work. The interested reader can pursue this issue by consulting Whitford, *op. cit.,* pp. 72–76, and Frederick A. Olafson, *Principles and Persons: An Ethical Interpretation of Existentialism* (Baltimore: The Johns Hopkins Press, 1970), pp. 162–174.

376. Cf. the passages cited in notes 331–335 above.

377. *Anti-Semite and Jew, op. cit.,* p. 90.

378. Jeanson, *op. cit.,* p. 180.

379. *Ibid.,* p. 208. See also *BN,* pp. 626–627.

380. Jeanson, *op. cit.,* p. 208 seems to conflate the two.

381. Sartre, *The Emotions: Outline of a Theory,* trans. Bernard Frechtman (New York: The Wisdom Library, 1948), pp. 78–79, emphasis added.

382. *Ibid.,* p. 91.

383. *TE,* pp. 100–101, emphasis added.

384. *TE,* p. 100.

385. *TE,* pp. 102–103.

386. *TE,* pp. 102–103.

387. *TE,* p. 106.

388. See section 1.2.1.1 above.

389. For Husserl's discussion of the natural attitude, sometimes called "the natural standpoint," see *I, #27–32,* pp. 51–62.

390. Compare Husserl's treatment of the reduction in the section of *I* cited in the preceding note with Sartre's radical conversion passages quoted in the present section.

391. Busch, "Sartre's Use of the Reduction: *Being and Nothingness* Reconsidered," in Silverman and Elliston, *op. cit.,* p. 27.

392. Cf. the works cited in note 306 above.

393. Busch, "Sartre: From Phenomenology to Marxism." *Research in Phenomenology* II (1972), p. 114.

394. A list of those who misunderstand *BN* because they fail to take into account Sartre's use of the reduction is provided by Busch in "Sartre's Use of the Reduction," *op. cit.,* pp. 17–18, note 7. On the other hand, passages which affirm the importance of the reduction in Sartre's thought can be found in de Beauvoir, *The Ethics of Ambiguity, op. cit.,* p. 14; Jeanson, *op. cit.,* p. 183; Sartre, *Cahiers pour une morale, op. cit.,* pp. 12–13, 489–490; and in much of Busch's work on Sartre.

395. This is substantially what we do in fact find in the posthumously published *Cahiers pour une morale, op. cit.*

396. *CDR,* p. 228, note 68.

397. *BN,* p. 514, emphasis added.

398. *BN,* p. 510, emphasis added.

399. *BN,* p. 510.

400. *BN*, pp. 523–524.

401. See Busch, "Sartre: The Phenomenological Reduction and Human Relationships," *op. cit.*, p. 58 on this point.

402. *Saint Genet, op. cit.*, pp. 45ff.

403. Karl Marx, "Toward a Critique of Hegel's *Philosophy of Right*: Introduction," trans. Loyd D. Easton and Kurt H. Guddat in *Marx Selections*, ed. Allen W. Wood (New York: Macmillan, 1988), p. 24.

404. *The Emotions, op. cit.*, pp. 62–63.

405. Robert V. Stone, "Sartre on Bad Faith and Authenticity," in Schilpp, *op. cit.*, p. 253.

406. *The Emotions, op. cit.*, p. 79.

407. Stone, *op. cit.*, p. 253. Sartre himself says as much in *Cahiers pour une morale, op. cit.*, p. 16: "One cannot achieve the conversion *alone*. In other words, morality is only possible if everyone is moral." I have here quoted Thomas Baldwin's translation of this passage from his "Sartre, *Existentialism and Humanism*," in Godfrey Vesey, ed., *Philosophers Ancient and Modern* (Cambridge: Cambridge University Press, 1986), p. 306.

408. *BN*, p. 453.

409. *BN*, p. 47, translation slightly modified (See *EN*, p. 85).

410. "The Itinerary of a Thought," *op. cit.*, p. 33.

411. *The Writings of Jean-Paul Sartre, Vol. 1, op. cit.*, p. 387.

412. "A Long, Bitter, Sweet Madness," *op. cit.*, p. 61.

413. *The Writings of Jean-Paul Sartre, Vol. 1, op. cit.*, p. 453.

414. *BN*, p. 580.

415. *BN*, p. 581.

416. *BN*, pp. 582–585.

417. Fell, *op. cit.*, p. 346.

418. *SFM*, p. 34.

419. "A Long, Bitter, Sweet Madness," *op. cit.*, p. 62.

Chapter Two: Values

1. *BN*, p. 38.

2. *BN*, p. 93.

3. "Materialism and Revolution," *op. cit.*, p. 235.

4. *BN*, p. 93.

5. *BN*, p. 93.

6. *BN*, p. 39.

7. *BN*, p. 38.

8. I have in mind principally Max Scheler, *Formalism in Ethics and Non-Formal Ethics of Values*, trans. Manfred S. Frings and Roger L. Funk (Evanston: Northwestern University Press, 1973) and, to a lesser extent, Nicolai Hartmann, *Ethics*, 3 Vols., trans. Stanton Coit (London: Allen & Unwin, 1932).

9. *I, #27*, p. 53.

10. *I, #27*, p. 53, emphasis altered.

11. *BN*, pp. 38–39.

12. See the descriptions of these experiences under section 1.2.2 above.

13. *BN*, p. 9.

14. Barnes, "Translator's Introduction" to *BN*, p. xxvi, emphasis added.

15. James Rachels, "John Dewey and the Truth about Ethics," in Steven M. Cahn, ed., *New Studies in the Philosophy of John Dewey* (Hanover, N.H.: The University Press of New England, 1981), p. 150.

16. For a similar characterization of objectivity in ethics, see A. C. Ewing, *The Definition of Good* (New York: Macmillan, 1947), pp. 1–3.

17. Bertrand Russell, as quoted in Germaine Brée, *Camus and Sartre* (New York: Delta Books, 1972), p. 15.

18. Zinn, *op. cit.*, p. 23.

19. This example is borrowed from Russell's "On Denoting," in his *Essays in Analysis*, ed. Douglas Lackey (New York: George Braziller, 1973), pp. 103–119.

20. Copleston, *A History of Philosophy, Vol. 9: Maine de Biran to Sartre, Part II: Bergson to Sartre* (Garden City, N.Y.: Image Books, 1977), p. 88.

21. Such a view is defended in G. E. Moore's famous *Principia Ethica* (Cambridge: Cambridge University Press, 1971), Chapter I, pp. 1–36.

22. For example, if "good" is a unique property, it must be possible for two objects to be exactly alike with regard to all of their other properties, and yet for only one of them to be good. It is possible, say, for two otherwise identical paintings to differ only in that one is good and the other is bad. Such a view seems bizarre, to say the least.

23. Rachels, *op. cit.*, p. 151.

24. David Hume, *A Treatise of Human Nature* (Baltimore: Penguin, 1969), 520.

25. These arguments are taken from R. F. Tredwell, "On Moore's Analysis of Goodness," in E. D. Klemke, ed., *Studies in the Philosophy of G. E. Moore* (Chicago: Quadrangle Books, 1969), p. 57.

26. Tredwell, *op. cit.*, p. 57.

27. On this point, see also Scheler, *op. cit.*, pp. 25–26.

28. Kurt Baier, "The Meaning of Life," in Morris Weitz, ed., *20th-Century Philosophy: The Analytic Tradition* (New York: The Free Press, 1966), pp. 375–376.

29. Anderson, *The Foundation and Structure of Sartrean Ethics, op. cit.*, p. 23.

30. *BN*, p. 433.

31. *BN*, p. 435.

32. *BN*, p. 38, emphasis added.

33. Cf. Anderson, *The Foundation and Structure of Sartrean Ethics, op. cit.*, p. 36.

34. *BN*, p. 625.

35. Sartre, "Consciousness of Self and Knowledge of Self," trans. Mary Ellen

and Nathaniel Lawrence, in Nathaniel Lawrence and Daniel O'Connor, eds., *Readings in Existential Phenomenology* (Englewood Cliffs, N.J.: Prentice-Hall, 1967), p. 129.

36. *I, #27*, p. 53.

37. Copleston, *A History of Philosophy, Vol. 9: Maine de Biran to Sartre, Part II: Bergson to Sartre, op. cit.*, p. 88.

38. *BN*, p. 38.

39. *BN*, p. 38.

40. *BN*, p. 38.

41. *BN*, p. 39.

42. *EH*, p. 33.

43. *EH*, p. 33.

44. *EH*, p. 33–34.

45. *EH*, p. 56, emphasis added.

46. See translator Stone's note 4 on p. 22 of Jeanson, *op. cit.*

47. *Sartre By Himself, op. cit.*, pp. 74–75. Note also the claim by Jeanson that Sartre considered the lecture "an error" (Jeanson, *op. cit.*, p. 22). For a sympathetic and plausible explanation of the lecture's faults, see Anthony Manser, *Sartre: A Philosophic Study* (New York: Oxford University Press, 1967), pp. 137–138.

48. Plato, *Euthyphro*. Cf. Hugh Tredennick's translation in *The Last Days of Socrates* (Harmondsworth, Middlesex, England: Penguin Books, 1978).

49. Alasdair MacIntyre, *A Short History of Ethics* (New York: Macmillan, 1966), p. 195. See also Cranston, *Jean-Paul Sartre, op. cit.*, pp. 34–36, who applies essentially this same point in connection with Sartre. It should be mentioned that the implicit premise of MacIntyre's argument is that right and wrong are defined independently of what the divine being commands. The consequences of rejecting this premise, and of simply *defining* the divine being's commands as "right," would include the trivialization of the claim that those commands are right, since one could with equal (in the sense of "equally arbitrary") justification define the divine being's commands as "wrong." Or, if one insisted on defining the commands as "right," it would follow that no matter *what* the divine being might command, including murder, rape, torture, etc., these commands would automatically be right.

50. Sartre, *The War Diaries of Jean-Paul Sartre,* trans. Quintin Hoare (New York: Pantheon, 1984), p. 108.

51. *EH*, pp. 35–36, 38.

52. *EH*, p. 49.

53. *EH*, p. 54, emphasis added.

54. *EH*, pp. 52–53.

55. *EH*, p. 53.

56. *EH*, p. 51.

57. *EH*, p. 51. See also Sartre's references to people who choose to live in bad faith as "cowards" and "scum" (*EH*, p. 52).

58. *EH*, pp. 29–30.

59. *EH*, p. 51.

60. Danto, *op. cit.*, p. 151.

61. *Ibid.*

62. *Ibid.*

63. W. D. Ross presents such a theory in his *The Right and the Good* (Oxford: The Clarendon Press, 1930), especially Chapter II, pp. 16–47.

64. Jeremy Bentham presents such a theory in his *An Introduction to the Principles of Morals and Legislation*. Cf. the anthology *The Utilitarians* (Garden City, N.Y.: Dolphin Books, 1961), pp. 8–398.

65. Frondizi, *op. cit.*, pp. 377–378.

66. *Ibid.*, p. 378.

67. MacIntyre, "Existentialism," in Warnock, ed., *Sartre: A Collection of Critical Essays* (Garden City, N.Y.: Anchor Books, 1971), p. 55. Regarding the accuracy of MacIntyre's intrepretation, see *BN*, p. 38.

68. MacIntyre, "Existentialism," *op. cit.*, pp. 55–56.

69. A. Phillips Griffiths, "Ultimate Moral Principles: Their Justification," in Edwards, ed., *The Encyclopedia of Philosophy, Vol. 8, op. cit.*, p. 178.

70. *EH*, pp. 49–50.

71. See the exchange between Naville and Sartre during the discussion at the conclusion of *EH* (pp. 69–70).

72. Cf. Frondizi, *op. cit.*, pp. 380–381. In the light of these considerations, one is inclined to sympathize with the complaints of Spiegelberg (who claims to "see no incompatibility between existentialism and a non-subjectivist phenomenology of values") regarding the "apodictic" nature of Sartre's "assertions about the subjectivity of all values in *Being and Nothingness*." "Certainly," Spiegelberg continues, "if it makes any phenomenological claims, existentialism has to undertake an unbiased and thorough examination of the evidence of value phenomena before rushing into a dogmatic subjectivism" ("Sartre's Last Word on Ethics in Phenomenological Perspective." *Research in Phenomenology* XI [1981], p. 105).

73. *Ibid.*, p. 380.

74. Warnock, *Existentialist Ethics, op. cit.*, p. 54.

75. *EH*, p. 52.

76. This example was suggested to me by Erazim Kohák.

77. Collins, *op. cit.*, pp. 83–84.

78. Lavine, *op. cit.*, pp. 373–374. Similar objections are raised by Luther J. Binkley, *Conflict of Ideals* (New York: D. Van Nostrand Company, 1969), p. 215; by Frondizi, *op. cit.*, p. 375; and by Leslie Stevenson, *op. cit.*, pp. 88–89.

79. Bernstein, *op. cit.*, p. 151. See also p. 161.

80. *Ibid.*, p. 152.

81. *BN*, p. 482.

82. Gilbert Harman, *The Nature of Morality* (New York: Oxford University Press, 1977), p. 4.

83. Føllesdal, *op. cit.*, p. 400, suggests that there are passages in which Sartre himself seems to recognize a coefficient of adversity with regard to ethical matters—that, in Føllesdal's words, "there are certain ethical limitations on how we may constitute reality." See also the discussion which begins in section 3.3.

84. *BN*, p. 554.

85. *BN*, p. 553.

86. Cf. *BN*, pp. 553–556; *Anti-Semite and Jew, op. cit.*; "The Responsibility of the Writer," *op. cit.*; Sartre's "Preface" to Frantz Fanon, *The Wretched of the Earth*, trans. Constance Farrington (New York: Grove Press, 1968), pp. 7–31; Sartre's *On Genocide* (Boston: Beacon Press, 1968), pp. 57–85; and the commentary of Thomas R. Flynn, *Sartre and Marxist Existentialism* (Chicago: The University of Chicago Press, 1984), especially pp. 213–214, note 30.

87. *BN*, p. 553.

88. "Preface" to *The Wretched of the Earth, op. cit.*, p. 25.

89. "The Responsibility of the Writer," *op. cit.*, p. 170.

90. *Ibid.*, p. 185.

91. *BN*, p. 580.

92. "The Responsibility of the Writer," *op. cit.*, p. 167.

93. *On Genocide, op. cit.*, p. 84.

94. *Anti-Semite and Jew, op. cit.*, p. 136.

95. Alvin Plantinga, "An Existentialist's Ethics," in Julius R. Weinberg and Keith E. Yandell, eds., *Ethics* (New York: Holt, Rinehart and Winston, 1971), p. 22.

96. *BN*, p. 29.

97. *EH*, p. 57.

98. *BN*, p. 479.

99. Plantinga, *op. cit.*, pp. 22–23.

100. *Ibid.*, p. 23. See also p. 24.

101. Gleicher, *op. cit.*, p. 20. Gleicher's reference is to *BN*, p. 24. See also Gleicher, pp. 21–22.

Chapter Three: Freedom as a Value

1. "Intentionality," *op. cit.*, p. 5.

2. *The War Diaries, op. cit.*, p. 88. See also pp. 50–51.

3. Spiegelberg, "Sartre's Last Word on Ethics in Phenomenological Perspective," *op. cit.*, p. 105.

4. Sartre, "The Historical Process," in *The Writings of Jean-Paul Sartre, Vol. 2, op. cit.*, p. 181.

5. *Life/Situations, op. cit.*, p. 85, emphasis added.

6. *What is Literature?, op. cit.*, p. 159, emphasis added.

7. *Ibid.*, pp. 159–160.

8. De Beauvoir, *Adieux, op. cit.*, p. 439.

9. *Ibid.*

10. *Ibid.*

11. *BN*, p. 627.

12. *EH*, p. 51.

13. *Cahiers pour une morale, op. cit.*, p. 16.

14. *SFM*, p. 34.

15. De Beauvoir, *The Ethics of Ambiguity, op. cit.*, p. 24. See also Anderson, *The Foundation and Structure of Sartrean Ethics, op. cit.*, pp. 42–44, 156–157.

16. Frondizi, *op. cit.*, p. 390.

17. Olafson, *Principles and Persons, op. cit.*, p. 206.

18. *BN*, p. 456.

19. See the passages cited in Chapter One, notes 156–158.

20. "Today's Hope," *op. cit.*, p. 172.

21. "Introduction to 'Les Temps Modernes'," *op. cit.*, p. 441.

22. Mill. *op. cit.*, pp. 7ff.

23. But see section 1.3.2.1.6 above.

24. *The Writings of Jean-Paul Sartre, Vol. 1, op. cit.*, p. 211.

25. *CDR*, p. 90.

26. *What is Literature?, op. cit.*, p. 49.

27. See Anderson, *The Foundation and Structure of Sartrean Ethics, op. cit.*, p. 59, and *CDR*, p. 800.

28. Mill, *op. cit.*, pp. 7ff.

29. De Beauvoir, *The Ethics of Ambiguity, op. cit.*, pp. 79–81.

30. *BN*, p. 581.

31. *BN*, p. 580.

32. Anderson, *The Foundation and Structure of Sartrean Ethics, op. cit.*, p. 58.

33. *SFM*, p. 34.

34. *SFM*, p. 34. See also *Cahiers pour une morale, op. cit.*, pp. 421–442, 487.

35. De Beauvoir, *The Ethics of Ambiguity, op. cit.*, p. 81.

36. *Life/Situations, op. cit.*, pp. 83-84.

37. *BN*, p. 172.

38. *BN*, p. 172.

39. *BN*, p. 172.

40. Lewis Carroll, "What the Tortoise Said to Achilles," as quoted in Peter Winch, *The Idea of a Social Science and its Relation to Philosophy* (London: Routledge & Kegan Paul, 1967), pp. 55–57.

41. *Ibid.* A similar argument is advanced by Ewing: "The need for admitting intuition is by no means confined to ethics. This we can show by a simple logical argument to the effect that some intuition is necessarily presupposed in all reasoning. Suppose I argue A,∴ B,∴ C. Now the argument is invalid unless B does really follow from A, but how can I know that it does so? I may be able to interpolate an intermediate proposition D which itself follows from A and from which B follows, but this only puts the problem further back. I must know that D follows from A, and though I might perhaps be able to interpolate a further intermediate stage, I obviously cannot go on in this way *ad infinitum*. Sooner or later, and probably very soon indeed, I must come to some link between A and the

next term in the inference which I see immediately to hold without being able to prove this by further argument. We may take it then that, if we are to have any knowledge by inference, intuitive knowledge must occur, and the same is true if we substitute for 'knowledge' in both places 'justified (rational) belief.' . . . The mere fact that intuitions have to be admitted in ethics cannot be made an objection against ethics, since it has been shown that we have also to admit intuition with all knowledge outside ethics that involves inference" (*Ethics* [New York: The Free Press, 1965], p. 120).

42. Of course, it does not follow from this that intuition is *sufficient* to give knowlege.

43. If we need a criterion for distinguishing accurate intuitions from inaccurate ones, than we will also need a criterion for distinguishing a correct criterion for doing so from an incorrect criterion; we will need a criterion for distinguishing a correct criterion for doing *this* from an incorrect one, and so on *ad infinitum*. The only way to halt this regress, it seems, would be to admit, at some point or another, that intuition is adequate to yield knowledge.

44. *I*, #19, pp. 36–37.

45. *I*, #24, p. 44.

46. It is interesting to note than even such hard-core ethical subjectivists as Russell and Ayer endorse this argument. Both, in my view, simply forget this argument when they are engaged in defending ethical subjectivism. See Ayer, *The Problem of Knowledge* (Harmondsworth, Middlesex, England: Penguin, 1979), pp. 20–21, and Russell, "The Elements of Ethics," in his *Philosophical Essays* (New York: Clarion, 1968), pp. 14–15.

47. Kohák, *op. cit.*, pp. 16, 143. See also *I*, #66–70, pp. 151–160.

48. Kohák, *op. cit.*, pp. 119–120. See also *I*, #79, p. 181–190.

49. Kohák, *op. cit.*, p. 120.

50. Warnock, *Existentialist Ethics, op. cit.*, p. 55, emphasis added.

51. Richard Price, quoted in J. N. Findlay, *Axiological Ethics* (New York: Macmillan, 1970), p. 5.

52. Zinn, *op. cit.*, p. 23.

53. Findlay, *op. cit.*, pp. 8–9. See also *I*, #52–54, pp. 117–128, and Kohák, *op. cit.*, pp. 94–95.

54. William Gass, "The Case of the Obliging Stranger," in Maurice Mandelbaum, Francis W. Gramlich, Alan Ross Anderson, and Jerome B. Schneewind, eds., *Philosophic Problems* (New York: Macmillan, 1967), pp. 525–526.

55. Ibid., p. 529.

56. Barnes, *An Existentialist Ethics* (New York: Vintage Books, 1971), p. 24.

57. Ewing, *Ethics, op. cit.*, p. 111.

58. Russell, *Religion and Science, op. cit.*, pp. 229, 238.

59. *I*, #19, p. 37.

60. *I*, #19, p. 37.

61. Cf. P. H. Nowell-Smith, *Ethics* (Harmondsworth, Middlesex, England: Penguin, 1965), pp. 44–47.

62. Ewing, *Second Thoughts in Moral Philosophy* (London: Routledge & Kegan Paul, 1959), p. 64.

63. In any case, it is irrelevant to the issue since, as Ewing points out, "The proposition that there is no further explanation needed as to why something is true because it is just evident is not identical with the proposition that there is no causal explanation of a man's ability to see its truth" (*Second Thoughts in Moral Philosophy, op. cit.,* p. 65).

64. Cf. Moore, *op. cit.,* and Ross, *op. cit.*

65. Anderson, *The Foundation and Structure of Sartrean* Ethics, *op. cit.,* p. 46.

66. *BN,* p. 627, emphasis added.

67. De Beauvoir, *The Ethics of Ambiguity, op. cit.,* p. 24.

68. Anderson, *The Foundation and Structure of Sartrean Ethics, op. cit.,* p. 47.

69. *EH,* p. 51, emphasis added. This interpretation also explains Sartre's reference on the same page to "men of good faith."

70. Barnes, "Introduction," to *SFM,* p. xv.

71. *The Writings of Jean-Paul Sartre, Vol. 1, op. cit.,* p. 211.

72. *Ibid.*

73. *SFM,* p. 34.

74. See also de Beauvoir, *The Ethics of Ambiguity, op. cit.,* pp. 90–91.

75. Sartre, "Conversation with Jean-Paul Sartre." *Oui* 4 (June 1975), p. 70, as quoted in Anderson, *The Foundation and Structure of Sartrean Ethics, op. cit.,* p. 42.

76. Kohák, *op. cit.,* pp. 80–81.

77. Olafson, *Principles and Persons, op. cit.,* p. 219.

78. *BN,* p. 488.

79. Anderson, *The Foundation and Structure of Sartrean Ethics, op. cit.,* p. 139, makes much the same point.

Bibliography

The best bibliography of Sartre's writings is: Contat, Michel, and Rybalka, Michel, eds. *Les Ecrits de Sartre*. Paris: Gallimard, 1970. This work has been translated into English as: *The Writings of Sartre*. 2 Vols. trans. Richard C. McCleary. Evanston: Northwestern University Press, 1974. Readers interested in the secondary literature on Sartre should consult: Lapointe, François, and Lapointe, Claire. *Jean-Paul Sartre and His Critics: An International Bibliography*. Bowling Green: Philosophy Documentation Center, 1981; and Wilcocks, Robert. *Jean-Paul Sartre: A Bibliography of International Criticism*. Edmonton: University of Alberta Press, 1975. Useful shorter bibliographies on Sartre can be found in many books on Sartre, but especially in: McMahon, Joseph H. *Humans Being: The World of Jean-Paul Sartre*. Chicago: The University of Chicago Press, 1971; Schilpp, Paul A., ed. *The Philosophy of Jean-Paul Sartre*. La Salle, Illinois: Open Court, 1981; and Silverman, Hugh and Elliston, Frederick, eds., *Jean-Paul Sartre: Contemporary Approaches to His Philosophy*. Pittsburgh: Duquesne University Press, 1980. The following list is limited to items that are actually mentioned or cited in the text.

Adler, Mortimer J. *The Idea of Freedom*. 2 Vols. Garden City, N.Y.: Doubleday, 1958 and 1961.

Anderson, Thomas C. *The Foundation and Structure of Sartrean Ethics*. Lawrence: The Regents Press of Kansas, 1979.

———. "Is a Sartrean Ethics Possible?" *Philosophy Today* 14, No. 2 (Summer 1970).

Ayer, Alfred J. *Language, Truth and Logic*. New York: Dover, 1952.

———. "Novelist-Philosophers V—Jean-Paul Sartre." *Horizon* XII, No. 67 (July 1945).

———. *The Problem of Knowledge*. Harmondsworth, Middlesex, England: Penguin, 1979.

Baier, Kurt. "The Meaning of Life." in Morris Weitz, ed., *20th-Century Philosophy: The Analytic Tradition*. New York: The Free Press, 1966.

Baldwin, Thomas. "Sartre, *Existentialism and Humanism.*" in Godfrey Vesey, ed., *Philosophers Ancient and Modern.* Cambridge: Cambridge University Press, 1986.

Barnes, Hazel. *An Existentialist Ethics.* New York: Vintage, 1971.

———. *Sartre.* Philadelphia: J.B. Lippincott, 1973.

Beauvoir, Simone de. *Adieux: A Farewell to Sartre.* trans. Patrick O'Brian. New York: Pantheon, 1984.

———. *The Ethics of Ambiguity.* trans. Bernard Frechtman. New York: Citadel, 1970.

———. *Force of Circumstance.* trans. Richard Howard. New York: G.P. Putnam, 1964.

———. *The Prime of Life.* trans. Peter Green. New York: Lancer, 1966.

———. *Privilèges.* Paris: Gallimard, 1955.

Bentham, Jeremy. *An Introduction to the Principles of Morals and Legislation.* in *The Utilitarians.* Garden City, N.Y.: Dolphin Books, 1961.

Berlin, Isaiah. *Four Essays on Liberty.* New York: Oxford University Press, 1969.

Bernstein, Richard J. *Praxis and Action.* Philadelphia: University of Pennsylvania Press, 1971.

Binkley, Luther J. *Conflict of Ideals.* New York: D. Van Nostrand, 1969.

Block, Haskell M. and Salinger, Herman, eds. *The Creative Vision: Modern European Writers on their Art.* New York: Grove Press, 1960.

Bowes, Pratima. *Consciousness and Freedom: Three Views.* London: Methuen, 1971.

Brée, Germaine. *Camus and Sartre.* New York: Delta, 1972.

Burkle, Howard R. "Jean-Paul Sartre: Social Freedom in 'Critique de la raison dialectique'." *Review of Metaphysics* 19, No. 4 (June 1966).

Busch, Thomas W. "'La Nausée': A Lover's Quarrel with Husserl." *Research in Phenomenology* XI (1981).

———. "Sartre: From Phenomenology to Marxism." *Research in Phenomenology* II (1972).

———. "Sartre: The Phenomenological Reduction and Human Relationships." *Journal of the British Society for Phenomenology* 6, No. 1 (January 1975).

———. "Sartre's Use of the Reduction: *Being and Nothingness* Reconsidered." in Hugh Silverman and Frederick Elliston, eds.,

Jean-Paul Sartre: Contemporary Approaches to His Philosophy. Pittsburgh: Duquesne University Press, 1980.

Cahn, Steven M., ed. *New Studies in the Philosophy of John Dewey.* Hanover, N.H.: The University Press of New England, 1981.

Catalano, Joseph S. *A Commentary on Jean-Paul Sartre's "Being and Nothingness."* Chicago: The University of Chicago Press, 1980.

Caws, Peter. *Sartre.* Boston: Routledge & Kegan Paul, 1979.

Champigny, Robert. *Humanism and Human Racism: A Critical Study of Essays by Sartre and Camus.* The Hague: Mouton, 1972.

Charlesworth, Max. *The Existentialists and Jean-Paul Sartre.* London: George Prior, 1976.

Collins, James. *The Existentialists.* Chicago: Gateway, 1968.

Contat, Michel and Rybalka, Michel, eds. *Sartre on Theater.* trans. Frank Jellinek. New York: Pantheon, 1976.

————. *The Writings of Jean-Paul Sartre.* 2 Vols. trans. Richard C. McCleary. Evanston: Northwestern University Press, 1974.

Copleston, Frederick. *A History of Philosophy.* 9 Vols. Garden City, N.Y.: Image Books, 1964–1977.

Craib, Ian. *Existentialism and Sociology: A Study of Jean-Paul Sartre.* Cambridge: Cambridge University Press, 1976.

Cranston, Maurice. *Freedom: A New Analysis.* New York: Longmans, Green and Co., 1953.

————. *Jean-Paul Sartre.* New York: Grove Press, 1962.

Cumming, Robert D., ed. *The Philosophy of Jean-Paul Sartre.* New York: Vintage, 1972.

Danto, Arthur C. *Sartre.* London: Fontana, 1979.

Desan, Wilfrid. *The Marxism of Jean-Paul Sartre.* Garden City, N.Y.: Doubleday, 1965.

————. *The Tragic Finale: An Essay on the Philosophy of Jean-Paul Sartre.* New York: Harper Torchbooks, 1960.

Descartes, René. *Meditations on the First Philosophy.* trans. John Veitch. in *The Rationalists.* Garden City, N.Y.: Anchor Books, 1974.

Dufrenne, Mikel. "Sartre and Merleau-Ponty." in High Silverman and Frederick Elliston, eds., *Jean-Paul Sartre: Contemporary Approaches to His Philosophy.* Pittsburgh: Duquesne University Press, 1980.

Edie, James M. "Sartre as Phenomenologist and as Existential Psychoanalyst." in Edward N. Lee and Maurice Mandelbaum, eds., *Phenomenology and Existentialism*. Baltimore: The Johns Hopkins Press, 1969.

Edwards, Paul, eds. *The Encyclopedia of Philosophy*. 8 Vols. New York: Macmillan, 1967.

Ewing, A. C. *The Definition of Good*. New York: Macmillan, 1947.

————. *Ethics*. New York: The Free Press, 1965.

————. *Second Thoughts in Moral Philosophy*. London: Routledge & Kegan Paul, 1959.

Fanon, Frantz. *The Wretched of the Earth*. trans. Constance Farrington. New York: Grove Press, 1968.

Fell, Joseph P. *Heidegger and Sartre*. New York: Columbia University Press, 1979.

Findlay, John N. *Axiological Ethics*. New York: Macmillan, 1970.

Flynn, Thomas R. *Sartre and Marxist Existentialism*. Chicago: The University of Chicago Press, 1984.

Føllesdal, Dagfinn. "Sartre on Freedom." in Paul A. Schilpp, ed., *The Philosophy of Jean-Paul Sartre*. La Salle, Illinois: Open Court, 1981.

Fretz, Leo. "An Interview with Jean-Paul Sartre." in Hugh Silverman and Frederick Elliston, eds., *Jean-Paul Sartre: Contemporary Approaches to His Philosophy*. Pittsburgh: Duquesne University Press, 1980.

Frondizi, Risieri. "Sartre's Early Ethics: A Critique." in Paul A. Schilpp, eds., *The Philosophy of Jean-Paul Sartre*. La Salle, Illinois: Open Court, 1981.

Gass, William. "The Case of the Obliging Stranger." in Maurice Mandelbaum, Francis W. Gramlich, Alan R. Anderson, and Jerome B. Schneewind, eds., *Philosophic Problems*. New York: Macmillan, 1967.

Gleicher, Jules. *The Accidental Revolutionary: Essays on the Political Teaching of Jean-Paul Sartre*. Washington, D.C.: University Press of America, 1982.

Griffiths, A. Phillips. "Ultimate Moral Principles: Their Justification." in Paul Edwards, ed., *The Encyclopedia of Philosophy, Vol. 8*. New York: Macmillan, 1967.

Grossmann, Reinhold. *Phenomenology and Existentialism*. London: Routledge and Kegan Paul, 1984.

Gurwitsch, Aron. *Studies in Phenomenology and Psychology*. Evanston: Northwestern University Press, 1966.

Harman, Gilbert. *The Nature of Morality*. New York: Oxford University Press, 1977.

Hartmann, Nicolai. *Ethics*. 3 Vols. trans. Stanton Coit. London: Allen & Unwin, 1932.

Hume, David. *A Treatise of Human Nature*. Baltimore: Penguin, 1969.

Husserl, Edmund. *Cartesian Meditations*. trans. Dorion Cairns. The Hague: Martinus Nijhoff, 1977.

———. *Formal and Transcendental Logic*. trans. Dorion Cairns. The Hague: Martinus Nijhoff, 1969.

———. *Ideas Pertaining to a Pure Phenomenology and to a Phenomenological Philosophy: First Book*. trans. F. Kersten. The Hague: Martinus Nijhoff, 1982.

———. *Logical Investigations*. 2 Vols. trans. John N. Findlay. New York: The Humanities Press, 1970.

———. "Phenomenology." trans. Richard E. Palmer. in Peter McCormick and Frederick A. Elliston, eds., *Husserl: Shorter Works*. Notre Dame: University of Notre Dame Press, 1981.

Jeanson, Francis. *Sartre and the Problem of Morality*. trans. Robert V. Stone. Bloomington: Indiana University Press, 1980.

Jones, W. T. *A History of Western Philosophy*. 5 Vols. New York: Harcourt Brace Jovanovich, 1970-1975.

Kaufmann, Walter. *Without Guilt and Justice*. New York: Delta, 1973.

Klemke, E. D., ed. *Studies in the Philosophy of G. E. Moore*. Chicago: Quadrangle Books, 1969.

Kohák, Erazim. *Idea and Experience: Edmund Husserl's Project of Phenomenology in "Ideas I."* Chicago: The University of Chicago Press, 1978.

Kruks, Sonia. "Simone de Beauvoir and the Limits to Freedom." *Social Text* 17 (Fall 1987).

Kwant, Remy C. *The Phenomenological Philosophy of Merleau-Ponty*. Pittsburgh: Duquesne University Press, 1963.

Langer, Monika. "Sartre and Merleau-Ponty: A Reappraisal." in Paul A. Schilpp, ed., *The Philosophy of Jean-Paul Sartre*. La Salle, Illinois: Open Court, 1981.

Lavine, T. Z. *From Socrates to Sartre*. New York: Bantam, 1984.

Lawrence, Nathaniel and O'Connor, Daniel, eds., *Readings in Existential Phenomenology*. Englewood Cliffs, N.J.: Prentice-Hall, 1967.

Lee, Edward N. and Mandelbaum, Maurice, eds., *Phenomenology and Existentialism*. Baltimore: The Johns Hopkins Press, 1969.

Lévy, Benny. "Today's Hope: Conversations with Sartre." trans. Lilliam Hernandez, George Waterston, and Claire Hubert. *Telos* 44 (Summer 1980).

McCormick, Peter and Elliston, Frederick A., eds. *Husserl: Shorter Works*. Notre Dame: University of Notre Dame Press, 1981.

MacIntyre, Alasdair. "Existentialism." in Mary Warnock, eds., *Sartre: A Collection of Critical Essays*. Garden City, N.Y.: Anchor Books, 1971.

———. *A Short History of Ethics*. New York: Macmillan, 1966.

McLeod, Norman. "Existential Freedom in the Marxism of Jean-Paul Sartre." *Dialogue* 7 (June-July 1968).

Mandelbaum, Maurice, Gramlich, Francis W., Anderson, Alan R., and Schneewind, Jerome B., eds. *Philosophic Problems*. New York: Macmillan, 1967.

Manser, Anthony. *Sartre: A Philosophic Study*. New York: Oxford University Press, 1967.

Marcuse, Herbert. *Studies in Critical Philosophy*. Boston: Beacon Press, 1973.

Marx, Karl. "Toward a Critique of Hegel's *Philosophy of Right*: Introduction." Trans. Loyd D. Easton and Kurt H. Guddat. in Allen W. Wood, ed., *Marx Selections*. New York: Macmillan, 1988.

Merleau-Ponty, Maurice. *Adventures of the Dialectic*. trans. Joseph Bien. Evanston: Northwestern University Press, 1973.

———. *Phenomenology of Perception*. trans. Colin Smith. New Jersey: The Humanities Press, 1962.

———. *Signs*. Evanston: Northwestern University Press, 1964.

Mill, John Stuart. *Utilitarianism*. Indianapolis: Hackett, 1979.

Molina, Fernando. *Existentialism as Philosophy*. Englewood Cliffs, N.J.: Prentice-Hall, 1962.

Molnar, Thomas. *Sartre: Ideologue of Our Time*. New York: Funk & Wagnalls, 1968.

Moore, G. E. *Principia Ethica*. Cambridge: Cambridge University Press, 1971.

Muller, Herbert J. *Issues of Freedom*. New York: Harper and Brothers, 1960.

Nowell-Smith, P. H. *Ethics*. Harmondsworth, Middlesex, England: Penguin, 1965.

Odajnyk, Walter. *Marxism and Existentialism*. New York: Double-day, 1965.

Olafson, Frederick A. *Principles and Persons: An Ethical Interpretation of Existentialism*. Baltimore: The Johns Hopkins Press, 1970.

———. "Sartre, Jean-Paul." in Paul Edwards, ed., *The Encyclopedia of Philosophy, Vol. 7*. New York: Macmillan, 1967.

Partridge, P. H. "Freedom." in Paul Edwards, ed., *The Encyclopedia of Philosophy, Vol. 3*. New York: Macmillan, 1967.

Plantinga, Alvin. "An Existentialist's Ethics." in Julius R. Weinberg and Keith E. Yandell, eds., *Ethics*. New York: Holt, Rinehart and Winston, 1971.

Plato, *Euthyphro*. trans. Hugh Tredennick. in *The Last Days of Socrates*. Harmondsworth, Middlesex, England: Penguin, 1978.

Poe, Edgar Allan. *Collected Works of Edgar Allan Poe*. 3 Vols. Cambridge, Massachusetts: The Belknap Press of Harvard University Press, 1978.

Poster, Mark. *Existential Marxism in Postwar France: From Sartre to Althusser*. Princeton: Princeton University Press, 1975.

Rachels, James. "John Dewey and the Truth about Ethics." in Steven M. Cahn, ed., *New Studies in the Philosophy of John Dewey*. Hanover, N.H.: The University Press of New England, 1981.

Reinhardt, Kurt F. *The Existentialist Revolt*. New York: Frederick Ungar, 1972.

Ross, W. D. *The Right and the Good*. Oxford: The Clarendon Press, 1930.

Russell, Bertrand. *Essays in Analysis*. ed. Douglas Lackey. New York: George Braziller, 1973.

———. *Philosophical Essays*. New York: Clarion, 1968.

———. *Religion and Science*. New York: Oxford University Press, 1968.

Ryle, Gilbert. *The Concept of Mind*. New York: Barnes and Noble, 1949.

Salvan, Jacques L. *The Scandalous Ghost*. Detroit: Wayne State University Press, 1967.

Sartre, Jean-Paul. *Anti-Semite and Jew*. trans. George J. Becker. New York: Schocken, 1974.

———. *Being and Nothingness*. trans. Hazel E. Barnes. New York: Philosophical Library, 1956.

———. *Between Existentialism and Marxism.* trans. John Mathews. New York: William Morrow, 1976.

———. *Cahiers pour une morale.* Paris: Gallimard, 1983.

———. "Consciousness of Self and Knowledge of Self." trans. Mary Ellen and Nathaniel Lawrence. in Nathaniel Lawrence and Daniel O'Connor, eds., *Readings in Existential Phenomenology.* Englewood Cliffs, N.J.: Prentice-Hall, 1967.

———. *Critique of Dialectical Reason.* trans. Alan Sheridan-Smith. London: Verso, 1982.

———. *The Emotions: Outline of a Theory.* trans. Bernard Frechtman. New York: The Wisdom Library, 1948.

———. *L'être et le néant.* Paris: Gallimard, 1943.

———. *Existentialism and Humanism.* trans. Philip Mairet. Brooklyn: Haskell House, 1977.

———. "The Historical Process." in Michel Contat and Michel Rybalka, eds., *The Writings of Jean-Paul Sartre, Vol. 2.* trans. Richard C. McCleary. Evanston: Northwestern University Press, 1974.

———. *Imagination: A Psychological Critique.* trans. Forrest Williams. Ann Arbor: Ann Arbor Paperbacks, 1972.

———. "Intentionality: A Fundamental Idea of Husserl's Phenomenology." trans. Joseph P. Fell. *Journal of the British Society for Phenomenology* 1, No. 2 (May 1970).

———. "Introduction to 'Les Temps Modernes'." trans. Françoise Ehrmann. in Eugen Weber, ed., *Paths to the Present: Aspects of European Thought from Romanticism to Existentialism.* New York: Dodd, Mead & Company, 1962.

———. "Letter-Foreword." in Francis Jeanson. *Sartre and the Problem of Morality.* trans. Robert V. Stone. Bloomington: Indiana University Press, 1980.

———. *Life/Situations: Essays Written and Spoken.* trans. Paul Auster and Lydia Davis. New York: Pantheon, 1977.

———. *Literary and Philosophical Essays.* trans. Annette Michelson. New York: Collier, 1962.

———. "A Long, Bitter, Sweet Madness." trans. Anthony Hartley. *Encounter* 22, No. 6 (June 1964).

———. "A More Precise Characterization of Existentialism." in Michel Contat and Michel Rybalka, eds., *The Writings of Jean-Paul Sartre, Vol. 2.* trans. Richard C. McCleary. Evanston: Northwestern University Press, 1974.

————. *Nausea*. trans. Loyd Alexander. New York: New Directions, 1964.

————. *No Exit and Three Other Plays*. New York: Vintage, 1949.

————. *On Genocide*. Boston: Beacon Press, 1968.

————. "Preface." in Frantz Fanon, *The Wretched of the Earth*. trans. Constance Farrington. New York: Grove Press, 1968.

————. *The Psychology of Imagination*. trans. Bernard Frechtman. New York: Washington Square Press, 1968.

————. "The Responsibility of the Writer." trans. Betty Askwith. in Haskell M. Block and Herman Salinger, eds., *The Creative Vision: Modern European Writers on their Art*. New York: Grove Press, 1960.

————. *Saint Genet*. trans. Bernard Frechtman. New York: Mentor, 1964.

————. *Sartre By Himself*. trans. Richard Seaver. New York: Outback Press, 1978.

————. *Search For a Method*. trans. Hazel E. Barnes. New York: Vintage, 1968.

————. *Situations*. trans. Benita Eisler. Greenwich, Conn.: Fawcett Crest, 1969.

————. *The Transcendence of the Ego*. trans. Forrest Williams and Robert Kirkpatrick. New York: Noonday, 1957.

————. *The War Diaries of Jean-Paul Sartre*. trans. Quintin Hoare. New York: Pantheon, 1984.

————. *What is Literature?* trans. Bernard Frechtman. London: Methuen, 1978.

————. *The Words*. trans. Bernard Frechtman. Greenwich, Conn.: Fawcett, 1966.

Scheler, Max. *Formalism in Ethics and Non-Formal Ethics of Values*. trans. Manfred S. Frings and Roger L. Funk. Evanston: Northwestern University Press, 1972.

Schilpp, Paul A., ed. *The Philosophy of Jean-Paul Sartre*. La Salle, Illinois: Open Court, 1981.

Schrag, Calvin O. *Existence and Freedom: Towards an Ontology of Human Finitude*. Evanston: Northwestern University Press, 1961.

Sheridan, James F. "On Ontology and Politics: A Polemic." *Dialogue* 7, No. 3 (December 1968).

————. *Sartre: The Radical Conversion*. Athens, Ohio: Ohio University Press, 1969.

Silverman, Hugh and Elliston, Frederick, eds., *Jean-Paul Sartre: Contemporary Approaches to His Philosophy*. Pittsburgh: Duquesne University Press, 1980.

Solomon, Robert C. *From Rationalism to Existentialism*. New Jersey: Humanities Press, 1978.

Spiegelberg, Herbert. *The Context of the Phenomenological Movement*. The Hague: Martinus Nijhoff, 1981.

————. *The Phenomenological Movement*. The Hague: Martinus Nijhoff, 1982.

————. "Sartre's Last Word on Ethics in Phenomenological Perspective." *Research in Phenomenology* XI (1981).

Stevenson, Charles L. *Ethics and Language*. New Haven: Yale University Press, 1960.

Stevenson, Leslie. *Seven Theories of Human Nature*. Oxford: Clarendon Press, 1974.

Stone, Robert V. "Sartre on Bad Faith and Authenticity." in Paul A. Schilpp, ed., *The Philosophy of Jean-Paul Sartre*. La Salle, Illinois: Open Court, 1981.

Tredwell, R. F. "On Moore's Analysis of Goodness," in E. D. Klemke, ed., *Studies in the Philosophy of G. E. Moore*. Chicago: Quadrangle Books, 1969.

Vesey, Godfrey, ed. *Philosophers Ancient and Modern*. Cambridge: Cambridge University Press, 1986.

Wahl, Jean. *Phénoménologie-Existence*. Paris: Arthaud, 1947.

Warnock, Mary. *Ethics Since 1900*. New York: Oxford University Press, 1966.

————. *Existentialism*. New York: Oxford University Press, 1970.

————. *Existentialist Ethics*. New York: St Martin's Press, 1967.

————. *The Philosophy of Sartre*. New York: Barnes & Noble, 1967.

————, ed. *Sartre: A Collection of Critical Essays*. Garden City, N.Y.: Anchor Books, 1971.

Weber, Eugen, ed. *Paths to the Present: Aspects of European Thought from Romanticism to Existentialism*. New York: Dodd, Mead & Company, 1962.

Weinberg, Julius R. and Yandell, Keith E., eds. *Ethics*. New York: Holt, Rinehart and Winston, 1971.

Weitz, Morris, ed. *20th-Century Philosophy: The Analytic Tradition*. New York: The Free Press, 1966.

Whitford, Margaret. *Merleau-Ponty's Critique of Sartre's Philosophy.* Lexington, Kentucky: French Forum, 1982.

Wilson, Colin. *Introduction to the New Existentialism.* Boston: Houghton Mifflin Company, 1966.

Winch, Peter. *The Idea of a Social Science and its Relation to Philosophy.* London: Routledge & Kegan Paul, 1967.

Zinn, Howard. *The Politics of History.* Boston: Beacon Press, 1971.

Index